Gendering the Vertical Mosaic

FEMINIST PERSPECTIVES ON CANADIAN SOCIETY

Gendering the Vertical Mosaic

FEMINIST PERSPECTIVES ON CANADIAN SOCIETY

Roberta Hamilton

Queen's University

COPP CLARK LTD.
Toronto

An honest attempt has been made to secure permission for all material used, and if there are errors or omissions, these are wholly unintentional and the Publisher will be grateful to learn of them.

ISBN: 0-7330-5537-1

Publisher: Jeff Miller
Editor: Barbara Tessman
Designer: Sharon Foster
Cover: Gordon Robertson
Typesetter: Carol Magee
Printing and binding: Metropole Litho Inc.

Canadian Cataloguing in Publication Data

Hamilton, Roberta
Gendering the vertical mosaic

Includes bibliographical references and index.
ISBN 0-7730-5537-1

1. Feminism - Canada. 2. Women - Canada - Social conditions. 3. Feminist theory.
I. Title

HQ1453.H35 1996   305.42'0971   C95-933237-5

COPP CLARK LTD.
2775 Matheson Blvd. East
Mississauga, Ontario
L4W 4P7

Printed and bound in Canada

1 2 3 4 5   5537-1   00 99 98 97 96

To my parents
Betty and Cy Russell

CONTENTS

CHAPTER 3

CHAPTER 4

CHAPTER 5

CHAPTER 6

PREFACE AND ACKNOWLEDGMENTS

In December 1976, when I sent my first manuscript to the publisher, I began my acknowledgments by recognizing my debt to the women's liberation movement. Today, my acknowledgment is similar, though in deference to the times, I invoke the collective work of generations of feminists who created the immense, diverse scholarly literature and intellectual environment that made possible critical research on gender, racism, sexuality, class—the list continues. Like the late poet and feminist activist Bronwen Wallace, I feel strongly that mine "is only one voice in a huge community" (1983, 295). In an interview with Janice Williamson in February 1989, only six months before she died, Bronwen stressed that this community included the dead as well as the living. For this reason, she started every public reading with a poem by someone who had died recently.

It is with great deliberation, then, that I recall Bronwen Wallace, her political commitment, her sensibilities, her power to evoke the best in others. In my copy of *The Stubborn Particulars of Grace,* she wrote what she must have written in many other copies: "For Roberta. Grace. Woman to woman through our own stubborn particulars." Bronwen told Janice that her book was "an attempt to begin to talk about spiritual matters in a political context and to say that if we're going to live in a state of grace, if we're going to live with wholeness or integrity in the world, we have to pay attention to the particulars and politics of where we are going." In writing *Gendering the Vertical Mosaic,* a book that presumptuously deals with so much, I keep Bronwen's vision in view, as well as her healthy scepticism toward academic feminism. My illustrations are intended to remind readers (and myself) that complex theoretical ideas needs to be understood through the prism of the small events of everyday life and evaluated in terms of their ability to illuminate, rather than obfuscate, our own stubborn particulars.

This book was written over the course of several years while I taught a large introductory class in sociology. My primary commitment as a teacher is to encourage students to understand their society and the social relationships in which they participate by using a range of theoretical perspectives—intellectual tools, as it were. I have never thought that this meant simplifying complex systems of thought. Indeed, this approach would provide a false sense that knowing is an easy matter, hardly worth the trouble. But conveying complexity, ambiguity, contradiction, and open-endedness puts the onus on the teacher to interact with students in accessible and challenging ways. Convincing my students that there is no simple formula for understanding the social world, and encouraging them to see this as intellectually exhilarating, rather than an occasion for regret, is great fun, and many of them have responded in kind, engaging in critical discussion with me, with each other, and, from what they tell me, with their housemates, friends, and partners.

In writing this book, I have tried to pursue a similar course. This proved far more difficult than teaching in a classroom where perplexed faces, body language, hands in the air, nodding heads and closing eyes, people lined up at the microphones, and the odd shout provide ongoing indications about the level of clarity and comprehension. Moreover, students find their way to my office and challenge me to explain, justify, or recant. But I have written this book with an eye to making complex ideas comprehensible. Many times I have sat before my keyboard imagining myself in front of two hundred and fifty undergraduate students, most of them less than half my age, waiting to be convinced (or at least entertained). And I have written for them. I trust that this book will be useful to introductory students in sociology, women's studies, and political studies. And because the ideas that animate this book are complex, I believe that it may be helpful as well to those who have considerably more background.

Because this book has taken so long to write—and even longer not to write—there are many people who contributed to making my environment supportive and stimulating. First, I must express my deepest gratitude to Barbara Tessman of Copp Clark. She persuaded me to write this book; she gave me a great deal of help; she was patient; and she shared my feminist convictions. The book would not have been written without her, and now, at the end of the project, I can say that I am very happy that she was willing to endure the wait. She deserved a more disciplined author, and she got me. But for my part, I am eternally grateful to have had the opportunity to work with this knowledgeable, competent, and indefatigable editor. I also want to thank her colleagues, Brian Henderson and Jeff Miller. Brian helped launch the project, and Jeff provided crucial support about halfway through.

I am grateful to several readers of the first chapters of the manuscript and especially to Dawn Currie who provided a thorough and incisive critique. Pat Armstrong and Deborah Gorham reviewed the whole manuscript, and I want to thank them very much. Not only were their comments very helpful, saving me from many errors, overgeneralizations, and excesses, but I appreciate that their schedules are frantically busy without such time-consuming additional tasks. I am also grateful to Karen Dubinsky for reading chapter 6, and to Jessica Hamilton, Elizabeth Russell, Susan Russell, Emma Whalen, and many graduate students in my feminist theories seminar for reading and commenting upon chapter 1. Two of those students, Adam Givertz and Alison Forrest, started the journal *left history* the year after taking that seminar. They invited me to submit an earlier version of chapter 1 for their inaugural issue, and it appeared as the first article. The response that I received helped spur me on to finish this book, and I am very grateful to them for going to such lengths to offer support! Another former student, Phyllis Bray, provided me with an amazing newspaper clipping service and much encouragement.

My research assistants have served me very well indeed. Patti Phillips offered critical readings of several chapters; Lore Fredstrom gave me the benefit of her rich and extensive background while doing a prodigious amount of research for several chapters; and Shelley Reuter made it possible for me to meet my final deadlines. Like all good researchers, she was a wonderful detective; she provided insightful response to all the chapters, and saved me from many an inappropriate turn of phrase. My great thanks to all of them.

During the 1990–91 academic year, I was fortunate to be associated with the Beatrice M. Bain Research Group at the University of California, Berkeley. In particular, I am grateful to Ilene Philipson and Carla Golden who provided warm friendship as well as critical readings of an earlier version of chapter 1. Janor Tuck and Ted and Susan Wright gave me wonderful places to stay in the Bay Area. I thank all of them for making my sabbatical a happy and productive time.

At Queen's University, I am very fortunate to have many colleagues in sociology and in women's studies whose personal support and encouragement for this project have sustained me through times happy and sad. In particular, for friendship and kindnesses over many years, I want to thank Rob Beamish, Annette Burfoot, Beverley Baines, Elspeth Baugh, Roberta Lamb, Colin Leys, Haideh Moghissi (now at York), Christine Overall, June Pilfold, Vincent Sacco, Terri Easter Sheen, Pamela Dickey Young, and (my Diana) Mary Morton. My new friends and colleagues in the Faculty Office have been so kind and supportive, as well as tolerant of my obsessive desire to finish this book; in particular I thank Natalie Forknall for helping in the preparation of the manuscript.

Jane Errington has been an ongoing source of love and confidence. Her perseverance, resilience, and scholarship are worthy of emulation, and I have tried. Olga Kits chose me to be her supporter when things were tough, and I am very happy she did. She taught me some new lessons about patience and possibility and loyalty. In an earlier incarnation, my colleague and friend, Karen Dubinsky, was my student. It is a sweet thing when intellectual and personal interests become so intertwined, as indeed they have with my own mentor and dear friend, Hubert Guindon. I have relied on all these relationships during all the machinations of personal life and university politics, and they make possible the finding of time and energy for writing.

For a person who has been so unremittingly critical of family in contemporary society, I have been remarkably blessed in my own familial relationships. In particular, I want to acknowledge how much I have learned from my son Joe and my daughters Susan and Jessica. Their experiences—as seen through my eyes—have long provided illustrations for my lectures, and they have never completely stopped speaking to me for this. They have worked hard to try and keep me informed about themselves and about life. They tease me about all that I don't seem to know and don't seem to want to know. Their interventions alone would save me from dogmatism about masculinity, racism, aerobics, music, sexuality, popular culture, work, and play. I have written much of this book with them in mind: Could I explain and justify what I have written to Joe, Susan, and Jessica? When the answer seemed to be no, the delete key on my computer was activated. Their support for me and for this project moves me greatly. Because they are my children, I don't suppose that they will ever know how much this mattered.

They must have learned a lot about support from their father, Neville Hamilton. I am also thankful for the close relationship I have with my brother, Jim Russell, and our sister, Susan, who is cited more than once in the pages that follow. I have learned so much from them both.

Finally I want to mention my partner, the irrepressible and loving Geoffrey Smith. Shulamith Firestone wrote that successful lovers give each other another window on the world. Looking through that other window has helped me see connections that I would not have seen (and may not be there), to shift my gaze, to reflect again. Living with someone who is politically and intellectually engaged, in ways different but not usually incompatible, may not have rushed this book along, but it altered the content, in ways subtle and various. Certainly living with Geoff has helped destabilize categories. As a dog lover, he often barks at dogs on the street; they often bark back. Once I went to the Syracuse Airport to pick him up. When I couldn't find him, I went to the Information Desk. The attendant picked up the Intercom: "Would Geoffrey Smith please come to the Information Desk." Seconds later, I heard barking from the other side of the airport. "Did you know it was me?" Geoff asked later. "Oh no," I replied. "There were lots of people barking." After that incident, I realized that I live with a man who thinks he's a dog, and a dog, Tuborg the Dog, who thinks he's a man. Together they have helped me write this book, although only Geoff did some serious proofreading. What can I say? They make me happy when skies are grey.

In the fall of 1962, I was a student in John Porter's course, "Class, Stratification and Power" at Carleton University. In retrospect, it is clear that his lectures became the basis of *The Vertical Mosaic* (1965). I wish that I could say that I realized, as a student, that he had not gendered his vertical mosaic. Looking back, I am flabbergasted by how much I didn't see what was to become—starting in the revolutionary winter of 1970—a central preoccupation in my life. This helps explain, I suppose, why one of the great joys of teaching for me has been introducing students to the ways of thinking that had not been presented to me, ways of thinking that turned out to be so important for every aspect of my life, including, and especially, my return to sociology as a graduate student ten years after my course with Professor Porter.

It is with humility and delight that I borrow John Porter's title for this book. I want to speculate briefly on what he might think about contemporary politics in Canada. For Porter, the way forward was to dismantle the vertical part of the vertical mosaic by providing equality of opportunity. The primary route would be access to education, particularly university education, and the precondition for this was a reasonable standard of living for all. What we are witnessing today in Ontario and much of the rest of the country is the dismantling of the educational opportunities in place since *The Vertical Mosaic* appeared. This is part of a larger agenda which, whatever the motivation, is most assuredly making the rich richer, the middle class smaller, and the poor poorer and more numerous. This agenda has been made acceptable precisely by declaring that more and more people have, to paraphrase Judith Butler, "bodies that don't matter" (1993). Declared outside the realm of the worthy are the poor, those on welfare, especially mothers and children, those with a physical or mental disability, mothers who work and mothers who don't work, fathers who don't work, and persons who are incarcerated. Not far removed are those who work for government whether in offices, classrooms, hospitals, universities, many of whom will be joining the ranks of the former. We must find ways to name this process of savage othering for what it is, a mean-spirited, racist, and misogynist rationale for buttressing existing privilege and power. We need to resist the hegemonic, multimedia message that each person stands alone, and that the best anyone can do is cling to a place inside the loop. Feminists have much to contribute to mobilizing resistance at every level to this absurd and unjust conception of social life, and I hope that *Gendering the Vertical Mosaic* makes this clear.

THIS BOOK provides an introduction to Canadian society from feminist theoretical perspectives. Yet it must be said immediately that neither *Canadian* nor *feminist* are used as though their meanings were self-evident. Controversies about the nature of Canadian society abound, and there is little agreement among scholars, activists, and citizens about just what this society is, or if it exists at all. Canadian society is not simply "there" awaiting feminist interpretation, nor is there any agreement on what might constitute feminist perspectives. As a result, my approach throughout this book is to examine critically the very concepts that constitute the book's themes, namely Canadian society and feminist perspectives.

Through this approach, I hope to encourage readers to critically analyze the interpretations offered here. Writing this book involved a constant process of selection, ranging from the questions posed and the interpretations presented to the research discussed. Readers must realize that textbooks—no less than other books—reflect the judgments, conscious and unconscious, informed and not-so-informed, of the authors. This book needs to be read critically, not for the ten major points from every chapter, but for the viability of interpretations. How do these interpretations stand up against other books you have read and the ideas presented by your professors? To what extent do they confirm or challenge your own experience, your mother's, your daughter's, or what you read in the newspaper? This book is intended, in line with the spirit of much feminist scholarship, to open many subjects for discussion rather than to provide some new received wisdom.

Most feminist scholarship proceeds from an understanding that knowledge is not prepackaged, that it is never simply a given. Rather, feminists seek to demonstrate that what passes for knowledge is historically specific and enmeshed in discernible ways with existing relations of power. Feminists have argued that men of the elites have had privileged access to creating knowledge—that is, to developing the descriptions and interpretations about the world that are deemed important for educated people to know. This means that dominant groups have also had the power to omit, to ensure that what they have deemed trivial has been omitted from the list of indispensable works—the *canons*—of various disciplinary knowledge. These omissions constitute the corollary, or underside, of knowledge—that which is too irrelevant to formulate, to pass on, or to explain. When such omissions are questioned by those who do not share the belief in their triviality, both the omissions and their advocates are often dismissed as too subjective, emotion-laden, or narrow.

Feminists have addressed what has been left out, filling in the silences. In this process, they depose, from its privileged location, that which was previously considered knowledge, and they call into question the assumptions and methods through which that knowledge has been created and shared. This point may be elaborated by looking more closely at the title of this book—*Gendering the Vertical Mosaic: Feminist Perspectives on Canadian Society.*

In 1965, Carleton University sociologist John Porter published a book entitled *The Vertical Mosaic.* A long-standing cliché comparing Canada and the United States described the former as "mosaic," the latter as "melting pot." This distinction drew attention to the idea that the many peoples from all over the world who had populated Canada maintained their various cultural identities. In the United States, the emphasis was upon assimilation: regardless of origin, all peoples would become American, not only in citizenship but in their way of life. Without commenting on the viability of the comparison—which has been contested by critics in both countries—Porter drew upon nearly two decades of research to demonstrate that Canada's ethnic mosaic was hierarchically arranged. In his words:

> Because the Canadian people are often referred to as a mosaic composed of different ethnic groups, the title "The Vertical Mosaic," was originally given to the chapter which examines the relationship between ethnicity and social class. As the study proceeded, however, the hierarchical relationship between Canada's many cultural groups became a recurring theme in class and power. . . . The title . . . therefore seemed to be an appropriate link between the two parts of the book ["The Structure of Class" and "The Structure of Power"]. (xii–xiii)

Although Porter's evidence on the nature of the relationship between ethnicity and power has been the subject of controversy within sociological literature (see chapter 4), many of his findings have been confirmed. Porter's book was also the first full-scale study to demonstrate that Canada was a class society; indeed, the media seized on the study as a news story, thus helping to dispel the common myth that nearly all Canadians were middle class, or just about to be.

The concept of a vertical mosaic also proves an apt metaphor for Canada as a racialized country. Indeed, the most enduring and dramatic divisions in Canadian society—which Porter mainly subsumed under "ethnic" differences—are those informed by the ways in which certain sectors of the population have been racialized. The term *race* becomes a code for *non-white*. Recent scholarship attends to the ways in which *whiteness* is constructed as the other side of *non-whiteness*, and how distinctions referred to as "race" shape power relations and the distribution of resources. My borrowing of the phrase *vertical mosaic*, therefore, also draws attention to a central theme of this book, namely the intersection of class and racialized hierarchies in Canada.

Let me turn to the first word in the title of this book—*gendering*. Porter's vertical mosaic acknowledged that the Canadian population came in two sexes. In particular, he called attention to the relationship between education, professional opportunities, and gender: "It is [women's] traditional exclusion from the higher professions which is a measure of the society's intellectual wastage" (179). Nonetheless, writing before the second wave of feminism, the Royal Commission on the Status of Women, and the explosion of feminist scholarship, Porter did not consider how the vertical mosaic was gendered in all of its manifestations.

Gender is a word that many feminist scholars use to indicate that sexual difference and sexual hierarchies are socially constructed. By using gender as a verb—*gendering*—I indicate that gender is not a thing but a process. Gender cannot be added on, as in "Gender *and* the Vertical Mosaic." Rather, gendering may be understood as ongoing action that plays out on every terrain from the psychic structures of individuals to the ways in which power is deployed in all organizations, institutions, and relationships. Gendering focuses on masculinity and femininity as continuously shifting social phenomena that intricately and variously inform all social interaction. Gendering the vertical mosaic involves using feminist perspectives to study Canadian society.

This brings us to the first words of the subtitle of this book. *Feminist perspectives* offer various, sometimes competing, explanations for the pervasiveness of relationships of domination and subordination between men and women, for different perceptions of the relevance of class, racial, and ethnic differences among women, and for a range of understandings about the changes required to redress exploitative and oppressive relationships. Feminists have explored the nature of reproductive labour and male control of female sexuality searching for the roots of male domination and female subordination. They have refashioned Marxism in their attempts to understand the relation between class and gender. Feminists of colour have insisted that white feminists acknowledge and dismantle their own racism, including the racism inherent in the theories that they have developed. Psychoanalytic theories have been reread for what they reveal about power, control, misogyny, and internalized oppression. Lesbians and gay men have put the oppressive system of heterosexism on the agenda and have related it to male privilege, racial stereotypes, and class exploitation. Feminists have been drawn to the theories of poststructuralism and deconstructionism and have turned them into powerful ways of examining how language creates, sustains, and constrains our sense of who we are and, at the same time, how language, by its volatility and flexibility, may open up the spaces for challenges to dominant discourses. Taken together, feminist theories involve a massive critique of every aspect of societies, past and present: relationships, institutions, behaviours, discourses, thoughts, and ideas.

Chapter 1 presents an overview of the current feminist theoretical perspectives that were used to develop the subsequent chapters on Canadian society. By first presenting the theoretical discussions, my aim is to provide readers with sufficient theoretical background to anticipate and appreciate the kinds of challenges that feminists have raised about Canadian society. In addition, the theoretical discussions should enable readers to understand and critically assess the particular interpretations of Canadian society offered in this book. Which theoretical questions are used to raise issues about Canadian society? Which questions are ignored? All selections involve exclusion, but to what extent have spaces been created to permit readers to consider for themselves what has been excluded? Readers may also raise the reverse question. To what extent do the historical and contemporary interpretations of Canadian society offered here suggest theoretical roads not followed in this text? I hope that readers who are encountering feminist theory for the first time will be attracted by the range of questions and perspectives that may be used to explore the areas of social life that most interest them.

Feminist theories offer to make visible, analyze, and critique the hierarchical social relations between men and women in all societies and in every aspect of society from the level of macroeconomics and international politics through to sexuality and the intimate social practices of everyday life. They expose the socially constructed nature of those relations and try to explain how they are sustained at the intra-psychic and inter-subjective levels. Feminist theories always offer an explicit or at least implicit critique of relations of domination and subordination. If these theories can explain why and how things are as they are, they also provide the possibility of transformation to societies no longer informed by exploitative and oppressive relations between the sexes.

In the subsequent chapters of this book, my task is to use feminist theoretical questions to study major aspects of *Canadian society*, the last part of the book's subtitle. But this task is more difficult than it may at first appear: there is no entity known as Canadian society that can simply be assumed to exist. Just as feminists have disagreed (at some point about almost everything), so have those historians, political scientists, sociologists, journalists, and bureaucrats who have written about Canadian society. Not only have their interpretations changed over the decades, but there are complex and ongoing debates about the nature of this society. Is Canada a land of opportunity for all (men) or a class-divided society, rent further by racism and ethnocentrism, a society that reserves its positions of power and wealth for self-perpetuating elites? Do the regional disparities reflect the vagaries of nature or the actions of political and economic leaders? Are we composed of one nation? Or two, as many Québécois would have it? Or at least three, as Aboriginal peoples argue? Or many, as some versions of multiculturalism would suggest? Are we a nation at all? Do the differences between Canada and the United States amount to little more than political fiction?

These profound disagreements about the nature of Canadian society mean that a feminist interrogation of the literature must also decide which (prefeminist) interpretations appear the most viable, which are most worth critiquing, elaborating upon, and appropriating. The voluminous prefeminist literature on Canadian society—including, for the most part, Porter's *Vertical Mosaic*—has generally taken the relations between the sexes as given, natural in some sense. Feminist questions undercut these assumptions and, as a result, the original interpretations are revealed more as sexist descriptions than explanations. The old interpretations do not completely disappear, however. It is rather like turning a kaleidoscope. There is familiarity about the new image, but the pieces are arranged quite differently, and, more especially, some that were hidden in the first arrangement come into full view in the second.

There is truly no aspect of life in Canada that has not been, or could not be, subjected to feminist interrogation, to a turn of the kaleidoscope. How then to decide what to discuss in this book? What criteria would be used for selection? My decision has been to organize the chapters around some of the major themes and issues that have been raised within women's movements in Canada in the past thirty years. After all, women's movements offer the sustained challenges to the sexual hierarchies that pervade Canadian society, as well as providing the initial and often continuing impetus for feminist research and theoretical development (Adamson, Briskin, and McPhail 1988).

There is a rich historical interrelationship between feminist theories and women's movements. Theories don't spring from the (disembodied) brains of women and men; they develop in the context of people's lives, and most especially from people's understandings of their lives. Feminist theories proliferated as feminists challenged women's subordination to men. But, in many cases, the theories took on a life of their own, in academic niches that often appear far from the activist locations where they were first spawned. There is, therefore, no simple relationship between feminist theories and movements, yet they develop, as I hope will become clear, in some sort of dialogue with each other.

Chapter 2, therefore, provides an interpretation of women's movements in Canada, with most of the attention given to what has been called second wave feminism. What have feminist activists in Canada heralded, through their mobilizations, as the most important themes and issues? Once again, the reader is called upon to assess the answer to this question as well as to judge the way that the issues have been constructed in the succeeding chapters. By presenting the women's movement as a chapter in itself, I intend to provide the reader with a broad historical interpretation as well as some grounds for assessing the process of selection. Chapters 1 and 2 provide the questions, the analysis, the broad subjects, and the particular issues that are explored in the last four chapters of the book.

Chapters 3 and 4 discuss feminist challenges to the Canadian state. Perhaps the primary reason why we speak about Canadian society is because of the internationally accepted legal set of relations encapsulated in the Canadian state. The Canadian state is generally treated as having the legitimacy to organize social and political relations within the territory recognized as Canada. There is a country called Canada on the map of the world. It is, however, a slippery slope from here to the concept of Canadian society.

Feminists have disagreed profoundly about the nature of the Canadian state, and about just what might be expected from this socio-political set of relations in terms of remedy for past injustice and inequality. Despite these disagreements, feminists have continually pressured the state for change. In the early twentieth century, the women's movement campaigned for suffrage, rights to property and child custody, and access to politics, education, and professions. The second wave has struggled for birth control, abortion, daycare, equity in employment and pay, and the end to violence against women and to discrimination on the basis of sexual orientation.

Understanding these campaigns involves an appreciation of the various feminist theories of the state. Liberal feminists have held that the state is pluralist in nature, open to the lobbying of pressure groups, and thereby avoiding capture by any particular set of interests. If feminists mobilize sufficiently, laws and policies will be altered to reflect their interests. Although Marxist feminists have not rejected such tactics, they hold that, in a capitalist society, the state will promote primarily the interests of private capital and those who own and control that capital. Socialist and radical feminists have argued that the state is patriarchal in conception and interests, formulating laws and policies that systematically privilege men and disadvantage women. Chapter 3 deals with these feminist theories of the state and the kinds of campaigns and issues that feminists have directed towards the state.

Chapter 4 continues the discussion about the Canadian state by documenting the challenges that have been offered to the very legitimacy of that state by Aboriginal peoples, the Québécois, and people of colour. In all of these locations, women have worked alongside men to further shared political goals. At the same time, they have organized independently to transform their subordinate status within each of these political forma-tions. The criterion for inclusion in this chapter is whether women seek to undo their historic and contemporary disadvantage in their own commu-nities, even as they demand more autonomy and/or resources for those communities from the Canadian state. The struggles of women in all of these locations have challenged feminists to recognize racist, class, and national barriers to transforming the relations of domination and subor-dination between the sexes. There is, therefore, ongoing dialogue and debate among the various feminist challenges to the state.

Feminists from all over the political and social map have challenged the Canadian state, especially during the past twenty-five years. Feminist nationalists in Quebec want that province to separate from Canada; Aboriginal women are among the vocal proponents of self-determination for their peoples; Canadians and immigrants disadvantaged by racism argue that their children remain destined for second-class status; many people, poor for generations, have ceased to imagine a better life; and feminists have argued that the October 1929 decision of the Judicial Committee of the British Privy Council recognizing women as "persons" (thus overturning the decision of the Supreme Court of Canada) has never been delivered in law or in practice (Baines 1993, 253–58).[1]

In their efforts to transform the organization of social life in Canada, feminists have challenged the gendered division of labour, how women (and men) are represented or portrayed, and how women and men per-ceive themselves, their characteristics, abilities, and goals. These three aspects of life—activity, representation, and subjectivity—are densely interrelated, and they can only be untangled for analytical and political purposes. These themes—what we do, how we are portrayed, and how we experience ourselves—constitute the tapestry of daily life. They are discussed in chapters 5 and 6.

Chapter 5 discusses first and second wave feminist challenges to the sexual division of labour, both in the paid labour force and in the home. Feminists have insisted on women's right to access to all areas of paid and unpaid work. They have challenged prevailing definitions of what constitutes work and have revealed how work has been gendered, sexu-alized, racialized, and differently valued depending on the ascriptive characteristics of those doing the work. They have demonstrated the fundamental incompatibility between the current organization and practices of the workplace and the requirements of childbearing and rearing, as well as the contradictions between profit making and the imperatives for sustained life on the planet. Chapter 5 elaborates upon many of the issues raised in chapter 2 on the women's movement, and continues to show the relationship between various theoretical perspectives and the issues that are constructed and perceived as most salient.

In chapter 6, the focus shifts to issues of representation and subjectivity, and feminist challenges to the sexual objectification of women. We look at just what seemed to be at stake in the various issues around sexual objectification and the ensuing debates among feminists. By examining the perspectives on sexual objectification that have been articulated at various times by Aboriginal women, black women, women with disability, older women, and lesbians, the diverse positions within feminism come into bold relief.

The feminist interest in representation has been linked with concerns about how girls and women understand and feel about themselves, the kinds of work they can imagine doing, the kinds of partners and relationships they dream of having, and how they think about and live their sexuality. All these questions have been encapsulated in explorations of gendered socialization: How do we come to think of ourselves in profound ways as male or female, as lesbian, gay, bisexual, or heterosexual? The discussions of these questions in chapter 6 are drawn primarily from feminist appropriations of psychoanalysis and poststructuralist understandings of gender and sexuality. In these theories we find provocative understandings of masculinity and femininity as constructions and performances that buttress not only misogyny but also homophobia and racism.

It is very difficult to write of many things all at once. As a result, we divide up the indivisible so that we may proceed in some sort of systematic fashion. It will be the reader's task to relate many of the different subjects in this book to each other. The concept of Canadian society disappears before our eyes as we focus upon the conflicting interests of Aboriginal and non-Aboriginal peoples, the English and the French, the rich and the poor, men and women, heterosexuals and gays and lesbians, the young and the old, the able-bodied and those with disability, and those who are advantaged and disadvantaged by racism. Yet I continue to use the words *Canadian society*, both as shorthand and as a sign of hope that by acknowledging and appreciating diversity, justice, and equality we might work towards such a reality. Feminists of many persuasions provoke ongoing challenges to oppressive and exploitative relations that exist within and beyond the geopolitical borders of Canada.

There is always a utopian aspect to these challenges: things could be better, much better.

In figuring out how the "better" or "much better" could be achieved, readers are asked to consider the various levels of analysis in which feminists have engaged. For example, the women and men who participate in creating the Canadian state, and provide grounds for ensuring its perpetuation or promoting its demise, all have gendered, sexualized, and racialized histories that shape their sense of the possible, their understanding of self and other, the fear or enjoyment they take in their own company and in the company of others.

Some of the theories about how we become gendered are presented in chapter 6, and it must be remembered that the consequences of gendering are felt not only in our intimate lives, but also in the kinds of work we do, wish to do, and are prevented from doing, as well as in the kinds of citizens of the Canadian state that we become. At the same time, the laws, social policies, and practices of the Canadian state shape the lives of the children and adults living within its boundaries. The right-wing agenda of the mid-1990s, whatever its motivations, is most assuredly making the rich richer, the middle class smaller, and the poor poorer and more abundant. Many of the gains made by feminist organizing in the 1970s have proved transitory and easy to dismantle. Feminist theories and strategies make links between the macro-politics of the Canadian state and the gendered socialization of children, yet such thinking remains marginalized to dominant political rhetoric in Canada.

This book presents a feminist introduction to Canadian society. The presenting questions are drawn from feminist theories, broadly considered, the issues from women's movement activists in many spheres. My hope is that it will encourage readers who are introduced to this material for the first time to engage in their own lines of questioning, and those who have pondered many of these issues before to continue to ask feminist questions and seek feminist solutions to the problems that beset those who live in Canada and elsewhere.

Notes

1. We should note here that this case concluded that women should be treated as persons for the purposes of membership in the Senate. This case did not extend a *carte blanche* invitation to personhood. For a history of women's claim to legal personhood see Baines (1993), 246–58. Baines concludes her analysis with this statement: "Women are not yet perceived as persons, always and everywhere" (258).

Feminist Theories

THEORY IS A WORD that sends most mortals rushing from the room, convinced that what is coming is too rarefied, too pretentious, too difficult, or completely irrelevant. But I want to argue three things: first, that theory is very much intertwined with how we make sense of the world in an ordinary, day-to-day way; second, that we can gain something from being more systematic and probing about this activity of making sense; and third, that feminists have made very good use, indeed, of this more systematic process.

Feminists have produced an enormous, diverse, and eclectic range of interpretations in their attempts to explain how sexual hierarchies are created and sustained as well as to provide strategies for confronting these hierarchies. Taken together, these interpretations constitute an unprecedented historical challenge to the organization of social life and the categories through which that life previously has been apprehended. This challenge involves examining the ways in which sexual oppression informs and is informed by the many social practices through which people are privileged and disadvantaged, included and excluded, wield and submit to power. Feminist literature in its diversity, complexity, internal debates, and many languages defies summary. Yet all of it is provoked by unease with current social arrangements. My concern is that we not lose sight of its origins within feminist movements that seek to transform our relationships to each other on the intimate, local, and global levels. This chapter delineates the contours of contemporary feminist theories and their relationship to each other, and emphasizes their collective indebtedness to past and present feminist movements.

Let us begin by examining the proposition that we all use theory and, further, that our lives would be well-nigh impossible to live if we did not. In making decisions, in our interactions with others, in carrying out our activities, we proceed on the basis of past experience and some form of conscious or unconscious speculation or prediction about the future. Through this process, we provide ourselves with explanations about why things turned out as they did, and whether and how future outcomes will be similar or different.

In such ways, we navigate our way through our relationships with parents, friends, children, teachers, store clerks, employers, employees, as well as through what we have come to think of as bureaucratic red tape: applications for university, jobs, and unemployment insurance, returns for income tax, and so on. We make decisions about whether to study or go to the movies; whether to start, continue, alter, or end relationships; whether to use contraception, terminate a pregnancy, or have a child; whether to cook a meal or eat out. We don't do all of this blindly, although we may often wonder why we did what we did. We know what will irritate our parents, and why; what will enrage our children, and what will give them some reason to believe they are understood. We have some understanding of why there are deadlines for university applications, and what kinds of marks or skills are needed for admission. When we approach the job market, we have some idea of what sort of work we will be offered. To make all these decisions, we have at our disposal diverse sets of experience, information, and interpretations ranging from ideas about why we behave as we do through to explanations about how goods, services, and power are distributed in our society.

Often, however, we feel perplexed. We wish we knew more so that we could feel more confident about our decisions. Often we may not comprehend how people behave or how "the system" works. In these situations we have choices: to allow the world to remain a mystery, to accept "common sense" understandings that are readily available in our own milieu, or to engage in a more conscious and coherent process of observing, researching, reading, thinking, discussing, and interpreting. If we choose this third way, we will encounter a body of literature—whether about the physical world, power and politics, human psychology, bureaucracy, law, ethics and morality, or sexuality—that others have produced. The answers we find will always be tentative, and we may have to choose between very different answers or interpretations. Sometimes controversy will have given way to consensus. For a very long time, people believed the world was flat; then some iconoclasts came along and made the perfectly ridiculous statement that the world was round. Imagine the surprise of those who once prosecuted these people as heretics if they were to find out that everyone, including present-day members of the same church that conducted the prosecutions, now believes that the earth is round.

Sometimes you may ask a question that no one seems to have asked before. And if there haven't been any questions, then there will not be any answers. You may be a pioneer. More likely, however, some people will have asked the questions before, but they may not be the ones who wrote the books; they may not be those who were in a position to decide that they were "good" questions. Further, those who are in a position to decide may have a good deal to gain if *nobody* asks those questions. They may even prosecute those who do as heretics, dissenters, or enemies of the state. The famous Norwegian playwright Henrik Ibsen wrote a play entitled *An Enemy of the People* (1882) about a doctor who worked in a small town known for its healing baths that brought visitors from everywhere. When Dr Stockmann discovered that the waters were contaminated, that "the whole Bath establishment is a whited poisoned sepulchre, . . . the gravest possible danger to the public health," he was condemned by the powerful as a traitor. But he first had to ask the question:

> Last year there were a number of curious cases of sickness among the visitors. . . . [T]yphoid and gastric fever. . . . It was thought at the time that the visitors had brought their infections with them. But afterwards . . . during the winter . . . I began to have other ideas. So I carried out a few tests on the water. . . . (Ibsen 1967, 43)

The same author wrote another play called *A Doll's House* (1879). At the end of that play, the heroine, Nora, thoroughly disillusioned with her husband, prepares to leave him and their two children. To her incredulous husband she declares: "I must try and educate myself—you are not the man to help me in that. I must do that for myself. And that is why I am going to leave you now" (1967, 64). Until then, conventional wisdom both. Ibsen caused a scandal by making emotional, intellectual, and political sense out of Nora's decision.

As Gertrude Stein lay dying, she apparently sat up suddenly and asked "What is the answer?" When she received no answer, she rose one last time to ask, "What then is the question?" The key to viable and convincing answers is in the question. Although there is more to theory making than asking, "What is the question?" it is a reasonable place to begin. Marx asked, What is the innermost secret of capitalism? If people get paid for what they *make,* where do capitalists get their profit for further investment? The innermost secret, according to Marx, was that people do not get paid for what they produce. That is an assumption; it seems to be true, but it is not true. They actually get paid for selling their ability to labour—Marx called it *labour power*—to someone who owns the factory or the mine—the *means of production*—for the going wage rate. Capitalists try to keep this wage as low as possible in order to maximize their profits. Over time, Marx argued, the wage cannot fall below *subsistence*—below what it takes to keep body and soul together—for working people as a whole, or workers would die and never reproduce a new generation. Workers do what they can, through collective action, to raise the wage above subsistence. But workers will be paid for their ability to labour, not for what they have actually produced: this is the form of exploitation that defines capitalist relations of production.

Unravelling this secret of capitalism formed an integral part of Marx's theoretical enterprise: his task was to understand how capitalism worked, what it was that brought workers together to resist exploitation, and how capitalism itself might be superseded by socialism. But the theory didn't just come out of his head. He studied history; he read what economists and philosophers had already written; he observed contemporary German, English, and French society; he participated in politics; he read newspapers. People have been arguing about the viability of different aspects of his observations and predictions—his theory—ever since. But many agree that, at the very least, his questions took us a giant step forward in understanding our economic system and capitalist society.

So theory writing (about human society) is about constructing informed interpretations of what has been, of how we arrived where we are, of the meaning this has for different participants and then, on that basis, attempting to draw informed predictions about the possible outcomes and the consequences of each. This last element will always be contingent, for it will depend on what people *choose* to do. Sociologist Philip Abrams (1982, xiii) chose the expression "the paradox of human agency" to convey the idea that what people choose to do is never straightforward. We live in particular times and places and face varying sorts of constraint and possibility; even what we can imagine we would like to do is shaped by these circumstances. This may not seem like a contestable proposition. But this way of understanding the individual and society actually stands against the ideology of the rational, autonomous individual "man" that has dominated Western thought in the past two or three centuries. These dominant ideas had their origins in the Enlightenment and have had powerful adherents throughout this age of capitalism. Marx's challenge to this ideology is encapsulated in his famous passage, "Men make their own history, but they do not make it just as they please; they do not make it under circumstances chosen by themselves, but under circumstances directly encountered, given and transmitted from the past" (Marx 1969 [1869], 398). As Marx indicates, we are born into particular, if always shifting, sets of relationships, within families and households, communities and states. Such relationships confer obligation and responsibility and shape access or lack of access to everything from economic power and privilege to care and intimacy.

Feminists have had different ways of conveying the important idea that we are born into particular arrangements that shape all aspects of our lives. Indeed, the question of who and what constrains, oppresses, and subordinates women, and how, not only unites feminists but also divides them.

Feminists and the Debate About Human Agency

THERE ARE MANY PROLIFERATING AND OVERLAPPING feminist perspectives. My intention is not to contribute to the drawing of firm boundaries between them, boundaries that may only imitate conventional disciplinary boundaries and make it more difficult to ask questions about the origins and perpetuation of hierarchical relations between the sexes. Yet for students of feminist scholarship, it is necessary to know something about the nature and history of these differences. The labels have been used a good deal and, even if labels are increasingly abandoned, it is important to know what is being abandoned and why.

Let us return to Marx's statement and see how feminists of differing persuasions—liberal feminists, socialist feminists, radical feminists, lesbian feminists, lesbian separatists, black feminists, and feminists of colour—would elaborate, modify, or overturn it. We also have to consider the ways in which feminists (who might also be in one or more of the above categories) have drawn on the insights of psychoanalysis, poststructuralism, and linguistic theories in considering this question of (wo)men making their own history but not under conditions chosen by themselves.

Liberal Feminism

Feminism's history is intertwined with the individualistic ideology of liberalism. When Mary Wollstonecraft wrote *A Vindication of the Rights of Woman* in 1792, she was in broad agreement with the liberal democratic slogan—Liberty, Equality, Fraternity—of the French Revolution. She argued that women, like men, are rational beings with the potential to be fully responsible for their own lives. For her, and for the liberal feminists who came after her, including those of our own time, the circumstances that shaped women's lives were the laws and prejudices that excluded them from the public sphere. During the next two hundred years, with much ebb and flow, women struggled for the right to higher education, entrance into the professions, the right to own property and hold public office, and for suffrage, the right that came to symbolize full citizenship. For liberal feminists, the laws that decreed that women were lesser beings than men were a product of ignorance. The expectation was that as men and women educated themselves on this subject, these laws and the prejudices that underwrote them would gradually be replaced by extending equality of opportunity to women.

Embedded in Wollstonecraft's later writings and in her personal biography, however, are painful clues that this public road to emancipation might not be the whole story (Eisenstein 1981; Snitow 1990; Sydie 1991). Pregnancy, childbirth, and childcare posed perplexing obstacles for Wollstonecraft's economic independence, while the unequal investment made by her and her lover, Gilbert Imlay, in their relationship left her devastated. According to Rosalind Sydie, Wollstonecraft's experience, as revealed in her writings, "illustrates her gradual realization of a critical basis for female subordination—sexual passion. Her own recommendations for social change become more radical as her understanding and personal experience of the nature and consequences of the sexual control of women developed" (1991, 36). These aspects of her thought moved to centre stage in later feminist theory.

Marxism and the Woman Question

The issue of economic independence figures prominently in Marx and Engels' theory on the subordination of women. Like other socialists, they conceptualized this as the "woman question." The problem was important, but clearly secondary to the central issue of social class.[1] Engels argued that our early ancestors lived in a state of primitive communism: everyone had to labour to survive and all that was available was shared. With the invention of cultivation and animal husbandry, people created the possibility of accumulating surplus. This development was of monumental importance in human history. It opened up the possibility of longer, more secure lives. But the underside was that this surplus could be controlled by some and used in the interests of the few against the many. The surplus would be claimed by the few as their private property. Some would labour so that others might prosper. Those men with a surplus wanted their own children to inherit the wealth they had amassed. But how would men know who were their own children? Only women have this assurance. The solution was to turn women themselves into private property. If a man owned a woman, she would labour for him, and she would be permitted to have sexual relations only with him. Thus the idea of *legitimacy* was born. Legitimacy means that a man's legal children are the biological children of his wife. They are assumed to be his biological children because he owns their mother.

In this interpretation, class society and male dominance enter onto the world stage together. For Engels these developments constituted the "world historic defeat of the female sex" (1948 [1884], 57). It followed, then, that with the abolition of private property (under communism), women would be emancipated. Under capitalism, Engels detected a first step towards women's emancipation, as economic desperation forced working-class women to become wage labourers, and hence propelled them into de facto equality with their husbands. Economically dependent bourgeois women, on the other hand, remained the property of their husbands. For Marxists, then, the circumstances that shape women's lives are the relations of private property and, in our era, capitalist relations. They are the same relations that shape the lives of men, albeit in different ways.

Historically, liberal feminism and the Marxist perspective on the woman question not only had different explanations for, and solutions to, the subordination of women but also occupied different, and sometimes hostile, political territory.[2] Marxists accused feminists of being "bourgeois," interested only in ensuring that women would share in the privilege (or destitution) of their class. Feminism was potentially dangerous to working-class struggles because sex-specific ideas about oppression would pit working men and women against each other and might create (false) grounds for class collaboration between upper- and working-class women. Feminists, for their part, often accused left-wing men and their political parties of being as uninterested, if not as hostile, as their class enemies in the rights of women.

Not until the late 1960s did another feminism develop that put liberal feminism and the Marxist perspective on the woman question into dialogue with each other and made fully visible the hitherto unexplored fragments in Wollstonecraft's writings. For this feminism launched a critique not only of the public world but also of the private world—the world of family, love, sexuality, pregnancy, and childcare. Furthermore, these feminists argued that the interconnections between public and private worlds were pivotal for understanding the sexual hierarchy. Women's liberation, therefore, depended upon the transformation of both worlds.

But these second wave feminists soon divided along political and theoretical lines into those calling themselves *socialist feminists* and those calling themselves *radical feminists*. For the purpose of this discussion, the difference between them centred upon the question of explanation: who and what oppressed women and why.

Socialist Feminism

Socialist feminists argued, with Marxists, that the relations of capital, and therefore class relations, are pivotal for understanding women's oppression. But they differed from Marxists in insisting that the oppressive relations between the sexes are not simply derivative of class. They argued that the interconnections between sex oppression and class exploitation had to be addressed. In other words, for socialist feminists, it was no longer enough to talk only about the woman question, and they did not assume that the basis for women's oppression would disappear automatically with the overthrow of capitalism. These feminists focused upon the ways in which the labour done by women in the household—which they called *domestic labour*—helps to sustain the capitalist system. On both a daily and generational level, women contribute to the reproduction of labour power by having and rearing children and by looking after husbands between their wearying days (or nights) in mines and factories (Armstrong and Armstrong 1994; Luxton 1980). As a result, both capitalists and individual men benefit from the unpaid and personal service of women in the home.

Socialist feminists analyzed the interconnections between the public sphere of capitalist and state relations and the private sphere of the family/household. Not only did the complex range of tasks done in the home prop up the capitalist edifice and allow the system to function at a fraction of its real cost, but in many ways the *appearance* of the distinction between private and public created and sustained the unequal relations between men and women throughout society. Challenging the dominant interpretation that men in the work force "bring home the bacon" and that nurturing women at home provide sustenance, socialist feminists uncovered the historically specific development of this relationship during the rise of industrial capitalism. Men of capital, together with middle-class philanthropists and social reformers and the better-paid male skilled workers, engaged in diverse, but mutually reinforcing, strategies to push women out of the labour force with promises of a family wage for male workers. For women, the results of this long historical manoeuvre were doubly exploitative and oppressive. First, denied access to higher education and the professions, women were also pushed out of the better-paying jobs; only the worst-paid and least-protected jobs remained open to them. Second, most men never earned a family wage but were nonetheless expected to support a wife and children. Women compensated for inadequate wages by increasing household labour, taking in boarders, laundry, and other people's children, and putting the needs of others before their own. Third, men earned the (main) wage, and this relative privilege reinforced their power over their wives and children. Men were exploited in the work force, and many responded by flexing their muscles, literally and figuratively, at home.

Socialist feminists pointed to the final irony that when men deserted their families, women, encouraged from birth to believe that men would care for them and their children, had to earn a living in the capitalist marketplace with "one hand tied behind their back" (Liddington and Norris 1978). Most women had no marketable skills, they were denied access to education and better-paying jobs, and they had no social supports for childcare. The family wage, portrayed as a form of security for working-class people, was unmasked as a fraud. Primarily, the *idea* of a family wage functioned as a rationale for excluding women from better-paying jobs and secure incomes, for paying them less, hiring them last, and firing them first (Connelly 1978). It served as a justification for women's sole responsibility for childcare and housework coupled with a lifetime of personal service to a particular man. No wonder that sociologists and socialist feminists Pat and Hugh Armstrong wanted to call *The Double Ghetto* (their path-breaking book on women's work in Canada) *Everyone Needs a Wife*.

During the 1970s, socialist feminism developed through heated debates and open dialogue with radical feminism, quickly taking up many of its insights while eschewing many of its explanations.

Radical Feminism

Radical feminists did not dispute the exploitative nature of capitalist relations, but they argued that, buried deeper in human society, both historically and psychically, are the relations of domination and subordination between the sexes. Writing at the dawn of the contemporary women's movement, Shulamith Firestone (1970) located these differences between men and women in nature's unequal allotment of reproductive tasks. Women bore, suckled, and raised children, while men had the time and opportunity to develop social institutions—including the family—through which they were able to appropriate power and control over women and children. The bottom line was that men oppress women. Overthrowing that oppression constituted the primary struggle in which feminists should engage.

Radical feminism was neither static nor monolithic. As its critique developed, many radical feminists began to locate men's power over women in their ability to control women sexually and to develop the institutions that ensure continuing control (Eisenstein 1984). Adrienne Rich (1980) coined the famous phrase *compulsory heterosexuality* to encapsulate the social and cultural imperatives that close off all sexual options for women except monogamous heterosexual permanent coupling, usually called marriage. In a world of unequal power relations between men and women, compulsory heterosexuality ensures not only women's sexual dependence upon men but also their economic, social, and psychological dependence. From this perspective—sometimes called *lesbian feminism*, though it was by no means confined to lesbians—women's lives in patriarchal society are shaped by the myriad legal institutions and cultural messages that enjoin women (from the time they are young girls) to look to men for sexual satisfaction, personal validation, and life-long companionship, and to accept their subordination to men in general and their husbands in particular as part of the bargain (Martindale 1995; see also *Resources for Feminist Research* 1990). From this critical position, some lesbian feminists took the short but dramatic step to a lesbian separatist position that women should no longer try to change the whole society but rather find ways to live apart from men and build a society alone.

More generally, early radical feminism was eclipsed by what has been called *cultural feminism*—overlapping with, but not confined by, a separatist perspective (Echols 1989). Women should build their own institutions from health clinics and women's shelters to small businesses, art galleries, publishing houses, and magazines. The rationale for these developments varies widely: for some it is a way of building a permanent women's world; for others it is a refuge from the pain of day-to-day struggle with men; for still others, such autonomous organizing is intended to build a power base from which the whole society could be transformed.

What is key for the discussion on human agency is that radical, lesbian, and cultural feminists argue that women are born into arrangements that force them to live their lives in subservience to men. These feminists might alter Marx's statement to something like "*Men* make their own history; women have no history of their own." Socialist feminists agree that most men of all social classes have the opportunity in both their intimate and work lives to dominate and oppress women. Yet they also argue that men's and women's lives are shaped by the relations of capital, which privilege a few at the expense of the many.

Anti-racist Feminisms

Women of colour led the way in insisting that liberal, socialist, and radical feminists failed to identify the key circumstances produced by racism; that is, racism produces lives of privilege for some and brutal oppression and exploitation for others (Brand 1984; Tynes 1987; 1990). For these feminists, an understanding of what shapes women's lives must intertwine an analysis of racism with the Marxist focus on class and the radical feminist focus on the sexual hierarchy. The "circumstances directly encountered, given and transmitted from the past" must include those relations that are the living legacy of colonialism, imperialism, and slavery. Furthermore, they have argued—in opposition to the radical feminist perspective on sexual hierarchy—that, while these relations of racism shape the lives of men and women differently, they do not necessarily privilege men over women (*Feminist Review;* hooks 1988; Lorde 1984; Silvera 1986; Williams 1991).

This challenge initially seemed to create irreconcilable differences among feminists. Michèle Barrett, for example, argued that the proposition that racism must have equal billing with class and sex dislodged the claim of socialist feminists to have a coherent theory of inequality. "Existing theories of social structure, already taxed by attempting to think about the inter-relations of class and gender, have been quite unable to integrate a third axis of systemic inequality into their conceptual maps" (1988, xii). Yet a response to anti-racist feminisms has been taken up by feminists from across the spectrum who have redrawn their theoretical perspectives and political agendas. For example, by looking at the lives of men and women in particular historical and social contexts, some feminists have abandoned the question of whether class, race, or sex is the more salient relation for analysis in favour of understanding the historical specificity of complex relations of power (Adamson, Briskin, and McPhail 1988).

Feminism and Psychoanalysis

Some feminists have turned to psychoanalytic theories to explain how resolutely we are born into particular arrangements (Barrett 1992; Gardiner 1992). Starting from Freud's assertion that "women are made, not born," the focus is upon how infants become gendered, how their sexual preference is shaped, and how they take their place within the hierarchical gendered order. What is particularly pertinent here is how we come to feel ourselves to be men or women as an intrinsic part of our being. This means that we are not just forced to be dominant or submissive, but that we are complicit in our subordination; we collaborate because it feels more comfortable than it would to resist. To put it more strongly, women who resist feel anxiety and therefore guilt, and women who resist make men feel anxious about their masculinity (Benjamin 1988).

Freud's emphasis was upon the key role played by the Oedipus complex in the making of male identity. Little boys take their mothers (because they are the primary caregivers) as their first love object. When they realize unconsciously that these feelings bring them into potential conflict with their fathers, they experience great anxiety—castration anxiety—that their stronger and more powerful fathers will do them some injury for daring to compete with them. In the typical Freudian formulation, the small boy gives up his love for his mother, incorporates his father's standards within himself (the superego), and is bought off, if you like, by the promise of a woman of his own when he grows up. Freud (1965) was much less sure about what happened to the girl child during this period but, nonetheless, he came to believe that little girls also have their first love affair with their mother. They soon realize, however, that they cannot possess the mother because they lack the necessary organ, the penis. Hence Freud's famous, even notorious, insistence that women's identity is shaped profoundly by penis envy.

Feminists working with the insights of psychoanalysis have not simply accepted Freud's formulations. Rather, they have situated them within a societal context that announces to girl and boy children alike that one needs a penis to have power in a patriarchal world. They argue that all children desire everything—penis, breasts, to have a baby (a wish often expressed by little boys as well as girls). Only in a patriarchal world will the desire for a penis become overvalued, and the desire for breasts and pregnancy become undervalued (Hamilton 1986; Horowitz 1977).

Some feminists, following the work of French psychoanalyst Jacques Lacan, have located the formation of masculine and feminine identities not in the process of bodily maturation and Oedipal complexes, but in the child's introduction to what Lacan called the *symbolic order* (Mitchell 1974). This symbolic order includes language—for words are the symbols through which we name everything around us, and are perhaps the most important way in which we communicate with others. What conveys power in this symbolic order is not the penis as such but rather its symbol, the phallus. For the boy child the phallus represents the power that he comes to realize will accrue to him because he is male; the girl child's identity is designated by the boy child (and by her) by what she "lacks." What is important here is that there is no essential meaning or power attached to maleness. Rather this power is defined and conveyed by the whole system of *discourse* in a society—that is, the language, gestures, and all the symbols that convey power for some and lack of power for others. For example, if a father has a special chair in the living room that is bigger and more comfortable than anyone else's including the mothers's, this is not lost on the child; this is part of the discourse that defines not only the hierarchy of male–female power but also introduces the child to his/her own place in this order.

Discourse Analysis

Lacan's ideas have been extremely influential, in part because they merge with those of other major late-twentieth-century theorists, notably Jacques Derrida and Michel Foucault, in highlighting the importance of discourse not only in creating human societies, but in providing whatever access we can have to discussing or understanding society. But discourses, which include but are not restricted to language, do not tell us the truth about the world. They are thoroughly informed not only by prevailing power relations—of class, race, sex, age, sexuality—but also by a kind of common-sense rationale for accepting those power relations as given, as the only way things could be (Belsey 1980).

This discourse also provides the possibilities and constraints for constructing our own identities, identities that are not fixed—as in the expression "the real me"—but rather are fragmented, changing, and contradictory. Freud argued that our psyches are a kind of lifelong battleground among the id, ego, and superego—or, put differently, among desire, possibility, and conscience. More recent theories of discourse accept Freud's idea of the fragmented self. But they shift the ground for explanation away from the body as such to the way that the body—including need and desire—is constituted by the discourse, again as a lifelong, fragmented, contradictory, illusory process. Why illusory? Because discourse can never capture "reality." This is an impossible task for two related reasons. First, the terms of a discourse are always time-bound, space-bound, culture-bound, bound by the multiplicities of power relations that inform daily life. Second, there is no "pure" reality outside of what is represented in discourse. There is no "something" outside of that which is already interpreted, except that which is to be interpreted in some future moment. In this sense, discourse does not represent reality; it shapes and creates that-which-is-believed-to-be-reality.

Central to understanding how this works is to notice that words do not simply describe or identify. Words make distinctions and create oppositions. They tell us what is encompassed in a symbol and, by implication, what is not. Think of the words *hot* and *cold*. These words structure how we describe everything from soup to sex. Yet, as we know, temperature comes on a continuum, and hot and cold are always relative. Hot and cold, when applied to sexual activity, still carry with them the connotations of lust and evil that have so informed Western civilization and the presumed identities of men and women. Medieval Catholic writers depicted women as full of lust, waiting to tempt unsuspecting men into a life of sin. Later, Protestant writers developed a language about women that described them as asexual; it was men who had to control their own lust (Hamilton 1978). A discourse that uses opposing concepts like hot and cold, rational and irrational (emotional), or aggressive and passive to distinguish men from women depicts each sex as either one way *or* the other, and ignores all the points on the continuum that are in between.

Some feminists have drawn upon this critique of the binary oppositions of language, which define the world in terms of opposites, to expand upon the idea of fragmented and shifting identities. Our language helps create the sense that our identities are not only fixed, but gender-determined. When feminists deconstruct this language, they open the space for consideration of identities that are not bound by biological sex, race, age, sexuality, ethnicity, or any other category that we use to fix and freeze identities. If we come back to the Lacanian idea that woman is defined by what she lacks—that is, by what is *not* male—we can see how this works more generally at the level of language.

Women are what men are not. If we say that men are aggressive, we are comparing them directly and indirectly to those—women—who are not. In like manner, if men are rational, women are irrational; if men independent, women are dependent. The point is not that men and women "really" are this way, although in particular times and places they may behave so or they may be believed to be so. Let us reiterate that the discourse does not convey "reality"; rather it constitutes what appears to be reality. Furthermore, women who are not perceived to be passive and emotional may be defined as "not real women," and men who are not perceived to be aggressive may be called effeminate. In such ways, the discourse permits acknowledgment that men and women do not always conform to these oppositions. But the point is that this acknowledgment is made only in the terms of the discourse itself: the categories are retained, but the individual people are labelled as deviants. In this sense, we can speak of discourses as "closed systems"; they make thought that is not consonant with the prevailing discourses difficult.

Using this kind of analysis, feminists have argued that identities are not fixed, but rather are continually constructed in particular times and places. They are not unified, but rather are fragmented: in some circumstances, we feel ourselves to be strong and powerful, in others weak and fragile, in others perhaps creative, stupid, lackadaisical, determined—the list is yours to make and remake. If this is so, the argument goes, how can we then talk about women and men as if these categories mean something that we can all agree upon? The kind of analysis that explores the ways in which language constructs thought has been called poststructuralism.

Feminism and Poststructuralism

For feminist poststructuralists the task has been to

> unmake the chain of binary oppositions—masculine/feminine, market/non-market, public/private, waged/non-waged—and rethink the categoricalism that cantonizes gender, class, race, ethnicity and nationality, so as to see past the conceptual signage, which has illuminated the previously invisible but now threatens to obstruct our view of the living space beyond. (Parr 1990, 8)

The argument in this excerpt from Joy Parr's *The Gender of Breadwinners* is two-pronged. She acknowledges that it was necessary for feminists to use the category of woman in order to "illuminate the previously invisible." Women had been invisible, present only in what was left unexamined, unexplored, unstated. But her main point is that this process of making visible must "see past the conceptual signage." We must not simply recapitulate the pattern of androcentric perspectives and continue to use the categories men and women as though they really described the world.

For by doing this, we fall into two errors. First, we perpetuate the categories of the discourse that once left women invisible. We refer to women and men as if we knew what they were, and we perpetuate the oppositional character of those identities. Women still are defined by what men are not, even though we may now place more value on what-men-are-not. Second, we assume that when we use the word woman we are referring to all women; we collapse the differences among women that accrue from class, racism, heterosexism, imperialism, even the idiosyncrasies of taste and talent. In this way, the theoretical challenges to second wave feminism from women of colour, disabled women, lesbians, bisexuals, and older women converged with those of poststructuralism. The command is "do not tell me what I am."

How might feminist poststructuralists respond to the issue of human agency, and in particular to Marx's statement that we make our history "under circumstances directly encountered, given and transmitted from the past"? The difference from Marx could be located in the definition poststructuralists might give to "circumstances": they want to look at the process through which the categories of male/female, black/white, work/home, public/private are constituted in time and place, and how those categories, as they are defined at any particular time, contribute to the range of possibility and constraint. Furthermore, unlike Marx and most feminists before them, they argue that the ways in which male and female are defined are also implicated in all other categorization, whether of class, race, or sexual preference. How, for example, has "working-class" as a category in the language informed shifting definitions of masculinity and, through inclusion and exclusion, shifting definitions of femininity? At the same time, how are gender definitions infused by notions of class?

Language appears innocent, in that it appears simply as an instrument through which our ideas can be expressed. Students often express this with the statement "I know what I think, but I just can't get it down on paper." But let us take a familiar example to see how language does not express our pre-existing thought, but actually shapes that thought. The term *working mother* has come into the language in the last twenty years with the great influx into the formal waged economy of women who have children. Embedded in the phrase, implicitly, are a whole host of shifting, value-laden, gendered, and classed characters. Counterposed to working mother are *women who don't work* (and who "just" keep house and look after children) and the victims of working mothers, *neglected children* (those whose mothers do not "just" look after them). Implicit in the phrase working mothers is a cast of male characters. Whoever heard of a *working father*, or children who were neglected because their father worked? Working mother can also designate those women who take jobs away from men, therefore contributing to the category *unemployed men*—fathers who don't work and therefore are, by definition, *bad fathers*. Furthermore, working mother is more likely to be used with reference to women who do certain kinds of *class-related* occupations that have relatively low monetary rewards and little status. Women who work in other sorts of class-related occupations may be defined as *professionals* rather than working mothers. Here we see the operation of a kind of implicit override clause: sometimes gender terms take precedence, other times class terms, or racist terms, or terms referring to women's sexual lives.

Words do not just say what they appear to say; they carry and create shifting identities, possibilities, and constraints. Joy Parr's description of gendered identities during a 1949 garment workers' strike in Paris, Ontario, captures the feminist poststructuralist perspective: "gendered identities were masks that changed in the shifting light and shadow of the dispute—mercurial, unpredictable in the effects upon public sympathy" (Parr 1990, 113).

Feminist Theories and Social Change

Feminist theories about human society are also, explicitly or implicitly, theories about the possibilities for social transformation and, in particular, for emancipation for the subordinated, oppressed, exploited, and excluded. Indeed, these theories play a role in producing or complicating their own predictions about the future. This is because theories that present ideas confirming peoples' sense of grievance also help to legitimate their resistance. For example, Marx's theories provided people throughout the world with an ideological legitimation to engage in revolution. Catholics in Latin America intertwined their religious beliefs with an understanding of Marxism to argue that the church should be on the side of the oppressed in this life as opposed to simply promising them an eternal reward after a life of suffering—"the preferential option of the poor" (Baum 1986). This complex set of beliefs, called *liberation theology*, contributed to widespread forms of social protest as a new generation of church workers challenged the church's age-old admonition that entrance into heaven depended upon acceptance of the hierarchy of this world. While few theories—perhaps none—have unsettled the powerful as much as Marxism, feminism arguably is running a close second. As women the world over increasingly question their subordination, victimization, and exclusion, they appropriate, revise, and develop theoretical perspectives to legitimate their struggles.

Social theories, then, address the question of how things change. Included in such theories is consideration of the role of conscious human intervention—*agency*—in bringing about social change. Marxist theory argues that the working class has the potential to become a conscious agent of liberation. The initial site for the development of a shared consciousness of exploitation is the point of production—that is, the workplace. But socialist feminists have argued that women's collective and specific oppression is located in the private sphere and in the interrelationship between private and public. This suggests that Marxism, left to its own devices, does not provide sufficient legitimation, let alone an adequate strategy, for the "rising of the women" (Tax 1980). Socialist feminists insist that women organize around their own interests in the workplace and that their demands address their interests as mothers and wives as well as their interests as waged workers. These considerations involve a critique not only of relations between workers and employers but also of the relations between men and women in both public and intimate spaces.

Some radical feminist theorists draw such an unyielding account of women's subordination and victimization that they have difficulty explaining how women ever came to resist, indeed how the women's movement itself could ever have mobilized. Where was the space for the development of rebellious ideas, let alone the possibility for acting upon them? In a similar way, those feminists who have drawn upon, elaborated, and critiqued Lacan's idea of the child's linguistic entrance into the symbolic order seem, at times, to create a closed system, impervious to change. Luce Irigaray has argued that women are excluded from the discourse of the symbolic order. If we are to glimpse what women think or feel, we must attend to the silences in their discourse, to the ways in which they may parody what men say. As a theorist, Irigaray repeats what male theorists have written, playing on their words to make her subtle point. From this perspective, we may have access to what women imagine, but even these triumphs of imagination are, necessarily, entangled within masculine discourse (Berg 1991). Does such a perspective leave a space for women's resistance?

Feminist poststructuralists have also been accused by other feminists of pulling the rug out from under the women's movement (Brodribb 1992; Hartsock 1990; Modleski 1991). If identities are fractured, if ideas of women and men must be deconstructed rather than accepted as given, what are the grounds for a feminist movement? If people are going to mobilize politically, they have to mobilize around something. In the women's movement the mobilization has been—it sounds self-evident to say it—around and about and for women. What happens when the rallying cries about women's oppression, their common interests and needs, indeed their victimization, are invalidated?

Although recent theoretical developments informed by poststructuralism challenge the concept of identity, and therefore of woman, in ways that appear, to some, to shake the foundations of the women's movement, the questions about what a woman is inform older perspectives as well. The category woman—what she is and what she should do—lies at the heart of most feminist analysis, albeit in different ways. Liberal feminists, dating back to the eighteenth century, argued that if women appeared less rational, less interested in the world, less given to philosophical thought and political activity, the explanation resided in the ways in which women were denied the opportunity for education. Women would be as rational as some men (and as irrational as some others) if they were treated similarly in social terms. Genetic makeup, biology, or reproductive capacities accounted for the essence of woman no more than for the essence of man. In the terms of the times, therefore, Mary Wollstonecraft challenged the category of woman and, also, although less systematically, that of man. Men, Wollstonecraft lamented, were disappointing in their inattention to love and emotional life. Contemporary liberal feminists argue that there are no tasks in the public sphere—including armed combat roles in the military—for which women are unsuitable. At the same time, they have argued for parental leave for fathers after birth, adoption, and in the case of children's illness. To the extent that we are defined by what we do, and what we have the capacity to do, liberal feminists have challenged dominant notions about women and men. Far from being discrete categories, women and men are more likely to overlap in their motivations, goals, and talents.

Socialist feminists go further than liberal feminists in challenging the concept of woman as a universal category. Following Marx, they argue that the consciousness of human beings reflects the activities in which they engage and the accompanying relationships they create. Women in different historical periods and different social classes are not only different from each other, but in some respects share more with the men of their time and station than they do with other women. Furthermore, by analyzing the interconnections between the private and public sphere, revealing and challenging the attempts to relegate women to the first, insisting that the tasks done in the household constituted "more than a labour of love," and renaming that activity domestic labour or work, socialist feminists challenged the dominant idea that held that male and female nature and identities were discrete.

Early radical feminists like Shulamith Firestone argued that the differences between men and women resided only in their different roles in reproduction. While these differences had been crucial in creating social inequality, increasing control over pregnancy and birth as well as the promise of reproductive technology could (and should) eliminate the social consequences of these differences. The categories of woman and man would cease to matter after the socialist feminist revolution. Some later radical feminists reclaim the category woman, suggesting that it possesses certain qualities and attributes that distinguish it in important and irreconcilable ways from the category man. At the same time, many radical feminist analyses increasingly address the question of diversity among women, diversity resulting from class, racism, age, ethnicity, religious conviction, and sexuality.

Some of the most trenchant criticisms of the assumption that there is a category called woman that may be used in theoretical discussions and political mobilization come from women of colour in the first world and women in non-Western societies. Their analyses expose the chasms between dominant ideologies about woman and the lives that women lead, the assumptions of white feminists about female exploitation and oppression, and the centrality of racism, imperialism, and cultural specificity in structuring their lives as women (White 1993). They have challenged any attempt to universalize the category woman and to counterpose the category woman to man. Paradoxically—paralleling the air-tight categories of man and woman created by some radical feminists—some of these writers produce discrete racialized identities of their own: categories of white and black, women of colour and white women. The title *Black Feminist Thought* implies another category, white feminist thought (Collins 1990). But most of these writers have an explicit goal: to challenge racism and the ways in which racism creates hierarchical categories of white and black. In their challenges to white feminists to confront their own racism, they insist that identities based on racial difference are politically and socially created. Furthermore, by looking at the ways in which racism and multinational capitalism inform people's lives, they also break down any sense of discrete categories of man and woman.

Seen in this light, the feminist poststructuralist assault on the concept of fixed identity of any sort—woman/man, white/black, straight/gay—does not go against the grain of most previous feminist analysis. When Denise Riley says at the end of *"Am I that Name?"* (1987) that there are times when we need to mobilize "as if" there were women, she puts into words an implicit assumption underlying much previous feminist analysis and action: women should not be defined by their biology; their life chances should not be defined by their relationships to men; the social constraints that have been legitimated by biological difference from men—whether women's size and physical strength or their role in reproduction—must be challenged. All this suggests, in line with Riley and other feminist poststructuralists, that human beings will be defined and will define themselves less than previously by ascribed characteristics of sex.

Perhaps the differences between poststructuralists and other feminists over the concept of identity have been overdrawn. Yet that is not the whole story. Poststructuralism does not focus on identities as the properties of human beings, but rather considers how identities are animated within and through discourses. The focus of analysis shifts from the subject in history and the relationships between people to an analysis of the discourse. This involves attending to how the structure of language informs thought and constructs identities. Not only what is said, but what is not said; not just what is said but how it is said; not just what can be said but that which cannot be said: this is what constitutes the focus for poststructuralist analysis. When Riley critiques the subject of woman in history, it is in the context of a perspective that dislodged the very concept of subject from a privileged place in social analysis.

Thus, it is very clear that there are major tensions within feminist theories. If the portrait of female subordination is painted in unequivocal terms, there is no way to explain or, indeed, hope for transformation. If, on the other hand, female identity across culture, time, space, situation, even moment-to-moment is completely contingent, what are the grounds or purposes of a women's movement (Butler 1993; Nicholson 1990; Riley 1987; Scott 1988)?

This question—about the grounds and purposes for women's movements—is a poignant one for feminist scholars. The remarkable and exponential development of feminist scholarship, perspectives, theories, and creative writing in the last twenty-five years originates with the questions, demands, and goals of the contemporary women's movement. Understanding this important convergence is also a theoretical/historical undertaking. In seeking answers, feminists have taken up the question of the origins of gender hierarchies, not just the contemporary questions about "in whose interest" such hierarchies are sustained, but also questions about ultimate origins. How contingent are the categories man and woman? To what extent do they encapsulate and describe biological and sociological realities? How do we begin to answer those who claim that feminists are tampering with the laws of God and nature when they critique and seek to transform the relations between men and women? How serious a challenge to hitherto existing, androcentric knowledge do feminists pose?

Origins of Gender Hierarchy

In seeking to explain the pervasiveness, and therefore the origins, of female subordination, feminists confront vast multicultural, theological, biological, archeological, and anthropological literatures that assume and justify gender hierarchy in terms of biological differences, sexual temperaments, divine ordinance, and natural proclivities. The argument about biological difference has been the most difficult to combat because such differences seem to be irreducibly natural. Indeed, a challenge to biological difference has often appeared ridiculous, a joke guaranteed to elicit laughter. In their practices and claims to domination, men appeared to have nature on their side. While assumptions about biological differences were once much easier to make, they are not without their vocal proponents today, both among the powerful and those with little power, among men and women.

Physical Size and Male Bonding

Let us look then at two different kinds of biological arguments—or rationalizations—for gender hierarchy that continue to enjoy broad consensus. On average, and in any particular society, men are bigger and physically stronger. This has led to a set of explanations that have insisted that men are more aggressive, and even that they have been genetically programmed to act collectively—through what has been called male bonding—in order to impose their will on women. Lionel Tiger is perhaps the best-known advocate of this position which, at times, appears strikingly disingenuous: even if women want to become political leaders they cannot "because males are strongly predisposed to form and maintain all-male groups, particularly when matters of moment for the community are involved" (1969, 75). This was clearly a message that many wanted to hear. If biology is necessary—and Tiger states (p. 46) that "sex differences are perforce related to male bonding and . . . male bonding is related to breeding advantage"—women and men may as well accept that the relations of patriarchy will be with us from here to eternity.[3]

Ideas like Tiger's, which attempt to explain gendered social practices in terms of biological differences—part of the whole field of *sociobiology*—tend to be used to confirm rather than question the socio-historical relations between the sexes. As a result, feminists have tended to reject not only the specific findings of sociobiology but the whole field of inquiry (Hubbard 1990). Sociobiologist Sarah Hrdy has argued that this is short-sighted and that there is a great deal to be learned from sociobiology about the evolution of human society (1981, 198). Sociobiology is not inherently sexist, she argues; rather its practitioners have been sexist: when the evolution of the female differs from the evolution of the male, the female is treated as an irrelevant deviation from the norm.

A good example, Hrdy argues, is the female potential to be multi-orgasmic. Sociobiologists have regarded this as an aberration, with no importance for the survival of the species. Hrdy argues that if they took their own precepts seriously—that there are no genuine flukes—they would have had to explore the reasons for this adaptation. Without going into her particular explanations, what is germane here is her argument that the female of the species has evolved in a way to maximize her survival and the survival of her children. This has involved the development of competition as an adaptation to environment. Males, she demonstrates, have no genetic monopoly on competitive forms of behaviour.

Feminist archaeologists and anthropologists have been in a good position to argue that the usual assumptions of sociobiology are the assumptions of an ideology of male supremacy. By approaching societies with a set of critical questions about the distribution of resources, the relations of power, and the division of labour, feminists have discovered that in many human societies women provide, in one way or another, most of the food necessary for the survival of themselves, the men, and their children. Feminist scholars were not as impressed as earlier observers that men hunted and occasionally brought back slaughtered animals for meat, particularly when hunting might supply as little as 10 percent of that society's food. Meanwhile, women and older children were gathering, and perhaps planting and cultivating, the rest. Furthermore, feminists noticed that the women often worked together to do this, developing co-operative strategies in order to care for children, provide the necessities of life, and create a material and social culture. Recently, some anthropologists have also speculated that men did not even have a monopoly on hunting.

The differences in physical size between men and women and the surmised differences in genetic aptitude for bonding have not impressed feminist researchers trying to explain the near universality of sexual hierarchies. But there is another set of biological differences that feminists have taken more seriously in their quest for explanations: namely, those differences related to the reproduction of the species.

The Sexual Division of Reproductive Labour

Women do almost all reproductive work. Men's role has been necessary, but so invisible that uncovering their participation was a rather late development in human history. That our early ancestors managed to link two events—conception and birth—that come nine months apart and are of such different order is quite mind-boggling. Most children, quite sensibly, do not believe it when they are first told how babies are made.

The process of pregnancy, childbirth, and lactation has meant that if women do not do the reproductive labour, it will not be done. Reproductive differences have underwritten an assumption that this natural division of reproductive labour has an autonomous life of its own, impervious to the social environment in which it occurs. Further, these differences have provided a point of departure for arguing that the hierarchical relations between men and women derive from this division of labour. There are several major problems with the leap that takes us first from "women have the babies" to "therefore women's lives are grounded in nature's imperatives," and from there to "therefore women are destined to be subordinate to men."

First, only women *can* have babies, but not all women choose to do so. Throughout the ages women have tried to control their fertility, and often these attempts were thwarted by religious teachings, law, and the suppression of information (Gordon 1976). In Canada it was illegal until 1969 for doctors to provide their patients with birth control information and for pharmacists to sell contraceptive devices (McLaren and McLaren 1986). Recent social programs in Quebec include financial incentives for parents for each child that they have (Maroney 1992). The historical record—particularly in France, which has a long record of providing such inducements—indicates that, if women have their price, it is more than any government has yet been prepared to offer. Clearly, women cannot always be counted upon to produce the number of children those in power wish them to produce (Vickers 1987). Women have remained celibate for life or for periods of time; they have loved women rather than men; they have developed and practised methods of birth control; they have self-aborted or sought help from others. African women, on board slave ships en route to America, are known to have killed their newborns rather than have them live the lives to which they were destined.

Second, while some women have refused to bear or suckle children or have been coerced or persuaded to do so, others have been encouraged or forced not to reproduce. State regulations have sometimes stipulated that women be sterilized before qualifying for social welfare; third-world women have been treated like laboratory animals by first-world pharmaceutical companies engaged in contraceptive research.

Third, the assumption of the naturalness of women's reproductive role neglects the enormous variations in the conditions under which women in different historical periods, cultures, and social classes have children (Armstrong and Armstrong 1986). Sometimes the economic and political organization of the society facilitates their reproductive work; other times there are enormous obstacles. In most cases, no special privileges greet pregnant women: if they are living in destitution, they will bear their children in destitution; if they live in countries at war, they will remain at risk; if they are subject to racist ideologies and practices, pregnancy will not alleviate them. Also, infanticide has been a widespread practice in many societies. We know little about how women have felt about this, but what we do know suggests that there is always a level of economic or political coercion involved in their decision. In Canadian society, pregnancy was considered sufficient grounds for dismissal from paid employment until recently, and these social practices die hard.

Fourth, there has been a related assumption that women's reproductive labour linked them more with the animal kingdom than with the productive labour of (primarily male) human beings. Mary O'Brien was the first to argue systematically that although women who carry their infants to term do not have a choice about engaging in reproductive labour, this does not mean that they do not actively and consciously engage in this labour. Through this labour, women mediate their relationship with their children, and more generally between the generations and continued life on the planet. Reproductive labour is human labour, actively entered into and, like productive labour, it shapes the consciousness of women so engaged (O'Brien 1981).

Fifth, although the link between women and childbearing was produced by nature, the link between women and childcare (outside of lactation) is humanly created. Men may actually do very little of the world's nurturing work. Their biology is not the reason; rather their biology has been invoked as the rationale for this lack of participation. Enough men have done enough of this work to indicate that their relative absence from this line of work is not a result of genetic programming.

Sixth, the link between childbearing and female subordination is clearly an invention—a highly ingenious invention—developed in most, though perhaps not all, human societies (Gough 1973; Leacock 1981). That the forms of female subordination are neither universal nor uniform constitute sufficient grounds for believing that the hierarchical relations between men and women are socially constructed. But even those feminists who insist most strenuously that women have always been subordinate, and that the roots of this subordination are to be found in the division of reproductive labour, argue that this does not mean that women must remain subordinate. In *The Dialectic of Sex,* Shulamith Firestone argued that women's subordination, stemming from nature's unequal allotment of reproductive tasks, was universal. But, in her words, "to grant that the sexual balance of power is biologically based is not to lose our case. We are no longer just animals. And the Kingdom of Nature does not reign absolute" (1970, 10).

It is difficult to avoid concluding that the sexual division of reproductive labour has made it possible, though not necessary, for men in many different kinds of societies to dominate and control women and their children. Indeed, the organization of contemporary Canadian society ensures that women who bear children will be at economic, political, and social disadvantage compared to the men of their social class, ethnic group, and age. But as this discussion of the sexual division of reproductive labour indicates, this hierarchy is not our natural inheritance, but rather is socially and historically constructed in ways that need to be explored in each situation (Parr 1990).

I am persuaded, however, that if we are to understand the subordination of women historically and cross-culturally, and understand why women have not resisted that subordination in great numbers throughout history, we must take into account the sexual division of reproductive labour. It has meant that most women have been dependent upon men for at least part of their adult lives, and that men have had more freedom—more time and energy—to consolidate their power over women. This question of the origins of the gender hierarchy and the role of the sexual division of labour is, I believe, necessary for understanding the broadest sweep of human history (back to its unrecorded beginnings), and why and how this history is so pervasively and variously shaped by gender hierarchies. But Firestone's vision that women's liberation would arrive with the development of test-tube babies (and therefore the end of the reproductive division of labour between men and women) appears naive, at best, less than three decades later.

Apart from simple methods of artificial insemination that permit women without male partners or with infertile male partners to conceive, much of the development of new reproductive technologies has been criticized by feminists (Overall 1993). Their research demonstrates that these technologies are primarily under the control of men, that women have highly unequal access to them depending on their social class and sexual orientation, and that these technologies are linked to forms of genetic engineering and systems of control that provoke prophecies of new forms of fascism rather than women's liberation. Sexual hierarchies are no longer dependent upon a division of reproductive labour but are thoroughly implicated with the complex relations of power that animate contemporary society. Indeed, new reproductive technologies develop *within* the context of those relations of power and threaten to serve and consolidate them.

Feminist theories are not just about explaining sexual hierarchies. They also aim to understand how and why women resist their subordinate status. This discussion requires a brief diversion into the more general question of how those in power retain—and eventually may lose—their power. This question hinges on the ability of the dominant to convince the dominated that the power relations between them are legitimate, even natural.

Legitimating Power, Challenging Power

Just as the kings of the Middle Ages and the aristocrats who lived off the court propagated the idea of the divine right of kings, so many men have insisted that their power is naturally or divinely ordained. A fairly new strategy undertaken by some men, including men in political elites, has been to deny that men have more power or resources than women. The result is similar, however, serving to consolidate the status quo: dominant groups do not willingly give up their prerogatives. About this much, at least, the historical record is clear. There may be a bit of cross-dressing: Friedrich Engels Sr owned factories; yet his son co-authored *The Communist Manifesto* with Karl Marx. Struggles for the abolition of slavery included white men and white women (though not many slave owners). There is evidence of some cross-class solidarity in feminist movements. Some men have allied themselves with feminist struggles, even in the early part of this century when it was a far less popular cause. Yet such exceptions serve to throw into relief that which is usually taken for granted: that the ideas developed, believed, and perpetrated by dominant groups legitimate their power. These ideas explain the relations of power and the distribution of resources in the society in ways that make them appear eminently reasonable and correct, not just to those whose interests they protect, but to those who are oppressed and exploited by them.

There is nothing necessarily conspiratorial about this. We all develop explanations for what we are doing that try to make sense of our behaviour and to justify our actions. But we all do not have the same opportunity to disseminate our ideas, to persuade others, and to pass laws that help produce the outcomes we wish. For example, the elites in the feudal world were well-served by the teachings of the Roman Catholic Church: kings and peasants alike were encouraged to accept their worldly conditions and to anticipate retribution or compensation in the afterlife. These teachings, drawn selectively from the Old and New Testaments, encouraged the rich to be charitable towards the poor and the poor to resign themselves to their fate. Peasants resisted increased impositions by church, state, or lords, but they seldom attacked the whole edifice. When they did, the results were bloody (Ladurie 1974).

The ideas of the dominant class or the elites are accepted, in large part, because they appear to describe everyday reality. Those in power *are* more articulate by the very standards that they are in a position to create, define, and enforce; they do have more formal education; and they do own most of the wealth. Dominant groups, then, tend to have a monopoly not just on societal resources and the means to attain and retain them, but also on the development and dissemination of ideas.

Challenges to dominant ideas do not come out of the air; they make their entrance onto the world stage with groups of people whose life activities and relationships are changing in ways that bring their needs and desires into conflict with the dominant social practices and ideas of the time (Williams 1981). All this happens in a most uneven sort of way. The power to effect change is highly variable; laws need to be enforced, not just made. The language encountered from the past and the meaning given to words must be renegotiated (Williams 1976). In aristocratic society, for example, the word work was pejorative; it implied that a man had insufficient income to live a life of ease and had to turn to trade or manual labour. Over time the word was redefined by the developing bourgeoisie. Work became a sign of virtue and worth; those who did not work did not deserve to eat. What is key here is that challenges to established authority and power occur, and in this process great transformations can be wrought.

Women's Resistance, Women's Movements

Exploring how and why women resist deprivation and oppression has intrigued feminist scholars from different theoretical and disciplinary perspectives. The next chapter explores how feminist theories developed within social movements, especially women's movements, as an integral part of their protests against the existing order. From these movements, feminist theories first made their way into the academy through both direct and circuitous means and, I would argue, their continuing presence in university curricula and politics depends upon their maintaining interconnections with emancipatory social movements.

Women's movements are explicitly political—that is, they aim to change social hierarchies, law, policies, and distribution of resources. In so doing, they constitute theoretical challenges to the relations of domination and subordination between men and women. An important aspect of feminist theories has been to seek explanations for women's subordination, the ways in which their subordination is maintained, and the ways in which they have tried to resist the consequences of their inferior status. This question of resistance is of great importance. For feminist theories themselves are products, manifestations, and tools of that resistance.

Chapter 2 provides an interpretation of the contemporary women's movement, which may be dated from the late 1960s, although this demarcation is contentious. Historian Veronica Strong-Boag has argued, for example, that there have been women's movements in Canada throughout the twentieth century. While there is certainly evidence for women's reforming activity throughout this period, I aim to show that books like this could not have been written before the 1970s because the questions had not been raised, the analysis not developed, the issues not publicly acknowledged.

My criteria for selecting the women's movement as an event, and for locating its origin in the late 1960s are simple. Not only did people look at each other and their society differently thereafter, but relationships, policies, perceptions, and public and private discourse changed, in almost every respect. These changes were neither straightforward nor linear; they produced new contradictions and dilemmas; and they certainly, in retrospect, represent histories of unintended consequences that were unanticipated by those who initiated them. But from this period on, whatever people *thought* about gender, gender relations, and gender inequality, these questions were up for discussion. No forum was too public or too intimate to preclude them.

My construction of this event is intended to demarcate a transition. As historical sociologist Philip Abrams (1982, 195) put it, "events are defined not by any measure of detail, specificity or concreteness within the chronology of happenings but by their significance as markers of transition." If we date the women's movement in Canada from the late 1960s, it becomes possible to speak about "before" and "after" on virtually every topic that has been raised by feminists. That does not mean that everything changed in the way that the participants and supporters of the movement intended. But there was a sea change, or so the next chapter aims to demonstrate.

Notes

1. In *Eve and the New Jerusalem*, Barbara Taylor (1983, xv–xvi) provides persuasive evidence that earlier Owenite socialists had called for a "multi-faceted offensive against all forms of social hierarchy, including sexual hierarchy." Marxists replaced this, she argues, with "a dogmatic insistence on the primacy of class-based issues, a demand for sexual unity in the face of a common class enemy, and a vague promise of improved status for women 'after the revolution'."
2. Within socialism, however, there is a history of feminist struggle that feminist historians have brought to light in their research. See, for example, Barbara Taylor (1979).
3. Monique Bégin, who served as executive secretary and director of research for the Royal Commission on the Status of Women, reports that Lionel Tiger was one of the unsuccessful applicants for funding from the commission. He sought funding for his work on male bonding (1992, 33).

The Women's Movement(s)

CHAPTER 2

IN APRIL 1977, *Weekend Magazine* ran a cover story entitled "Beyond Sisterhood," proclaiming that the women's movement was dead. A large wreath of the sort that is placed on tombstones graced the magazine cover (Dewar 1977). The accompanying article was not persuasive; the more interesting story is the continuing propensity of the media to declare the death of the women's movement and of feminism. Indeed, any consideration of the women's movement must deal with the range and scale of the counter-revolution or backlash that the movement has unleashed, including reports of its demise. There is a complex and ongoing history of women's resistance and the resistance to their resistance. As a result, any evaluation of the goals and strategies adopted by women's movement activists is very difficult. At times success in a particular area—abortion rights or daycare, for example—seems imminent, only to be replaced by profound defeat and remobilization.

This chapter begins with a consideration of the following questions: What were the conditions that help to explain the rise of the women's movement that began in Canada in the late 1960s? How was it possible for all the social movements of the 1960s, but in particular the women's movement, to go so unheralded—by the media and social scientists alike—in the preceding decades (Adamson, Brisken, and McPhail 1988; Black 1993, 151; Morris 1980; Phillips 1991, 763)? How can we explain women's resistance in this time and place?

Background to the Women's Movement

THE 1950S APPEARED TO BE A CONFORMING and, in many ways, complacent decade in Canada and, indeed, in the other Western capitalist countries. Postwar affluence and the expansion of capitalist enterprises and educational opportunities seemed to converge in an ideology of prosperity and conformity. In the United States, well-known sociologist Daniel Bell wrote a book called *The End of Ideology* (1960) in which he suggested that the days of causes, struggles, and revolutions were over. More than anything else, he argued, youth, working people, and racial and ethnic minorities aspired to share in the good life of middle-class affluence and security. Those already partaking in this good life—prominent among them university-employed social scientists like Bell—agreed that slowly, but inexorably, middle-class living standards, values, and lifestyle were spreading throughout society. The vehicle for this development was not the cries of anguish and concerted action of people in social movements, but the spirit of progress itself, propelling American society to fulfil its special destiny—a society on automatic pilot. As Bell put it, "the United States is probably the first large society in history to have change and innovation built into its culture" (1960, 35).

Textbooks on the family set out a model of companionate marriage, with men pursuing solid careers and women making apple pie and raising solid little children (Cheal 1991; Parsons 1959; Seeley, Sim, and Loosley 1956). Unions would be content to negotiate on economic issues—every man's salary should be enough to support him and his wife and children. If there were some people still left out, it was only a matter of time until the benefits of rational economic production and business-as-usual democracy spread slowly and painlessly throughout the country. No more stirring slogans, no more idealistic youth. With the communist dream revealed as a living nightmare in Stalin's Soviet Union, and German and Italian fascism defeated, America settled down to enjoy its eternal and unchanging place in the sun.

Canada appeared a pale but loyal imitation of the American Dream. There was less wealth but, as the closest neighbour of the United States, sharing the much-vaunted longest undefended border in the world, the standard of living would continue to rise just as surely as more American-made television sets brought more American-made programs into happy Canadian homes.

If social scientists made their livings according to the quality of their predictions, most would have lost their jobs during the subsequent decade. With the advantages of hindsight, the subterranean events that eluded educated middle-class observers in the 1950s become visible. To understand the development of the women's movement in Canada, we need to look at two distantly related events: first, the growth of the double day of labour for women coupled with the decline of the marriage contract and, second, the rise of the movements for social and economic justice.

The Double Day of Labour and the Decline of the Marriage Contract

In *The Hearts of Men: American Dreams and the Flight from Commitment* (1983), Barbara Ehrenreich makes the controversial but persuasive argument that the feminist revolt of the late 1960s was, in large measure, a response to an earlier male revolt. She posits that, by the 1950s, the men of the upper managerial ranks were twitching uneasily in their role as breadwinner, mostly absentee-father, and faithful husband. The *Playboy* alternative (the magazine was first published in 1953) recommended that men should pursue affluence in order to share their wealth with a series of beautiful women, rather than a permanent and boring wife with her boring and demanding children. *Playboy*'s first feature article was a "no-holds-barred attack on 'the whole concept of alimony' and, secondarily, on money-hungry women in general, entitled 'Miss Gold-Digger of 1953'." As Ehrenreich continues, "from the beginning, *Playboy* loved women—large-breasted, long-legged, young women, anyway—and hated wives" (1988, 43). How did all this feel to a young woman, growing up to believe that her goal was to marry a man who would support her forever in return for being a gracious homemaker, interesting bedmate, and perfect mother for his children? Women were to chase; men to run and finally succumb. Ehrenreich argues that affluent men were the first to tire of the deal. Hence the popularity of *Playboy*.

A young woman went to university in the 1950s and 60s, so it was said, to catch a man, thus earning her degree—an MRS. At Queen's University in Kingston, this idea was captured in the welcoming ceremony for co-eds: the women carried candles with a ribbon; the ribbon was said to be in the colours of the faculty of their future (and still unmet) husband. In retrospect, Queen's alumna Priscilla Galloway asked why she had married at nineteen, while still in the middle of her under-graduate work. In 1949, given that a woman and her children would be economically dependent on her husband, such a decision made sense. As Galloway put it, "marriage held the illusion of security" (1987, 109).

What was breaking down in these pre-women's-movement years was the social contract between men and women, a contract codified in law. The contract stipulated that men would share their wages with their wives in exchange for housekeeping, cooking, sex, and full-time care for their children. Ehrenreich argues that this contract was being attacked frontally by upper-middle-class managerial men. But it was also being eroded on several other fronts.

To begin with, most men had never earned enough to support their wives and children. Not only did most women married to working-class men do the domestic labour and childcare, they also supplemented wages in a variety of ways: taking in boarders, laundry, and other people's children, doing piecework distributed from factories, and exchanging services with friends and neighbours (Bradbury 1979; Cohen 1988). Yet the ideology about a man earning a family wage, despite its origins and material reality in the upper middle class, was applied to everyone. All husbands were judged (by others and often themselves) by those standards: a good man did not "send his wife out to work." As one retired male factory worker in Hanover, Ontario, remarked, "if the man is able to work, the man should be able to provide enough money to support his wife at home" (Parr 1990, 198). More liberal-minded men might "let" their wives go to work.

How did this ideology hold such sway when there were so many households to which it did not apply? This is a difficult question, but it is important to realize that ideologies are not just formulated by what they do say, but also, and more importantly, by what they leave out—by what some have called the silences in a society's common-sense discourse. In this case, the economic contributions of women were not referred to in a straightforward way. Far from indicating her accomplishments, a wife's waged work constituted evidence of her husband's inadequacy: her contributions referred directly or obliquely to that which her husband did not do. At best, her contributions were downplayed or rendered invisible by inattention, conscious and unconscious. A waitress, married to a farmer, told me in the summer of 1990, "I *only* have to earn enough for our food [my emphasis]." This seems a large "only."[1]

By the beginning of the 1960s, real wages were declining for many working men, and wives could no longer stretch the wages to cover all their families' expenses. As Armstrong and Armstrong demonstrate, "the requirements of households for cash income tended to increase faster than did the real wages of the men in them." There were several reasons for this: "Lengthening education, expanding services and changing ideologies made children more expensive. Taxes, mortgages, heating and transportation costs grew much more rapidly than those related to goods women could still produce in the home placing further stress on household budgets" (1988, 160–61). At the same time, more jobs were opening in the expanding service sectors, and more and more women added full-time waged work to their domestic responsibilities. Even then, the ideology of man the provider and woman the nurturer proved elastic: women were working for "extras," people said. This belief legitimated lower wages for women, perpetuated the idea of women's marginal economic contributions to their households, and assumed that women would continue to do the bulk of household work and childcare. It seems that men had quite a deal, the complaints of the followers of the *Playboy* message notwithstanding.

But women were also on the verge of calling this division of labour into question. By the 1960s, the contradictions involved in women being mothers first—"working mothers"—at the same time that they were doing full-time waged work ultimately were too great to be contained by the old ideology. Table 2-1 shows that the percentage of married women working for wages outside the home rose steadily until the late 1980s, as did the rates for women with children under six. Women began to pressure men for "help" at home and governments for new policies on childcare, maternity leave, and wages. The struggles that ensued at the household level were sufficiently intense and numerous that women's double day of work moved dramatically from what C. Wright Mills called *private trouble*—a personal problem for the individual to sort out quietly—to *public issue*—a societal dilemma requiring changes in laws and policies (1959, 8–11). The new ideas articulated through such struggles—public daycare, equal pay for work of equal value, shared parenting and household work, and control over reproduction, as well as a critique of the devastating consequences of economic dependence for many women—all shaped and found expression within the women's movements of the 1970s.

TABLE 2-1

Shifts in Labour-Force Participation of Women in Canada:
Women Who Work Outside the Home, 1931–91

	% of all women	% of married women	% of mothers with children under 6
1931	19.4	3.5	–
1951	24.4	11.2	–
1961	29.3	22.0	–
1971	38.3	37.0	27.7
1981	51.6	50.5	47.2
1991	53.0	55.9	56.5

Source: Adapted from McDaniel (1993), 428, and Statistics Canada (1993), 9, 10, 12.

Social scientists did not anticipate the societal changes involved in the rise of the women's double day of labour and the decline of the marriage contract. Nor did they predict the event—often referred to now simply as "the Sixties"—that provided a catalyst and context for the rise of the women's movements (Adamson, Brisken, and McPhail 1988, 38–42; Kostash 1980). For our purposes, we focus on the movements for social and economic justice that characterized that decade and beyond.

The Social Movements of the 1960s

Movements such as the civil rights movement, the student movement, the new left, the resurgence of the old left, the anti-nuclear and peace movement, the black power movement, and the anti–Vietnam War movement (which brought many American draft resisters and their wives and lovers to Canada) shared a rhetoric calling for economic and social justice. These movements, separately and together, exploded two related myths: that everyone was getting better off, and that getting better off was all anybody wanted.

There were many differences among the members of these overlapping movements: the scions of affluent families looking for more meaning than that provided by replicating their parents' lifestyle in suburbia;

American blacks seeking to overturn the de facto segregation that had existed in the South since the Civil War; urban blacks determined to blast their way out of geographic and economic ghettos; young men unwilling to accept the draft if it meant fighting and dying in a war in Vietnam; women determined to stop the proliferation of weapons of destruction (Adamson, Brisken, and McPhail 1988; Macpherson 1994).

The gap between the rhetoric of the male-dominated social movements and the way many women perceived their own treatment as activists *within* these movements provided, by many accounts, a significant catalyst for the women's movement (Bernstein et al. 1972; Burstyn 1990; Evans 1979; Mitchell 1971). By the late 1960s, there was a visible, active, and growing women's movement—first called the women's liberation movement—in all of the Western industrialized countries, including Canada.

During the same period, the numbers of younger feminist radicals multiplied as college-educated women began to recognize the huge gap between the rhetoric of equality that had underwritten their education and the choices (or lack of choices, more properly put) that awaited them upon graduation. Although they did not realize it at the time, they owed their right to an education and access to professions to those feminists who had struggled for these rights during the latter decades of the nineteenth and first two decades of the twentieth centuries. But first wave feminists—many without formal education or economic independence—had, for the most part, left the family untouched by systematic critique. Women needed men economically to support them and their children; men were the only meal ticket in town, and marriage the only socially acceptable way to acquire one. The bequest of first wave feminists to later generations of women was the right to a higher education, the possibility of economic independence, and some of the rights of citizenship.

During subsequent decades, when women came forward to make their claims, they discovered deeper obstacles: the double day of labour, economic dependence, and exclusion from political decision making. Women with college degrees were expected to marry and be interesting companions for their husbands and full-time mothers for their children. Those women who did not marry or tried to combine career and marriage found their careers blocked in which ever area of work they had chosen (Gillett 1981; LaMarsh 1968; Parr 1987). The Honourable Judy

LaMarsh, the only female cabinet minister in Prime Minister Lester Pearson's government, explained what finally drove her from politics:

> Scandal is the first weapon, the most continuous one, and the last weapon used against a woman anywhere, and particularly one of political prominence. I have had repeated to me by friends, families and foes the most horrendous stories of my personal life. I have been accused of the full spectrum of sensual impropriety—funny had it not been so malicious. Perhaps the curiosity is natural, but it was so intensified in my case that it became a cardinal factor in my decision to retire. (1968, 304)

The origins of discontent in women from all walks of life might have been noticeable in the late 1950s and early 1960s to a particularly astute observer. But who notices little ripples until they become enormous waves? Then people say, retrospectively, "Yes I remember feeling like this." For when I look back to high school in the 1950s, there were no signs that my friends or acquaintances were developing the skills, insight, or predispositions for life in the social movements of the next decade (Cebarotov 1995; Strong-Boag 1995). One of my friends, who was a great athlete, lamented that she had not been born a boy, but neither she nor I imagined a social movement that would insist on equal athletic opportunities for girls. More than that, when she grew up she realized she was a lesbian; it turned out that you did not have to be a man to love a woman. This we would have to learn for ourselves. In the 1950s, lesbian lives were closeted, and their histories yet to be written.

That was 1959. A short decade later, thousands and thousands of girls-cum-women like ourselves had been swept up in the women's movement. Together we created a movement that uncovered, explored, critiqued, and attempted to transform the hierarchical relations between men and women in every aspect of social life.

The Women's Movements

Throughout the twentieth century, women in organizations like the University Women's Clubs, the YWCA, the Business and Professional Women's Club, the Fédération Nationale Saint-Jean-Baptiste, and the National Council of Women submitted briefs to governments calling for reforms to improve the lives of women at home and in the work force as well as to claim women's equal rights as citizens (Black 1993; Lavigne,

Pinard, and Stoddart 1979). Indeed it is such activity at federal, provincial, and local levels—together with the work of other influential groups like the Voice of Women, founded in 1960 to oppose nuclear weapons proliferation—that provides the grounds for the argument that there has been a women's movement throughout this century (Macpherson 1994; Morris 1980; Williamson and Gorham 1989). This pressure, given voice and influence by two remarkable women—Laura Sabia, then president of the Canadian Federation of University Women and the Honourable Judy LaMarsh, then Secretary of State—culminated in Prime Minister Pearson's reluctant decision to strike the Royal Commission on the Status of Women (LaMarsh 1968; Morris 1980). Sabia had helped mobilize representatives of thirty-two women's organizations who formed, in 1966, the Committee on the Equality of Women in Canada. She told Pearson that, if he did not strike a commission, she would bring a million women to demonstrate on Parliament Hill, although she later admitted that she doubted if she could have rallied six women for such a protest (Morris 1980, 15).

The hearings of the royal commission took place over the next two and a half years. During that period, there was something of a sea change in Canadian life. In 1967, the press—everywhere but in Quebec—ridiculed setting up the commission (Morris 1982, 210; Newman 1969). Whatever could such a commission be about? The *Ottawa Journal* editorialized:

> By all means let the girls gather facts and opinions about women's rights in Canada and see how they can be strengthened where they need it. Bosh! But we suggest to them for their own good, of course, that they do it in the same way that they have advanced their cause in recent years—quietly, sneakily and with such charming effectiveness as to make men wonder why they feel they need a royal commission. (Quoted in Morris 1980, 27)

Angela Burke Kerrigan, public relations director for the commission, reported that "attitudes changed like day and night over a two-year period. At the beginning you couldn't even talk sensibly to people. The changes occurred because consciousness-raising was going on everywhere for men as well as women" (quoted in Morris 1982, 224).

The commission collected briefs from women across the country in every walk of life, documented their circumstances, and submitted its report complete with 167 recommendations for reform. The commission and its recommendations can primarily be seen as a reincarnation in Canada of liberal feminism (Kowaluk 1972), although, as we shall see, it was liberal feminism with a potentially radical future (Eisenstein 1981; Phillips 1991). In their report, tabled in 1970, the royal commissioners noted that in Canada there were not only equal rights feminists but "local units of the Women's Liberation Movement in 16 cities from Vancouver to Halifax." These units were made up of "increasingly diversified groups of women that try to improve their collective lot as well as to combat discrimination. . . . Some of them are not merely reformist but revolutionary in their aims, seeking radical changes in the economic system as well as in the institution of marriage and the nuclear family" (*Report* 1970, 2).

In Canada this radical movement was heralded by a short manifesto written by women in one of the many radical groups of the 1960s. This particular group had broken away from the Student Union for Peace Action (SUPA). The manifesto "Sisters, Brothers, Lovers . . . Listen . . . ," written in the fall of 1967, argued that male comrades put "women in SUPA in two categories or roles—the workers and the wives." This, the authors pointed out, "is a situation not unlike that of the dominant society—'behind every successful man is a successful woman.' While their real women are being women by earning money, cooking and housecleaning, their radical partners can be political and creative, write, think and ooze charisma" (Bernstein et al. 1972, 38).

The issuing of such manifestos, whether in written or verbal form, occasioned discussion, debate, breakaways, and splits in virtually all of the social movements of the late 1960s and 1970s. The outcomes were varied: some women sided with those men who argued that feminism was a "bourgeois" issue that should not concern real radicals; some stayed to try and change these original groups; others left these organizations and began autonomous organizing within the women's liberation movement; still others left to begin consciousness-raising groups, the hallmark of early radical feminist organizing. Like the equal rights feminists that sparked the royal commission and its aftermath, all these newer feminist radicals—identified by the commission as part of the women's liberation movement—developed analyses and strategies to transform Canadian society.

From the beginning, the women's movement in Canada was never a single organization, and much of it was never organized in the more traditional sense. First, there was an early—and never completely dis-crete—division between equal rights feminists and feminist radicals (Black 1993). Second, even in the first wave of feminism (after a short initial period of unity), there were separate equal rights movements in English Canada and francophone Quebec. While first wave franco-phone Quebeckers tried to accommodate the teachings of the Roman Catholic Church with regard to women's proper roles in society (Hamilton 1995; Lavigne, Pinard, and Stoddart 1979), many Québécoises in the second wave intertwined feminism and the struggle for an independent Quebec (Dumont 1992). Third, from the early 1970s there were—particularly in the United States but also in Canada—acri-monious and public struggles between women based on sexual orienta-tion (Vancouver Women's Caucus 1972). Lesbians wanted full acknowledgement of their numbers and indispensability to the move-ment and of the specific oppression that they faced. Some feminists, mostly heterosexuals, fought this, ostensibly on grounds that this issue would endanger the respectability of the movement and the chances for success of other campaigns. The implicit and explicit homophobia behind such fears fuelled dissension (Weir 1987). Fourth, Aboriginal women, black women, and women in various cultural groups had formed organizations to serve their members, gain state support for ser-vices, and fight discrimination (Adamson, Brisken, and McPhail 1988; Brand 1984, 42; Chunn 1995; Vickers, Rankin, and Appelle 1993, 305–19).

In Canada there was much overlap among feminists of different per-suasions and from different locations in their organizing efforts and strategies. Women organized at every level from the national through the provincial and local to their own backyards and kitchen tables (Walker 1990). Most assuredly there is not only one story to tell. The only femi-nist media stars were American imports, such as Gloria Steinem, Betty Friedan, and Kate Millett, or Australian Germaine Greer. Women in Canada did not declare themselves, nor were they declared, speakers for the whole movement. Part of the media's frustration with this move-ment, mushrooming as it did everywhere, was that they never seemed to be able to find it or its leaders. If this was a frustration for the media, there were clear advantages for organizing strategies. Individuals could be packaged, presented to the public, and dismissed; the amorphous and multifaceted organizing of women in all walks of life and of all political persuasions resisted such packaging, stardom, and dismissal.

One way to understand the rise of the women's movement is to try to see things from the point of view of the women who began to regard the world in new ways. Suddenly, instead of a series of unspoken assumptions, there were a lot of questions: "Why should . . . ?" or "Why shouldn't . . . ?" Why should women be blocked in their careers because they are women? Why should women be responsible for all the housework? For all the childcare? Why shouldn't women have control of their own bodies? Why should women be economically dependent on men— or, failing men, on welfare? Why should women's work be paid less than men's—or, worse still, go unpaid? Why should women stay with men who abuse them? Why should women who have been raped be the ones who are effectively put on trial? A series of slogans appeared that presented the world in new ways: "The personal is political"; "Every woman is one man away from welfare"; "Free abortion on demand"; "Every mother a willing mother; every child a wanted child"; "Equal pay for work of equal value." In some sense, what all this amounted to was that, for those looking for "it," the women's movement appeared to be everywhere and nowhere.

Forwarding Feminist Agendas

DURING THE 1970S AND BEYOND, feminists disagreed not only on the explanations for women's inequality, oppression, and subordination, but also on the means to transform their situation. In the interests of discussing a very complex set of activities, I have categorized these strategies as follows: lobbying groups, consciousness-raising groups, women's centres, women's caucuses, women's cultural and business initiatives, and feminism in the academy. All these activities went on at the same time, sometimes in open conflict, usually with overlapping groups of participants, and sometimes on apparently discrete playing fields. Only consciousness-raising groups no longer continue today, at least under that name.

Lobbying Organizations: The Struggle for Equality

The century-old struggle for women's legal equality was taken up on a vastly greater scale following the publication of the *Report of the Royal Commission on the Status of Women*. Many feminists believed that the commission's report with its recommendations would be shelved unless they actively intervened. Following the examples of women in the first wave of feminism who had organized the National Council of Women in 1893, and the more recent example of women in Quebec who had formed the Fédération des femmes du Québec (1966), they organized new lobby groups at the provincial and national levels. The National Action Committee on the Status of Women (NAC), created in 1972 to pressure government to bring the laws into conformity with the royal commission's recommendations, is an umbrella group that brings together women's organizations and groups from across the country. Its goal was equality of opportunity for women in all sectors of Canadian society, an apparently quintessentially liberal agenda. Radical and socialist feminists put less stock in the ameliorative effects of legal equality and devoted less time to lobbying. They often criticized liberal feminists for devoting themselves to these activities, which radicals saw as reformist at best, and more likely co-optive (Findlay 1987; Kowaluk 1972).

However, as Zillah Eisenstein argued in *The Radical Future of Liberal Feminism* (1981), if equality of opportunity were genuinely extended to women, it would require deep structural changes in society. In Canada this became clear as NAC moved far beyond its original mandate and lobbied for example, against free trade and the Charlottetown Accord and for issues ranging from reproductive freedom and daycare to the repeal of racist legislation (Vickers, Rankin, and Appelle 1993). In Canada there were feminists of all persuasions involved in NAC. Some of them put much effort into encouraging NAC to take more radical positions on questions of the economy, racism, national status for Quebec, and self-determination for First Nations people. As well, lobbying groups on particular issues, including abortion, daycare, violence against women, and constitutional equality, have conducted wide-ranging campaigns with members of Parliament and the public (Adamson, Brisken, and McPhail 1988; Kome 1983; McIntyre 1994).

Twenty years of formal lobbying has also convinced many feminists that the struggle for simple legal equality is indeed too simple. Socialist feminists pointed out that legal equality might be useful to some women of the middle and upper classes, but that women should not settle for a piece of the already-constituted pie. Their position has been taken up by feminist legal critics, anti-racist activists, and those using a poststructuralist analysis, all of whom argue that "equality for women" explicitly holds up men as the norm with whom women want equality. But women are not similarly situated with men, and legal equality may simply paper over existing hierarchies.

What does it mean, for example, to provide equality between men and pregnant women? Because men can't be pregnant, and because equality for women has been taken to mean equality with men, pregnancy has been likened to illness or disability, or even ruled beyond the scope of law. The fact that every person on earth is here because a woman somewhere was pregnant has not served to make pregnancy "normal" when it comes to questions of health and well-being, employment, or childcare. Lobbying efforts informed by notions of *equality of opportunity* are limited because they do not attend to this elementary fact: women and men are not similarly situated, and men's conditions—including their bodies—are considered the norm. Feminist lobbying efforts often embrace the goal of *equality of condition*, which addresses the different circumstances in which men and women find themselves.

Consciousness Raising: The Personal Is Political

Apparently borrowed from Mao Tse-Tung's early organizing strategy that encouraged peasants in the practice of "speaking bitterness," consciousness-raising (CR) groups began among feminists in a few large American cities. The idea spread quickly, and in the early 1970s hundreds of such groups met weekly in Canada. The groups were small, perhaps eight to fifteen participants, but the atmosphere was often electrifying as women shared experiences and feelings formerly considered too personal, shameful, or guilt provoking to discuss. Women talked about husbands, children, mothers, fathers, sex and sexuality, about double standards of sexuality, sexual harassment, rape, isolation, and full-time motherhood (Adamson 1995; Adamson, Brisken, and McPhail 1988; Bose 1972). In some ways, CR groups were confessional; but the response was more often anger than guilt, and the answer was not penance but personal exoneration and social change. In other ways, CR groups were similar to group therapy; but while individuals altered their lives, the problems were defined as collective and systemic.

While women from a range of political persuasions and social and economic backgrounds participated in consciousness-raising groups, such groups tended to be the flagship of radical feminism and were often critiqued, even spurned, by other feminists for focusing upon individual

solutions to collective problems (Mitchell 1971). But consciousness raising spoke to the ways in which oppressive conditions become internalized; CR groups provided the occasion for women to complain,
reinterpret, and change. With the support of their sisters and a revamped
consciousness, women changed their living arrangements, their priorities, their identities, their career goals, and their jobs. Beyond this, the
phrase consciousness raising slipped into everyday language, and the
analysis and strategy of making the personal political informed feminist
organizing more generally. No longer were the power relations that animated personal life accepted as private and therefore outside the purview
of open discussion and public policy (Young 1990, 120–21).

Women's Centres: From Private Trouble to Public Issue

During the 1970s, women in all parts of the country established women's
centres to respond to the growing numbers of women coming forward
to declare their private trouble as public issue. Feminists viewed such
centres not simply as service centres but as places where women would
connect with the women's movement and join forces with those already
seeking social and political change. Such women sought birth control
and health information, legal advice, feminist therapy, and referrals to
doctors who would perform abortions. Battered women were offered
counselling and were encouraged to leave abusive husbands. Yet such
centres were often criticized both by those who chose other strategies for
change and by participants as too service oriented and for losing sight of
critical explanations for why women found themselves in need in the
first place. During the 1970s, the federal government began funding such
services, and there were dire predictions that this would give traditional
social service administrators the power to call the shots within the once-
autonomous women's centres. Navigating such waters required creative
funding and strategy making.

Paralleling and sometimes succeeding the all-purpose women's centre were those organizations set up to respond to particular issues and
demands—shelters for battered women, rape crisis centres—and organizations set up by and to serve particular populations of women such
as immigrant women, domestic workers, specified ethnic groups, and
disabled women.

Over time, the workers in government-funded centres found themselves faced with all the problems of traditional social service work: low pay, burnout, and too few resources to serve the need (Walker 1990). Such problems continue, intensely aggravated by the cutbacks of debt-ridden governments who often included women's centres among their first targets. There is little question, however, that women's centres are multifaceted, respond to deep and immediate needs, accumulate and publicize the evidence of women's subordination and victimization, and engage in political organizing to transform these conditions.

Women's Caucuses: Autonomy and Integration

Women often had organized separately within trade unions and political parties, but most often this was done in the broader interests of the main organization. Women traditionally did "women's work": fundraising, support services, and office work. The usefulness of such women's caucuses to the organization was often considerable, but it was usually invisible or acknowledged in perfunctory—"thanks to the ladies"— remarks at conventions. Feminist-inspired women's caucuses had grander goals. They organized for two main reasons: to pressure for gender equity in leadership positions and to press for the inclusion of their demands on the main agenda. This strategy of autonomy and integration was pursued most often and systematically by liberal and socialist feminists (Briskin 1993). Their goal was to change the organization, to make it inclusive of the demands and needs of women. Most women's caucuses met resistance, sometimes short-lived, often prolonged, from men and women. Their impact on parties and unions has often been stunning, but the results are varied and specific (Maroney 1987). For example, in 1993 women headed two of Canada's three main political parties at the federal level. Women's caucuses had more to do with the election of Audrey McLaughlin as leader of the NDP than Kim Campbell as leader of the Progressive Conservatives (and Canada's first female prime minister), but it is difficult to imagine the election of either leader without prolonged organizing by women.

Women's caucuses exist now in many professional associations, and their initiatives encourage women to serve in leadership positions and change the priorities and practices of the main organizations. Charges that universities create "chilly climates" for women have been taken up by women's caucuses in the Canadian Association of University Teachers and in discipline-based organizations like the Canadian Political Science Association and the Canadian Sociology and Anthropology Association.

Early radical and cultural feminists eschewed such organizing: why should women put their efforts into male-dominated organizations? More recently, radical feminists have actively pursued their agenda for change within established institutions, most notably universities. At Queen's University in 1984, law professor Sheila McIntyre wrote a memo to her colleagues that eventually won front-page space in Canada's daily newspapers (1995). She described her experiences with both colleagues and students in unequivocal terms: harassment, misogyny, and plain lack of good will. Nine years later, Somer Brodribb authored a chilly climate report for her political studies colleagues at the University of Victoria. The report, because of the hostile responses it provoked, earned front-page coverage not only in local papers but in the *Globe and Mail*. A radical feminist analysis is reflected in the unequivocal stance of these reports: men have the power, and they use it to create and sustain the subordination of women; men have to be forced to change.

Women's Business and Cultural Initiatives

During the 1970s and beyond, feminists began small businesses and collectives, including book publishers, magazines and newspapers, art galleries, pottery guilds, and stores. The motivations were various. Publishing ventures aimed to bring the ideas of the women's movement to a broader public, to publish work that would likely have been rejected by the gatekeepers of mainstream—"malestream"—publications, to encourage women to write from their own experience, and to provide more amenable working conditions for women. Some hoped to—and did—make a living through such ventures. More often, they were collectively run and did not produce enough for salaries beyond one or two paid editors. As early as 1970, Toronto women founded the Canadian Women's Educational Press (now the Women's Press) to publish the papers and manifestos of the women's movement as well as feminist-informed studies, fiction, and poetry. By publishing their own material, such companies, along with magazines like *Fireweed*, *Herizons*, and *La vie en rose* and newspapers like *Broadside*, avoided the gatekeepers of existing publications. Birth control activists founded the Montreal

Health Press in the early 1970s and have sold millions of copies of their booklets on sexual assault, sexually transmitted diseases, and the menopause. Art galleries like Powerhouse in Montreal attempted to address the old question, Why are there no great women artists? Even when women had the time and resources to paint or sculpt, they seldom had the gallery space or the networks to convert their artistic creations into public showings. Moreover, those in a position to judge what is "great art" are still overwhelmingly male.

Women also started businesses with the primary aim of supporting themselves under conditions more of their own choosing (Dickie 1993). For some this meant not having to work for or with men (Nash 1995). For others, it meant providing goods and services that were tailored to their own community and that invested profits back in that community (Mackenzie 1986). Women started credit unions as the evidence mounted that banks heavily discriminated against women: women with husbands protested the fact that loans were granted only with their spouses' signature; women without husbands were outraged that they could not establish credit ratings.

Many of these entrepreneurial women were seeking financial independence from men. But they also had the effect of forcing policy changes in mainstream institutions. If banks wanted women's business, if publishing houses wanted the profits from the feminist-inspired book boom, if galleries wanted to show the work that was getting rave reviews and stirring controversy, they had to re-examine their attitudes and practices. Meanwhile women working in mainstream institutions—including universities—pressured for change from within.

Feminism in the Academy

There are many accounts of how women's studies began to develop within universities (Eichler 1992; Hamilton 1985; Strong-Boag 1983). At the most general level, we must start with the women's movements, where feminists first began to raise the questions that turned the "natural" world into socially constructed sets of relationships. Feminists began writing articles, starting small newspapers, and editing anthologies. The titles of some of these publications provide a clue to their contents: in the United States *Sisterhood is Powerful;* in Canada *Women Unite!* and *Mother Was Not a Person.* Books like Kate Millett's *Sexual Politics* and Shulamith Firestone's *The Dialectic of Sex* were best sellers.

Feminists began enroling in the university, determined to study the situation of women in a more systematic way. Others were already in the university, and their presence was reflected in a variety of ways: new kinds of thesis topics ("You want to study *what?*" was the response of scandalized, perplexed, and threatened professors); demands for new kinds of courses ("But we already have women's studies—isn't it like home economics?"); and a growing critique of the sexist assumptions that ran through traditional disciplines and normal professorial banter. A few feminists already teaching in the university initiated the first courses on women. Like every workplace, kitchen, and bar in the country, so could every classroom become a potential battleground—in this case between professors and their feminist students and among students themselves. What was up for debate was the long and glorious tradition of Western androcentric knowledge.

The debate escalated as feminist students graduated and began applying for and sometimes securing positions within the university. From this somewhat strengthened position, and in concert with a new generation of students, the struggle for changes to curricula, for new courses and programs, and for the hiring of more feminist scholars proceeded. One can now say that women's studies is well-established in the margins of academe. At some universities, it is possible to major in women's studies at the undergraduate and sometimes the graduate levels. Many departments in the social sciences and the humanities and many professional schools, particularly faculties of law, offer feminist courses taught by feminist teachers; a small number of departments in the physical sciences, particularly biology, are moving in that direction. There is a Canadian Women's Studies Association that meets at the Learned Societies every year. The Canadian Research Institute for the Advancement of Women, founded in 1975, brings together academics and policy makers to hold conferences and publish working papers (Vickers, Rankin, and Appelle 1993, 237). Posters of upcoming events on every university campus speak to the traffic in feminist scholars and activists. Most of all, there is a feminist literature that is growing at such a dizzying rate that it has become impossible to be familiar with all the new titles, let alone read them. At the same time, the feminist challenge to androcentric scholarship has barely touched the established curricula and the teaching practices of most of the professoriate. The debate between feminist and mainstream scholars contines to rage, and there is a great deal at stake.

We have looked briefly at some of the major ways in which second wave feminists have chosen to forward their agendas. The discussion of feminist theories in the last chapter makes it clear, however, that there were many—often competing—proposals for changing society. Furthermore, we should realize that the process for understanding what should be done is indeed that, a process. Only in retrospect can we compose a list of the various goals pursued by feminists in the past two decades. We are in the midst of a transition, and today's issues may be the next decade's assumptions, or they may have been bypassed, transformed, or defeated, temporarily or not.

Developing Analysis: Forwarding Agenda(s)

FEMINISTS OF EVERY PERSUASION and from every location analyze the relations of power in a society and seek to transform them. From the perspective of the 1990s, we may take a snapshot of the range of interpretations and consequent demands made by feminists from different theoretical and social locations. A discussion that makes such distinctions should try to obscure neither the manner in which the same issues were taken up in different ways and at different times by feminists in different locations, nor the amount of overlap there has been. Nonetheless, there is some advantage in presenting the issues from the perspectives of feminists in different locations. Some of this relates to giving credit where it is due. Issues may have first been raised from one perspective and then taken over, revamped or not, co-opted or not. More importantly, discussing them in the context in which they were raised serves to underscore the overall analysis that produced the questions and the demands.

The Campaign(s) for Equal Rights

To encapsulate briefly: liberal, or equal rights, feminists worked for a society of equal opportunity for men and women. They sought to complete the agenda of the first women's movement, and they directed their attention primarily to the public sphere, as had the women in the first wave of feminism. They wanted access to the professions as well as to the political arena, and support for women in the home. They urged reform of all laws that either explicitly or implicitly discriminated against women or had differing consequences for men and women. The recommendations of the *Report of the Royal Commission on the Status of Women* were grouped in the following areas: women in the economy; education; women and the family; taxation and childcare allowances; poverty; participation of women in public life; immigration and citizenship; criminal law and women offenders; and a plan for action (1970, 395–418). Equal rights feminists primarily saw before them a legislative agenda coupled with education to change attitudes (O'Neil and Sutherland 1990, 11).

The Family: Site of Women's Oppression

Establishing the conditions for equality of opportunity was, then, the hallmark of the royal commission and the feminists who initiated the National Action Committee. Radical and socialist feminists responded by asking, What does equality of opportunity mean on an unequal playing field? Second wave feminists zeroed in on the family as the unequal playing field *extraordinaire*. From the late 1960s, they argued that the key to women's situation—which they now labelled oppression or subordination—lay in the private sphere of the family and the links between this private sphere and the public sphere. As the feminists who wrote the "Sisters, Lovers . . . " manifesto argued, as long as women's primary role was to look after men, women would be subordinate to men in all aspects of society. Shulamith Firestone articulated the position of many feminist radicals when she wrote, "the family is neither private nor a refuge, but is directly connected to—is even the cause of—the ills of the larger society which the individual is no longer able to confront" (1970, 254). This critique of the family posed perhaps the greatest challenge—and threat—of this wave of feminism. The family appeared to many to be the bedrock of society. How could feminists argue that it needed to be transformed, even abolished?

The royal commissioners had argued that women should have the choice to work in the waged labour force or to be full-time homemakers. But radical and socialist feminists pointed to women's economic, sexual, and emotional dependence upon men, and the costs, at every level, of choosing the latter option. Like Engels nearly a century earlier, they targeted marriage as a property relationship in which women gave men the rights to their bodies, their reproductive capacities, their sexuality, and their labour. Within this perspective on the family, they raised many of the issues that, stripped of their radical context, gained wide support in succeeding decades. Many of the issues raised by feminist radicals were subsequently taken on and supported by liberal feminists and even by mainstream politicians. In this process, particular issues were isolated and lifted from an analysis of oppressive family structures (including the relationship between women's economic dependence upon men and their subordination to men) and redrafted as issues of equal opportunity and individual rights.

Let us look more closely at the major issues that emerged from feminist analysis of the family as oppressive to women. It is important to keep in mind that, within this analysis, all these issues are interrelated. Significant change in the relations between the sexes would occur only if they were all addressed as part and parcel of the relations of domination and subordination between the sexes. Still the following list gives a general idea of the scope of the feminist objections to contemporary society that were raised during the early 1970s: sexuality and reproductive rights; violence against women; women and work; romance, love, marriage, and motherhood; socialization and education; the construction of masculinity and femininity; and lesbian challenges to compulsory heterosexuality.

Sexuality and Reproductive Rights

In Canada, the first national campaign waged by feminist radicals was for free abortion on demand. As one group in Quebec put it, "Nous aurons les enfants que nous voulons." In 1970, women organized a cross-country caravan, destination the Parliament buildings in Ottawa, where they chained themselves to the seats in the visitor's gallery (Kostash 1980, 175–78). But the struggle for abortion was only the most dramatic aspect of a thorough-going reassessment of reproductive rights and female sexuality. Feminists demanded access to birth control for all women, married or not. It is hard to imagine at this point, with easy access to a variety of contraceptives, and with the AIDS epidemic making the advertisement of condoms such an everyday event, that birth control was ever a radical demand. But unmarried women were expected to eschew sexual intercourse until marriage. The penalties for premarital sexual activity were lost reputations and the alternatives of shotgun marriages or adoption if pregnancy should result. In radical feminist terms, women's sexuality passed from the guardianship (ownership) of their fathers to their husbands without interruption. Hence came the critique not just of marriage but of the Christian marriage ceremony—"Who gives this woman to be married?" asks the priest or minister. "I do," answers the father.

Feminists exposed the double standard of sexuality through which men were applauded for "sowing their wild oats" and women divided into "whores" (more recently "sluts") and "virgins." Critics insisted that women's sexual pleasure be a goal in itself, and some raised the argument that men were not necessarily the best sexual partners for women. The first years of the critique of sexuality elaborated upon the "pleasure" side of the sexuality debate. This discussion was influenced by the movement of the 1960s for sexual liberation, often called "free love." The emphasis was upon women actively pursuing sexual pleasure unencumbered by marriage—that is, by economic or sexual dependence upon men. The message in articles with titles such as "The Myth of the Vaginal Orgasm" was that patriarchal ideology and practices in various forms, including Freudian psychoanalysis, conspired to deny women access to pleasure from their own bodies (Koedt 1973). As long as women's sexual experiences were contained by genital encounters of the marital kind, so the new critique went, so long would women's sexuality be in the service of men's sexual pleasure and power. As one 1970 statement put it, "Society has conditioned women to be pleasure givers rather than pleasure seekers or receivers." The group went on to declare, "We feel that until women themselves determine their own code of sexuality based not, as in the past, upon the code of males or society, our myths will not be exposed and our fears will not be eradicated" (Gill et al. 1972, 169).

Violence Towards Women

The *Report* of the royal commission and feminist publications from the early 1970s were almost completely silent on the other side of sexuality, known as the "danger" side (Bégin 1992). Indeed, early feminist hopes that pursuing pleasure would eradicate women's fears turned out to be utopian, at least in the short term. If, in the first years of the 1970s, women's right to abortion symbolized feminist hopes for sexual emancipation, by the middle of that decade the focus on the danger of rape came as a grim reminder that sexual emancipation involved more than becoming active players in the sexual encounter.

Symptomatic of this shift are popular feminist book titles from the early and middle 1970s: in 1970 *Sisterhood is Powerful* and *Women Unite!*; in 1975 *Against our Will* and in 1977 *Rape: The Price of Coercive Sexuality*. More than internalized oppression and fear of economic destitution brought women to the sexual encounter aiming to please men, not themselves, authors like Susan Brownmiller and Lorenne Clark argued. Whether in war, in back streets and alleys, or in marriage beds, men had the strength and physical resources to rape women, resources backed in practice—if not always in theory—by law. In this way we learned that rape had been considered a crime only when one man raped another man's wife or daughter. For a woman could not charge her husband with rape; at her marriage ceremony, when she was "given away," she said "Yes" once and for all.

During the same period, it became clear that rape was not the only method of violence wreaked on women by their husbands. Indeed, the mounting public evidence that the family was a place in which men wielded power and, with impunity, vented their rage and anger against women began to make the radical feminist arguments about the family and oppression increasingly plausible to growing numbers of women. My experience at the New Woman Centre in Montreal was repeated across the country. In 1975 two researchers at the centre began a research project on battered women. There was much scepticism—including my own—about whether this was a problem that feminists should take up. Was this not a question of rare individual pathology? But the day the newspapers first reported the project, the phone began to ring, and it never stopped.

What was new about this analysis was not that women might be the object of violent attack or rape. Indeed, mothers had long warned their daughters about the dangers of being out on the streets alone at night, or of travelling in the wrong circles. The emphasis, however, had been on women behaving themselves, not wearing provocative clothing, not going out alone, and remaining sexually inactive until after marriage. In other words, women were responsible for keeping men in line and for not putting themselves in jeopardy. Feminists challenged this allocation of blame. Israeli prime minister Golda Meir seemed to capture the new mood when she stated that it was men, not women, who should be subject to a curfew. More than this, what was new was the realization, made public by the stories of many women, that women were in danger in their own families from their husbands.

The sheer empirical evidence for this violence helped extend the analysis that the family was a site—many said the primary site—for the oppression of women. There were disagreements about the explanations for male violence against women, particularly about which factors were more important. Socialist feminists looked to the exploitative nature of capitalism; radical feminists looked to men and the construction of masculinity. But for all, the list of explanations included women's economic dependence upon men. This dependence was particularly important for explaining why women didn't always leave abusive partners. How would they support themselves and their children? Where would they go? In response to crises, the immediate answers devised by feminists—shelters, counselling, and helping women to relocate—were intended as short term. The ultimate solutions would have to be revolutionary: an end to all forms of male domination, including the nuclear family—and, for socialist feminists, an end to capitalism.

Women and Work

The focus on domestic violence also drew sharp attention to issues that feminists had already raised: women's unpaid service to men in the home; their primary responsibility for twenty-four-hour childcare; the double day of labour; their confinement to underpaid job ghettos in the labour force; and their exclusion from better-paying jobs—those known as "nontraditional" (that is, those that were always the prerogative of men), from the professions, and from managerial and leadership roles in all sectors of the paid work force.

It is ironic that feminists have stood accused by right-wing groups, like REAL Women, of failing to value women's contributions to their families. A more accurate reading, historically speaking, would be that feminists insisted that housework and childcare were indeed *work*. Socialist feminists developed a sophisticated analysis that tried to demonstrate that capitalism itself was fundamentally indebted to and propelled by the unpaid labour of women in the home. Women not only reproduced and raised the next generation of workers but also, on a daily basis, provided the necessities of life, relaxation, and sex to the present generation—their husbands. What feminists objected to was that all this labour was done by women for men, that it was invisible and undervalued, and that it was unpaid, thereby leaving women in a situation of economic dependence, with all the dire consequences that it was now clear such dependence entailed.

Romance, Love, Marriage, and Motherhood

Feminists zeroed in on the ideology of romance, love, and marriage for its success in disguising the realities of family life, and for ensuring that women would interpret their discontent and their abuse as products of their own shortcomings. How could one explain the apparent anomaly that while few young women wanted marriages like their parents, almost all young women wanted to marry? The explanation seemed to hinge on the phrase "falling in love." In a society that ostracized young women who became pregnant out of wedlock, denied the unmarried (and, indeed, the married) access to birth control, and described the children of unmarried women as "illegitimate," there seemed to be only one response to falling in love—particularly when one became as old as twenty-two or twenty-three: get married. So went the words of the popular hit of the 1950s, sung by the soon-to-be-divorced couple Debbie Reynolds and Eddie Fisher:

> Love and Marriage; love and marriage;
> Go together like a horse and carriage;
> This was told by Mother;
> You can't have one without the other.

Once women were married, another set of ideas—which political leaders and others had taken up enthusiastically after World War II to push women out of their wartime jobs—came into play. Children, it was declared, required a full-time mother in the home in order to grow up to be happy, productive citizens. When women "had to" work for wages outside the home, they would do so in the face of the message that this was harmful to their children. Not only did governments close childcare centres that had been created to facilitate women's wartime waged work

(Pierson 1986; Prentice 1995), but their resistance to daycare was interpreted as in the best interests of children. Feminists called all this into
dispute. Children, it was argued, suffered along with their mothers when
confined to the isolated nuclear family (Cameron and Pike 1972; Killian
1972). Children were far too important to be segregated all day with
their captive moms; children should be the responsibility of the society
as a whole, of women and men. Based on their understanding of the
needs of children and women, feminists initiated the movement for universal state-supported childcare.

Nor was remaining at home all day with small children any life for
an adult human being. As Melody Killian wrote in 1969:

> Most working girls happily assume that they will work only until their
> first baby arrives. Often I see pregnant girls at work whose expectations
> are so high and so happy. At first it feels good to be away from a job
> that was probably poorly paid and dreary. But then, somehow, every-
> body forgets about her. Lonely and bored in her apartment with her
> baby, she senses that the rest of the world is going on without her. She
> begins to wonder why it is that she is not happy. Something is wrong,
> but she is not sure what it is. (1972, 90)

In the words of Betty Friedan (1963), this was "the problem that has no
name," with its symptoms of depression and even madness. Psychiatrists
and physicians who offered women valium to help them accept the
injunction that to be good mothers they should have no life of their own
came under feminist fire. And on the basis of historical and cross-
cultural comparisons, feminists argued that the idealized nuclear family
was an anomaly, a destructive location for children and an oppressive
site for women. Briefly put, the ideologies of love and romance, as well
as that speaking to the "real" needs of children, were re-interpreted as
part of the arsenal that kept women subordinate and oppressed within
the family.

Education, Work, and Family

Feminists did not explain young women's predilection for marriage and
full-time motherhood through these mystifying sets of ideas alone. They
argued that girls, from the earliest ages, were educated for marriage, boys
for the labour market. Boys were to grow up and be something; girls

were to grow up and marry boys who did something. Feminists became critics of every aspect of child rearing and education, from the identification of pink with baby girls and blue with baby boys, through early childhood years when girls were given dolls and boys trucks, to all aspects of the curriculum in public and high schools. In Quebec, the campaign to get little Yvette of the school readers out of the kitchen and onto the hockey rink, and little Guy to take his turn in the kitchen was propelled onto the front pages of newspapers—and into the centre of the 1980 referendum on sovereignty association—when René Lévesque's nationalist minister of state, Lise Payette, called the wife of the leader of the Opposition an "Yvette."

Liberal feminists concentrated upon changing school curricula and the attitudes that encouraged women to plan for full-time marriage and motherhood rather than full-time careers with or without motherhood. Meanwhile socialist and radical feminists undertook a far-reaching critique of the social construction of masculinity and femininity.

The Social Construction of Masculinity and Femininity

Feminists continued to search for explanations when faced with the array of ways in which men dominated and enforced their domination over women, with the incontrovertible evidence that many women were not taking up the feminist cause, and with the growing counterrevolution in response to the feminist movement. The liberal feminist campaign—underpinned by the belief in education and the efficacy of law—to change attitudes, provide role models for the young, and alter sexist child-rearing practices didn't seem to address the full measure of male brutality or the scope of male and female resistance to change. So fundamental did this intransigence appear that radical feminist interpretations veered close to genetic or biological explanations. The logical extension of such explanations suggested that men should be removed from child rearing, and that women should remove themselves from work or relationships with men. One feminist joke that expressed this attitude was, "If we know enough to put one man on the moon, why can't we put them all there?"

Negotiating their way through this interpretive thicket, other feminists cast about for explanations powerful enough to account for the full slate of male and female behaviours and interactions without lapsing into biological reductionism. The problem, they posited, was not men and women but masculinity and femininity. Their diagnosis came from various appropriations and developments of psychoanalysis. Not only the bad behaviours of brutal men but the range of characteristics of good men—real men—found themselves under the microscope. From infancy, boy children were taught to be in control, to hide signs of vulnerability, and to repress all those characteristics defined as "sissy-like"— that is, girl-like. This monumental task of repression meant that they would project all these despised characteristics onto those who were supposed to carry them, namely girls and women. More than attitudes needed changing, but the problem was not genetic: the diagnosis was misogyny, and this woman-hating permeated the practices and institutions of the whole society. This analysis lent credence to a parallel interpretation of male-female relationships: the developing critique of compulsory heterosexuality.

Lesbian Challenges and the Critique of Heterosexism

By the mid-1970s, lesbianism as alternative lifestyle had been superseded by a thorough-going critique of marriage, family, and what Adrienne Rich first called "compulsory heterosexuality." This analysis owed a good deal to the foregoing critique of the family as the site of women's oppression and was obviously predicated upon the demand for an end to all discrimination based on sexual orientation. Rich argued that by making heterosexual marriage the only legal location for long-term intimate relationships, for socially and legally sanctioned sexual activity, for the conceiving, bearing, and rearing of children, and the only means through which a woman might be guaranteed support for herself and her children, men had secured their power over women, their control over children and motherhood, their sexual access to women, and their right to lifelong personal service.

Such an analysis helped underwrite many of the demands for abolishing, altering, and reforming the myriad of laws and customs pertaining to marriage, family, children, education, and work, both paid and unpaid. In one way or another, this perspective provided the legitimacy for such diverse demands as custody rights for lesbian mothers, access to reproductive technology for lesbian couples and single women, and the end to the privileging of heterosexual partnerships—whether this be through employment benefits, the family reunification guidelines of immigration policies, or in public demonstrations of affection. More fundamentally, the argument that marriage, as currently practised, was a power relationship between a man and a woman buttressed by law, custom, attitudes, and force pointed to the necessity of transforming the whole system rather than attempting a piecemeal program of social reform.

From Revolution to Reform

Many of the issues raised by radical and socialist feminists were lifted, during the succeeding decade, from their overall analysis and taken up more generally by feminists, civil libertarians, legal reformers, social workers, social scientists, and police administrators. This helps explain why any particular reform did not have—from the point of view of a radical or socialist feminist agenda—the desired effect. Let us take a couple of examples.

The Royal Commission on the Status of Women recommended "that the Criminal Code be amended to permit abortion by a qualified medical practitioner on the sole request of any woman who has been pregnant for 12 weeks or less" and "for more than 12 weeks if the doctor is convinced that the continuation of the pregnancy would endanger the physical or mental health of the woman, or if there is a substantial risk that if the child were born, it would be greatly handicapped, either mentally or physically" (1970, 286–87). In 1988, after two decades of concerted feminist activity, the Supreme Court of Canada struck down section 251 of the Criminal Code, a federal law restricting the conditions under which abortions might be performed. At the moment, abortion is simply a medical procedure like any other. Whether women have access to the procedure, however, is determined by where they live and by their access to receptive medical resources. Doctors and hospitals are not obliged to perform abortions, unlike other procedures, and in many places there are no clinics. Thus, the feminist goal of free abortion on demand has proved elusive.

Moreover, the right to abortion was part of the campaign for reproductive rights. The goal was not simply the recognition that women have the right *not* to have a child, but also that they should have access to what they need to raise a child. Favourable conditions for raising children still do not exist for many women: Canada lacks a national daycare policy; the meagre social programs once in existence have been cut back; there is upwards of 9 percent "official" unemployment;[2] the poverty rate for women alone with children continues to soar; when they do have a job, women make, on average, 70 percent of what men make (Philp 1995); and the effects of pregnancy and childcare on jobs and career are punitive. None of this means that the decriminalization of abortion should not be hailed as a feminist victory, or that access to abortion is irrelevant for women's lives. But, as with the granting of suffrage in 1918, the winning of a single issue does not impinge greatly on the overall relations of power between men and women, or the distribution of resources between them.

The second example is the problem of wife beating. In the twenty years since such behaviour was targeted by feminists, there has been a general shift in attitude. Police departments are enjoined to take domestic disputes more seriously; social workers in mainstream agencies refer women who have been battered to shelters rather than sending them home with the promise of marital counselling; governments have funded shelters; politicians no longer laugh publicly when the issue is addressed. No feminist could fail to appreciate these changes. Yet, as Gillian Walker (1990) has demonstrated, when wife battery became one of a list of social problems, it was lifted, without ceremony, from the feminist analysis of male domination and women's subordination, from the analysis of the family as a site for creating and sustaining women's oppression, and from an understanding of the formation of masculine and feminine subjectivities. Instead, the problem of family violence is now widely perceived within a revamped functionalist perspective: the dysfunctional family, the violent male, and the female as victim. The social intervention that occurs—when it occurs—creates two new social actors: the criminalized male (the batterer) and the social welfare client (the female victim). Little or nothing is done for the woman—now victim—who lacks the skills or education to support herself or her children; little is done to provide young men in school with the information, skills, and understanding to become men for whom it would be inconceivable to have their way through violence (Currie 1989; Walker 1990).

The devastating critique of the family, first offered by socialist, radical, and lesbian feminists, has been accepted, in piecemeal form, by much of the population. It has also coincided with (and perhaps was a response to) massive demographic changes that dislodged the nuclear family from its place as the only unreservedly acceptable game in town. Many women raise children alone, and no longer only because they are widowed, divorced, or separated. Lesbians raise children alone or with partners, not just because they have children from earlier marriages, but because they make use of the new reproductive technology. Finally, the nuclear family, with father in the work force and mother at home, exists alongside households in which both parents work, only women work, or, in these days of high unemployment, no member of the household has a full-time paid job (Eichler 1988).

Many of the issues initially raised by liberal, socialist, and radical feminists have been taken up, elaborated upon, or challenged by women who insist that gender is only one—and sometimes not the most important—aspect of their oppression and exploitation. Socialist feminists, as we have seen, have always considered the intersection of class and gender; women of colour focus on racism; disabled women on disability; many Québécoises on national subordination; Aboriginal women on self-determination. All this has brought many feminists to new perspectives that do not rank one form of oppression over others, that always insist upon historically specific and local analysis, and that direct attention away from causes or origins to complex interrelationships (White 1993). You should keep this in mind as we look briefly at some of the challenges to the currents of Canadian feminism. These challenges will be taken up more fully in subsequent chapters.

Women and Disability

In the past decade, women with disabilities have organized autonomously to make politicians and feminist activists more aware of the needs of the disabled. In addition, disabled women have pointed out that much current feminist analysis cannot simply be extended to them (Doucette 1989). For example, family looks different if you live in an institution. Furthermore, abusive practices identified by feminists as family-sited are common occurrences in many group homes and residences for those needing assistance with daily life. Some disabled women argue that the literature on women as sex objects means nothing to women who have often been defined—because of disability—as asexual. Yet, at the same time, disabled persons are particularly vulnerable targets of sexual assault, violence, and theft.

The critique of the assumptions about normality resonates with the arguments of poor women, older women, lesbian women, minority women, indeed all women as we reconsider what is normal. But the disabled women's movement is also specific, with specific critiques and demands. For example, Judith Mosoff has explained why women with disabilities tend to reject new reproductive technologies, especially prenatal testing, more categorically than do many feminists. She points out that although "these tests purport only to provide additional information to women about [their] pregnancy, certain diagnoses lead almost inevitably to the termination of the pregnancy." Disabled people argue that "this reflects a value judgement on their own lives as 'not worth living,' thereby exacerbating the existing discrimination" against them (Mosoff 1993, 114).

Feminists have pointed out how mothers are perceived to be responsible for their children's health and character. With the pressure to undergo prenatal tests and to act on the results, however, "mothers can be blamed for the ways that their children turn out at an earlier point than ever before" (ibid., 121; see also Lippman 1989). How dare a woman knowingly produce a disabled child? Disability activists situate this kind of thinking within the attitudes that made possible the scientific and medical backing for "the most horrific modern program of eugenics, the Nazi program of racial hygiene" (Mosoff 1993, 115). As the Canadian Disability Rights Council has argued, embracing eugenics also shifts attention from environmental causes of disability and from the role of poverty, as reflected in poor maternal nutrition and health care, as a major cause of infant disability.

Feminism and Anti-racism

Women of colour, including black feminists, rewrote previous feminist scripts. What could female emancipation mean to women of colour in a racist society? Feminists who did not take on board the struggle against racism, they argued, were refusing to admit and dismantle their own racism and were, therefore, perpetuating their own power and privilege in relation to women of colour. Nor was it simply a question of adding anti-racist critiques to feminist struggles. First of all, anti-racist feminists produced trenchant critiques of the Canadian state. They argued that the reforms initiated by white feminists failed to address the state's racist practices and goals, which continuously disadvantaged and victimized them. Second, many women of colour rejected the central tenet of second wave feminist thought that the family was the primary site for the creation and sustaining of women's oppression, arguing instead that the family was often a site of support and resistance for women, men, and children of colour. Third, they demonstrated that every issue raised in the past by white feminists needed to be rethought from the various locations of women of colour—whether they be the descendants of Canadian citizens, immigrants, or refugees (Bannerji 1995; Brand 1984; Silvera 1986).

Feminism and Nationalism: The Women's Movement in Quebec

As we have seen, the women's movement has directed much of its energy towards pressuring the federal government—in other words, the Canadian state—to change laws and initiate policy. But many Québécois feminists have taken quite a different stance toward this state. A strong and influential wing of the feminist movement in Quebec linked women's equality to the nationalist struggle and the independence of Quebec. While English-Canadian feminists were enjoining the Canadian state to change laws, make laws, create new policy, and fund services, many Québécois feminists wanted powers transferred from the federal to the provincial government. They did not recognize the legitimacy of the Canadian state, so it made little sense to join with English-Canadian feminists in campaigns that were directed towards federal action (De Sève 1992; Dumont 1992). More than that, feminist *indépendantistes* pointed out that English-Canadian feminists were thoroughly entangled in, and privileged by, their dominant national status. Not to put too fine a point on it, they were the *maudits anglais*.

From the beginning of the second wave in Canada, sisterhood was as likely to be fractious as powerful. For when the sisters belonged to different hierarchically related nations, it meant that they could not always act in unison. Certainly, most English-Canadian feminists did not become supporters of the nationalist struggle, nor did most of them see why the Québécoises would not lend their support to the organizations described as national in character, the *National* Action Committee, for example. The Fédération des femmes du Québec (FFQ), the umbrella organization for liberal feminism that predated NAC by six years, did join NAC from 1972 until 1981 and again from 1984 to 1989. Both its withdrawals centred around constitutional disagreements: the FFQ supported the Meech Lake Accord; NAC did not. The FFQ was against the Charlottetown Accord, and although NAC was also against it, many of its member organizations were not. The bottom line was that English-Canadian feminists saw the federal government as potentially more responsive to their demands than were the diverse provincial governments. Furthermore, most failed to understand the fundamental objections of the Québécois to the Canadian state and their passionate desire for sovereignty. In Quebec, radical and socialist feminists, while they were likely to be *indépendantistes*, put much less stock in the power or will of *any* state to take on board their demands, not unlike their counterparts in English Canada. Thus, struggles within Quebec among liberal, radical, and socialist feminists tended to parallel those elsewhere in Canada.

Women and Self-determination: The Aboriginal Challenge

In 1956, Mary Two-Axe Early, a Mohawk woman from Kahnawake, raised the issue of discrimination towards Indian women before the Standing Committee on Indian Affairs and Northern Development (SCIAND). As an Indian woman who had "married out"—that is, married a non-Indian—she had lost her legal status as an Indian under the Indian Act, her band membership, and her right to transmit legal status and band membership to her children (Weaver 1993). Fourteen years later, the Royal Commission on the Status of Women recommended that the offending section of the Indian Act (12(b)) be repealed. In 1985, following a concerted struggle by the Native Council of Canada, Indian Rights for Indian Women, and NAC, and legal challenges by Jeannette Corbiere Lavell and Yvonne Bedard to the Supreme Court of Canada (they lost) and Sandra Lovelace before the International Covenant on Political and Civil Rights (she won), this section was removed from the Indian Act. The successor legislation, Bill C-31, sustained gender inequality, however, by establishing the second-generation cut-off rule. Nearly thirty years after her original public statement, Two-Axe Early appeared again before SCIAND to protest that the grandchildren of a woman who "married out"—unlike the grandchildren of a man—would not be eligible for reinstatement or band registration.

This struggle represents a long-term and successful joint endeavour by mainstream feminist organizations and (primarily) Indian women who had lost their status through marrying non-status men. On its surface, section 12(b) appeared as a straightforward patriarchal law. But as Aboriginal women and men have argued, the Indian Act was also a racist and imperialist piece of legislation that was imposed upon the indigenous peoples in ways that distorted their internal relations, structured their subordination to non-Aboriginal peoples, and threatened their extinction (Monture-Angus 1995). In recent years, Aboriginal women's major call has been for self-determination for their peoples and an end to the tragic results of colonization, imperialism, and what many consider the importation of Western practices of male domination. As with Québécois feminists, they argue that people who do not support their demands—feminists or not—are part of the oppressive relationships and structures that have brutalized and destroyed their peoples. The complicated nature of relationships of subordination and domination are here revealed: Aboriginal women direct their admonitions to French and English alike, to the Canadian state as well as to the government of Quebec, and to the nationalist aspirations of the Québécois that do not take account of Aboriginal prior claims.

No wonder, then, that the approach of Aboriginal women to the Canadian state differs sharply from that of English-Canadian feminists, and their approach to the government of Quebec differs from that of the Québécoises. In both cases, Aboriginal women and men look to self-determination for their peoples as their primary strategy and hope for the future. Furthermore, the radical feminist critique of family also left many Aboriginal women cold: "Our lives and our communities," said Theresa Tate, "include men and our children and we can't leave them behind" (Cowan 1993, 23; see also Castellano and Hill 1995). Just as socialist feminists have tended to focus upon the exploitative relations of capitalism to explain male brutality, so have Aboriginal women looked to the long history of Western imperialism and the dispossession of Aboriginal peoples from their land. They argue that Aboriginal men learned the advantages of patriarchy from their conquerors and that, in the context of the deprivation and state-initiated violence of their lives, they vented their frustration and rage on women, children and on themselves.

To the extent that there is a shared critique of patriarchal relations, there is some meeting ground for Aboriginal and non-Aboriginal feminists. Folk singer Buffy Sainte-Marie put it this way: "Native men get the same message as colonial men. Some men in the Indian movement have not wanted to hand the microphone to me and never wanted to give credit to women. . . . In not getting the credit sometimes our older and younger sisters don't get the encouragement of having role models" (1993, 31). But a more sustained meeting ground will have to be on different terrain. While "some aboriginal women have turned to the feminist or women's movement to seek solace (and solution) in the common oppression of women," Patricia Monture-Angus writes that for her such a turn does not provide "a full solution. . . . [I]t is not solely through my gender that I perceive the world, it is my culture (and/or race) that precedes my gender" (1995, 177).

The problem of and for feminism is serious in this context: Is such a meeting ground possible? Feminist critiques of capitalism, imperialism, and the state gain breadth, focus, and passion when reinterpreted from the location of Aboriginal women. Who controls land and development, and in whose interests? Who makes and enforces the criminal law, which sends Aboriginal peoples to prison out of all proportion to their numbers in the general population? In whose interests has the environment been rendered close to uninhabitable for plants, animals, and human beings? For many Aboriginal women, these must be feminist questions, or they will continue, largely, not to identify their own struggles as feminist. Until now, as Monture-Angus writes, "the women's movement has never taken as its *central* and long-term goal, the eradication of the legal oppression that is specific to Aboriginal women" (1995, 175).

Conclusion

THE SECOND WAVE OF FEMINISM was remarkable in many ways: the sheer numbers of women who shaped its ever-expanding agenda; the links that were drawn between aspects of life once considered discrete—economic life and the family, private and public, work and home, love and brutality; the interconnections between the feminist movement and movements for lesbian and gay liberation, peace, and ecology, and against racism; its development as women's studies within the academy; and, from the vantage point of 1990, its longevity. Indeed, of all the social movements of the 1960s, the women's movement, however diversified it became, however its strategies were adapted to new circumstances, continued to grow in countries throughout the world.

While it is widely agreed that the agenda of the women's movement of the 1970s largely was set by middle-class, white, educated women, the last decade and a half has witnessed a far more active mobilization of women from many other locations. This is particularly relevant for women's movements because many of these women also claim the term feminist, and in this sense we can say that the movement is far larger and more diversely located than it was a decade ago. Aboriginal women, women of colour, disabled women, lesbians, immigrants and refugees have often pursued a similar strategy with regard to the women's movement as have feminists with regard to mainstream institutions: one of autonomy and integration. In this process they seek to change existing feminist organizations—NAC, FFQ, women's presses and magazines, and women's studies programs—in two major ways. They insist that they be (at least) proportionately represented in the policy making and leadership positions of these groups, and they struggle to ensure that these organizations make their perspectives, practices, and goals their own. Certainly feminism—in its theoretical and organizational manifestations—is contested territory. This promotes the prevailing assumption, much propagated in the media, that the movement has become splintered and fragmented.

Two points should be made to qualify this idea that a once-unified women's movement has now self-destructed. First of all, in Canada, at least, the movement was never one. Second, for the media's descriptors like splintered and fragmented, we may wish to substitute terms like diversified, multifaceted, and enriched. Certainly, the women's movement appears as a fluid and open-ended event; those who have tried to draw boundaries or act as gatekeepers have been persuasively challenged.

This chapter has provided one interpretation of the questions, issues, and perspectives feminists in different and overlapping locations have raised in the past twenty-five years. The focus has been the women's movement in Canada. But, as we noted, feminists diverge widely in their relationships with, their assessment of, and the demands that they make of the Canadian state. Chapters 3 and 4 elaborate on some of these feminist critiques of the Canadian state.

Notes

1. The majority of farm women in Ontario now hold wage-earning jobs off the farm (Cebarotov 1995, 201).

2. "The *unemployed* include mainly persons who during the week before Census Day . . . were without work, had actively looked for work in the past four weeks, and were available for work in the reference week" (Statistics Canada 1995b). Such figures, therefore, leave out all those who are no longer looking for work because there is no work to be found. Long-term unemployment has worsened during the 1990s. For example, in 1990, persons whose unemployment had lasted more than a year accounted for only 6 percent of total unemployment. By 1994, this proportion had risen to 15 percent (Akyeampong 1995, 9).

The Canadian State: Feminist Perspectives

AS THE LAST CHAPTER SUGGESTED, feminist challenges to the Canadian state have come from many social locations and political perspectives. Gendering the history of the Aboriginal–European encounter, the formation of the Canadian state, the negotiations that shaped Confederation and the period thereafter, reveals specific and complex relations of domination and subordination between men and women. These gender relations shape and are shaped by class, regional disparities, national hierarchies, and racism. Chapters 3 and 4 explore feminist challenges to the state in terms of their theoretical alignments and their political goals.

Feminists have expanded upon various existing theories of the state: liberal pluralism, neo-Marxism, and anti-racist theories of colonialism and imperialism. They have also developed theories that include analyses of law, social policy, and state practices and that seek to demonstrate that the state is *patriarchal*; that is, that the state incorporates and sustains a system of male domination as an intrinsic, however variously expressed, aspect of its mandate and functioning. But, as many feminists have argued, this notion of a patriarchal state can not be taken as a given or as self-explanatory, but must be demonstrated in any particular context. Nor can the state's patriarchalism be singled out over its role in creating and consolidating the interests of capital or racism. Most of the recent emphasis focuses upon the intersection of sexual, racial, and class hierarchies in state formation, practices, and priorities.

This chapter explores feminist challenges that draw upon, extend, and alter liberal pluralist and neo-Marxist theories of the state. In this process, feminists began to conceptualize the state as patriarchal, and we will examine the debates around this understanding. In chapter 4 we turn to the anti-racist and nationalist challenges to the legitimacy of the Canadian state that have been issued by Aboriginal women, by women of colour more generally, and by feminists in Quebec.

Liberal Pluralism and the State

THE EARLIEST AND MOST SUSTAINED FEMINIST CHALLENGE to the Canadian state drew upon and extended a liberal pluralist understanding of the state. From the 1800s through to the present day, feminists have demanded that the state include women as full and equal citizens (Bacchi 1983; Errington 1993; Strong-Boag 1986). At first this appeared a reasonably simple proposal that required only the political will. Women should be granted the vote, the right to higher education, the right to hold property, and admission to the professions. For liberal feminists, the state was essentially neutral and could *in principle* extend the rights of citizenship to all.

This assumption regarding the state's neutrality has underwritten the dominant—that is, liberal—historical and political interpretations of Canada's past and present. The notion of neutrality went hand-in-hand with the idea that the state should not stand in the way of the development of trade and commerce, the growing strength of the bourgeoisie that had emancipated itself from feudal and aristocratic fetters, and the expansion of enlightened and progressive European societies (Whitaker 1977, 31). From this point of view, European explorers discovered Canada, developed relations with the Indians through offering the exchange of guns and trinkets for furs, fought the Indians and defeated them when their co-operation was not forthcoming or when they refused to accept the authority of the newcomers, and paved the way for the founding of Quebec and other colonies. In the battle for Canada between French and English, the latter won fair and square on the battlefield, a victory that was subsequently confirmed by treaty. From the point of view of traditional English-Canadian historiography, the battle of the Plains of Abraham in 1759 legitimized English rule over New France and, in the process, provided the basis for the eventual assimilation of Aboriginal peoples.

One hundred years later, the Fathers of Confederation met to forge political and economic links between the various colonies that made up British North America. Sobered by the states' rights rationale for the Civil War in the United States—when the southern states had seceded in protest against the federal law banning slavery—Canadian politicians sought to avoid a similar challenge to the legitimacy of the state they were creating. Canadian school children have been taught how the powers of the provinces were carefully delineated and all residual powers vested with the federal government.

Those who provide such an interpretation of Canada's past would not deny that there have been times when the state used force against sections of its own population: during the wars against the Indians and the Métis, the Rebellions in Lower and Upper Canada, and the Winnipeg General Strike, and with the use of the War Measures Act in 1970 in Quebec and the armed attack on Kanesatake in 1990. Liberal pluralism, however, accepts that the state has a monopoly on the use of violence for the purpose of maintaining—in the words of the British North America Act, the original constitution of Canada—"peace, order and good government." Those in power who order the deployment of force may be chastised for errors in political judgment, for using excess force, or for failure to compromise, but this does not change the overall rules of the governing game.

This kind of account provides a backdrop for what is usually called the politics of pluralism. Canada is a country made up of people of diverse origins: the Aboriginal peoples, the French, the English, and subsequent waves of immigrants. All levels of government are constituted by, and beholden to, different groupings of people who may lobby for their own interests. In such accounts, governments are power brokers; if they make enough people unhappy, they will be defeated in the next election (Albo and Jenson 1989, 181). In response to unpopular laws and policies, new lobby groups may mobilize and, depending on their strength, their demands will be gradually incorporated.

Liberal pluralist theory accepts that society is stratified but argues that equality of opportunity mitigates this unequal distribution of resources and ensures that the most able and motivated will rise to the top. As we saw earlier, John Porter's *The Vertical Mosaic* was the first major study of stratification in Canada. Porter demonstrated that social mobility occurred largely *within* well-organized strata based on country of origin and educational attainment of parents. Descendants of charter groups from England and Scotland not only occupied the majority of influential and well-paid positions, but were able, through a variety of well-honed strategies—private schools, clubs, camps, and other forms of networking—to carve out similar places for their children (1965, 293–95). Similarly, those dispossessed by the white colonizers, capitalists, and politicians passed on a legacy of poverty, ill-health, low life expectancy, high infant mortality, and marginal employment to their children. Those who arrived from non-English-speaking countries with little or no capital were able to accumulate little for their children, who tended to fill the same kinds of jobs as did their parents. Even with education, the sons of immigrants from these countries were less likely than sons of British charter members to attain the pinnacles of economic or political power.

Porter did not abandon the belief that a liberal democracy could produce equality of opportunity, and he argued for a system of education, open to all, in which the most able, rather than the most privileged, would rise to the top. Such a meritocracy would require a comprehensive system of social welfare so that the gifted children of all segments of the population could pursue a higher education. Whether such a meritocracy is possible in a liberal democracy has not been put to the test in Canada. Not only has the cost of university education risen, but the postwar expansion of social welfare and medicare provisions that Porter applauded in the 1960s has been eroded. The social and economic mobility that does occur is still more likely to be "within classes than between them" (Brym with Fox 1989, 102).

Liberal Feminism and the State

THE PREDOMINANT STREAM of feminist politics fits—although, some have argued, very uneasily—within the politics of liberal pluralism. We are going to explore the liberal feminist perspective on the state by looking first at the particular example of women's suffrage—the campaign and the consequences. Suffrage was key to the liberal feminist agenda, for it represented citizenship. A liberal democratic state rests upon the right of citizens to choose their government. As long as women were excluded from this right, the very notion of equality between the sexes remained moot.

Second, we look at the issue of equality of opportunity between men and women. While Porter's study demonstrated, and subsequent studies have only served to confirm, the limited social mobility in Canada, many feminists would argue that equality of opportunity between men and women might be possible *within* social classes. This possibility is investigated by comparing the numbers of men and women who have been in the federal cabinets since World War II and, in particular, during the period since the late 1960s when there has been concerted feminist effort to increase the numbers of women in political office. Third, we look at pay equity, a second wave feminist demand that appears as a liberal demand, yet may demonstrate, in Zillah Eisenstein's words, "the radical future" of liberal feminism.

The Meaning of Suffrage

The main goal of liberal feminism from the time of Mary Wollstonecraft, through the first wave of feminism that culminated in the vote, to the lobby that produced the Royal Commission on the Status of Women and beyond, has been equality of opportunity. Although liberal feminists increasingly have recognized the obstacles to achieving this ideal, they argue that society, as constituted, can accommodate equality of opportunity for women and men. Through education and political lobbying, archaic laws and attitudes can be changed, allowing women to achieve all levels of political, economic, and social power.

Like the first wave's struggle for the vote and women's right to a higher education, the lobbying efforts of groups like the National Action Committee on the Status of Women and the work of feminists within government bureaucracies have been predicated—at least until the late 1980s—on the fundamental idea that women can achieve equality in this society. From their perspective, the liberal democratic state exists beyond the interests of any particular group, yet is capable of shifting and responding to newly organized constituencies. The history of universal suffrage is often invoked as evidence for this conception: in the beginning no one had the right to vote; gradually, so the story goes, men of property, followed by most men, and finally most women were granted suffrage.[1]

In Canada, female suffrage for all British subjects was granted at the federal level and in all provinces except Quebec between 1916 and 1922. It had been a long struggle: "The campaign had taken some sixty years to win. . . . [T]housands of women and hundreds of organizations had been involved in the fight for political rights" (Prentice et al. 1988, 209). Does this success constitute evidence for the validity of liberal pluralist theory? Many historians argue that the granting of suffrage changed much less than feminists had imagined and their opponents had feared. Rather than proving the reforming potential of the liberal state, the granting of suffrage, they argue, illustrates the limits of liberalism. Other feminists (Bacchi 1983, 47–49), not necessarily in disagreement with this judgment, insist that we must evaluate the victory in the context of those times. As Ann Snitow has put it, "at a time when criticism of women's separate family role was still unthinkable, imagining a place outside the family where such a role would make no difference was—for a time—a most radical act" (1990, 26).[2] If the demand for the vote was, at one point, "a most radical act," and since that struggle was successful, we can see the grounds on which some would argue that liberal democracies can encompass gender equality. Yet there was an underside to the struggle for suffrage and to the reasons why it was granted that puts in a different light feminists of the time and the politicians who represented the state.

For there was a racist and francophobic dimension to the struggle for suffrage that reveals the divisions among women and raises questions about the state, as neutral arbiter, moving towards representing a new consensus of gender equality. Some English-speaking, middle-class suffragists engaged in racist and ethnocentric arguments that pitted women like themselves against immigrant men and women from non-English-speaking countries. Arguing that hearth, home, and nation needed protection from the foreign multitudes, they appealed to the male electorate and politicians to grant them suffrage in return for safe votes from like-minded women. As Isobel Graham of the Manitoba Political Equality League wrote in 1913: "Are we Western farmers so cultured, so steadfast, so loyal, so philanthropic that we can bear dilution by the ignorance, low idealism, and religious perversity of the average foreigner? . . . Keep aback the foreigner. Give us good, sound British stock—women already British, already civilized, already subjected to both earth and heaven for conduct" (quoted in Bacchi 1983, 52–53). For its part, the federal government first granted suffrage in 1917 to women nurses serving in the First World War, and later that year "extended the franchise to wives, widows, mothers, sisters and daughters of those, alive or deceased, who had served or were serving in the Canadian or British military or naval forces" (Prentice et al. 1988, 207–8). This selective franchise was calculated to shore up support for the re-election of Robert Borden's Union government and its mandate for conscription. The Conscription Crisis—like the war itself—had divided the country and the women's movement. In Quebec the war was unpopular: Why sacrifice the lives of young Quebeckers for a war among foreign powers, an ocean away? For them. Great Britain was scarcely the "mother country." The war was also opposed in principle by feminist pacifists.

The federal government's Wartime Election Act selectively enfranchising women drew both praise and outrage from suffrage advocates. Those who "in the wartime context, believed in the superiority of the Anglo-Saxon race and saw the vote as a way of reshaping society according to their values," welcomed the federal initiative (Prentice et al. 1988, 208). Opponents insisted that "valid change could only be achieved when all women acquired equal political rights with men" (ibid.). This history of the federal suffrage reveals that the neutral state had its own agenda, and politicians in power their own reasons for granting suffrage. They had committed the country to a war that was unpopular with a large segment of the population; selective female franchise was a small price to pay for electoral victory.

Yet within four years of the Armistice, women's franchise had been extended at the federal level to all women who were British subjects and in all provinces except Quebec. After decades of struggle, did women win? Or did politicians decide that women's franchise, despite all the extravagant claims made for and against it in previous decades, posed little threat to the status quo? Certainly what appeared as a radical demand in the first decades of the century quickly became incorporated into the ongoing electoral process. Indeed, extending the vote to women broadened the state's claim to legitimacy, since governments in power can claim victory in a free election in which almost all adults have the right to vote. Today even anti-feminists do not argue that women should not have the vote (Eisenstein 1981). Does this history sustain or challenge the liberal feminist perspective?

The Promise of Equality of Opportunity

Fifty years after the granting of suffrage, the Royal Commission on the Status of Women declared that equality of opportunity between the sexes was still elusive in Canadian society (see, for example, *Report* 1970, 12, 90–91, 97). The statistics seemed to speak for themselves. There were few women in Canadian parliaments, and there had never been more than one in cabinet. Corporate boardrooms seemed free of women. Indeed, when one of the major Canadian banks was challenged by the Honourable Marc Lalonde in 1976 to appoint a women to its board, the bank's president replied that there were no qualified women (Newman 1976). The right of women to pursue higher education had not resulted in a significant proportion of women professionals or academics.

Twenty-five years after the tabling of the *Report* of the royal commission, and as many years of concerted feminist mobilization, we may ask the question again—What about equality of opportunity between women and men? Since liberal democratic feminist theory locates decision-making power within government, it is germane to see how women have fared in their representation in federal cabinets, especially since successive federal governments have espoused the goal of equality between the sexes. Table 3-1 clearly reflects some changes. Until 1957, there had never been a woman in the federal cabinet. Prime Minister Jean Chrétien has appointed more women than his predecessors to cabinet, and several of them carry major portfolios.

Political scientists have argued that women's gains in party politics more generally have been marginal, and that it is too early to speak of anything like an irreversible progression toward women's equality (O'Neil and Sutherland 1990). Federally, women made up just over 6 percent of the candidates for election in 1972 and just under 20 percent in 1988. For the same years, their membership in the House of Commons was respectively 2 percent and 13 percent and had risen to 18 percent after the 1993 election (Trimble 1995, 100). The success rate of women candidates is about half that of male candidates. This does not mean necessarily that voters are less likely to vote for women. Rather, political parties have been more willing to nominate women in ridings that they expect to lose (Bashevkin 1993). In the provincial and territorial legislatures, women represent, on average, 18 percent of the membership, from a low of 6 percent in Newfoundland to a high of 25 percent in British Columbia (Trimble 1995, 100). Linda Trimble has shown that women are better represented on city councils and other elected offices

TABLE 3-1

Number of Women in the Federal Cabinet

Year	Prime Minister	Party	Number/Cabinet Total
1957	Diefenbaker	Conservative	1/22
1958	Diefenbaker	Conservative	1/23
1962	Diefenbaker	Conservative	1/22
1963	Pearson	Liberal	1/26
1968	Trudeau	Liberal	0/31
1972	Trudeau	Liberal	1/30
1974	Trudeau	Liberal	3/39
1979	Clark	Conservative	1/30
1980	Trudeau	Liberal	3/35
1984	Mulroney	Conservative	5/40
1988	Mulroney	Conservative	6/39
1993	Campbell	Conservative	3/25
1993	Chrétien	Liberal	8/33

Sources: O'Neil and Sutherland (1990); *Ottawa Letter* (1993); *Canadian Parliamentary Guide* (1995).

at the municipal level, and that their numbers are rising. She takes issue with those who have argued that this is because there is less power at the local level and that what happens there is less important. She suggests that "politics at the city level—'politics where we live,' is . . . more tangible, more immediate, and more rewarding than political action at the federal and provincial levels" (1995, 110).

Pay Equity and the Limits of Liberal Feminism

We may catch another glimpse of the liberal equality of opportunity perspective in action by looking at another feminist demand first raised in the early 1970s. Feminists were beginning to argue that the jobs that women did were paid less not because they required less education and skill but because they were done by women (Gaskell 1986). A major response to this reconsideration of women's traditional work has been the struggle at the federal and provincial levels for a set of policies that Ann Snitow has described as "humble and earthshaking, . . . this little brown mouse of a liberal reform"—policies that come under the rubric of the feminist slogan "Equal pay for work of equal value" (1990, 41). The main strategy for implementing this demand has been the struggle for pay equity legislation. Such legislation has been introduced at the federal level to cover workplaces under its jurisdiction, and in Quebec, Manitoba (in the public sector), and Ontario for firms with more than 100 employees (Burt 1993, 224). The legislation requires places of employment to develop job evaluation plans that compare, along a variety of dimensions, jobs usually done by men with those usually done by women. When such a plan is constructed and implemented conscientiously, the result is salary increases for those doing traditionally female jobs.

Such legislation was a clear improvement on earlier provincial and federal laws that applied only to identical or substantially similar work and could only be mobilized by an individual seeking redress (Burt 1993, 220–21). As Armstrong and Armstrong note, this legislation, mobilized by the slogan equal pay for equal work, "implied that pay inequality was a minor and individual problem for a few female employees who were discriminated against by a few misguided employers . . . and suggested that the widespread practice of paying women low wages was justified and necessary, a matter of women's productivity or women's choices" (1990a, 31–32).

In some ways, the newer formulation of equal pay for work of equal value is also informed by liberal pluralist theory. Feminists inside and outside government pressured public policy makers to enact laws that oblige employers to implement such plans. The working assumption behind such a strategy can still be a neutral state, open to assessing and resolving conflicting demands. In this case, the numbers of women in the workplace mean that they are in a position, as never before, to have their demands for equality at work mandated.

But it is striking that pay equity legislation also involves a departure from the liberal idea of the free and open marketplace, as corporate and business leaders have lamented. Their opposition clearly is not based only on philosophical grounds. The prospect of paying women salaries equivalent to those paid to men doing work of equal value provokes heated opposition, particularly from the owners of small businesses with narrow profit margins. The viability of small enterprises often rests on the low wages paid to women and visible minorities. But large corporations, employing huge numbers of women in clerical positions, also resist pay equity legislation. Such legislation challenges the liberal notion that society is made up of discrete individuals in competition with each other. When liberal feminists argue for legislation that would alter the conditions of work for most women, the inadequacy of traditional liberal theory for understanding and attaining liberal feminist goals becomes apparent. Rather than arguing that the best woman or man should get the jobs at the top, or that any woman should have an equal opportunity with every man to do nontraditional jobs, pay equity targets women as a group and allows what could be called sex action suits. This analysis declares women as a sex to be disadvantaged in the waged marketplace, not because they are less hard working, less intelligent, less motivated, less educated, less needy, less skilled, but because they are women. Pay equity legislation is motivated by an analysis that declares that women's work is undervalued compared to men's simply because women do it. Such legislation relies on an analysis of power relations that rests uncomfortably, if at all, within liberal pluralist political theory.

It is true that invoking the state to correct such inequities suggests that another part of liberal pluralist theory is retained: that the state is neutral arbiter and, if lobbied effectively, can be part of the solution. Yet so-called liberal reforms like pay equity challenge the liberal conception of society and state. For Ann Snitow, this "little brown mouse of a liberal reform" has potentially subversive consequences that contribute to the destabilization of gender hierarchies throughout the society. Comparable worth "erodes the economic advantages to employers of consistently undervaluing women's work and channelling women into stigmatized work ghettoes where pay is always lower. . . . [C]omparable worth undermines the idea that all work has a natural gender." More than this, "a woman earning [decent] money is an independent woman. She can change the family; she can consider leaving it" (1990, 42–43). Decent pay erodes the historical economic dependence of women on men and gives women more scope to choose living arrangements quite different from the traditional nuclear family; women with good salaries can choose to live alone, with children, with other women.

Despite these implications, feminist activists struggling for pay equity have been the first to admit the limitations of their strategy: "On its face, the proposal ignores the work women do in the family, ignores the non-economic reasons why women and men have different kinds of jobs, ignores what's wrong with job hierarchies and with 'worth' as the sole basis for determining pay" (Snitow 1990, 41). Liberal pluralist theory has proven inadequate for understanding and redressing the hierarchy between men and women in society. Most feminists would agree that the principal reason for this failure is that such a theory rests on the assumption that, in some important sense, everyone in society can compete for the most rewarded and influential positions, and that superior ability and drive will win out. Not only do these assumptions ignore head starts provided by privileged class and ethnic position, as John Porter first signalled, but they also obscure the power relations and gendered division of labour that structure familial relations.

Put simply, women cannot compete—even with men of their social class—in a free and open marketplace because that marketplace is predicated on the reproductive labour and childcare done by women somewhere else. Not only do women continue to do the lion's share of domestic labour and childcare, but also the work they do draws lower wages than men's work. No wonder, for many women, the right to work has been a mixed blessing. Laws governing property division in the event of marital dissolution have been rewritten to ensure more equitable distribution, yet, unlike men, women and their children are overwhelmingly poorer after separation and divorce (Morton 1988). From the vantage point of the 1990s, the entire attempt to legislate sexual equality seems like running an obstacle course in which the obstacles are constantly rearranged in ever more complex patterns. It is not that nothing changes; it is, rather, that the changes never occur in the form in which they were desired, and that their consequences often depart radically from what was envisioned by those who called for them. What Canadian society, presently organized, does not provide for women is equality of condition, even with men of their class.

For Marxist and socialist feminists, the primary issue has never been equality of opportunity. They argue that feminism must explain and transform the conditions and potential for all women and men, and in so doing they have engaged in useful adaptations of neo-Marxist formulations.

Neo-Marxism and the State

JOHN PORTER'S ANALYSIS of Canadian society as a vertical mosaic was both welcomed and challenged by Marxist scholars. They argued that Porter had accurately described a society in which rewards were differentially distributed according to ethnic and class background but that his explanation bypassed a crucial relation between those who owned capital and those who only owned their labour power. Wallace Clement (1975) and others agreed that the owners and managers of capital were largely members of the English and Scottish ethnic groups, but it was their ownership of capital that was crucial in sustaining and expanding their power and in excluding others. Their special and multifaceted links with the Canadian state were key to this strategy. In the eyes of neo-Marxists, the building of the Canadian state was not so much the work of enterprising business leaders, clever politicians, and industrious colonizers. Rather, it was the story of building an infrastructure that would make possible the easy movement of resources and people in the interests of accumulating profits. Central to this story was the creation of disciplined work forces (by making agricultural land scarce and expensive, importing labouring men from other countries, and using the military and police to quell revolt) together with raising and deploying capital (including taxes) (Teeple 1972). Reg Whitaker has called these developments "private enterprise at public expense" (1977, 43).

In *The Communist Manifesto*, Marx and Engels declared that "in the modern representative State," the bourgeoisie had "at last . . . conquered for itself . . . exclusive political sway." The role of the state, henceforth, was to manage "the common affairs of the whole bourgeoisie" (1969 [1848], 110–11). However, the growing power of the state in the succeeding century led theorists to develop more complex understandings of the relationship between economic and political power. Canadian Marxists argued that all capitalists did not have the same interests. Some made money from exporting resources; others through indigenous manufacturing and industry. The state had to be in a position to mediate conflicts and also to accommodate any strenuous popular movements. These ideas were encapsulated in the phrase the "relative autonomy of the state." If the state were to protect the long-term interests of capital while continuing to elicit consent from the governed, there had to be room to negotiate. Put crudely, the men of the state did not await marching orders from the men of capital (Panitch 1977, 3).

Feminism and the Relative Autonomy of the State

Socialist feminists found the neo-Marxist analysis of political economy and the notion of the relative autonomy of the state useful in explaining their involvement in struggles to pressure the state into changing laws or making new policies, including legislation like pay equity. Unlike liberal feminists, but like neo-Marxists, they held that the state is not neutral. However, unlike neo-Marxists, but like radical feminists, they argued that the state did not simply have a special relationship with capital: it also incorporated, created, and sustained patriarchal relations within its own networks and throughout the society.

This conception of the state ensures that feminists seldom treat the state as an ally. But since the state has the capacity to respond to the demands of popular movements—and indeed must respond in order to maintain its legitimacy—it followed that strategies aimed at transformation of policies and practices could have desirable results. At the same time, this analysis—and the resulting experience of feminist activists—indicated that the state would work to ensure that any resulting legislation was as narrow and uncostly as possible. Socialist feminists realized also, as neo-Marxists argue, that the struggle for such legislation might also benefit from the divisions within capital. Some large international corporations might be able to incorporate such legislation without cost, while smaller businesses might depend for survival on employing cheaper female labour. While feminists capitalize on divide-and-rule strategies, the state tries to formulate a new accommodation that does not aggravate those who own and control big capital and that defuses the popular movements that campaigned for the new policies.

This is why Marxist feminists Pat and Hugh Armstrong argues that the Ontario pay equity legislation *could* "legitimize women's right to better pay and transform the definitions of skill, effort, responsibility and working conditions while challenging established, hierarchical ways of organizing work" (1990a, 30). But the conditions for such success rest not on the existence of the new legislation itself but on foiling the attempt of the state and capital to pacify the organizers and their supporters. Feminist versions of the neo-Marxist formulation of the relative autonomy of the state allow for the efficacy of social movements originating within society and directed, at least in part, towards the state to change laws and develop new policies. Yet such a perspective spurns any belief that gains once won are secure—a notion that did not lessen the sense of outrage and betrayal when, for example, the Conservative government of Ontario premier Mike Harris, as one of its first acts in office, moved to repeal the province's employment equity legislation.

Feminists have also proceeded from neo-Marxist understandings of the state to examine the relations between men and women in the context of the regional disparities and differences within Canada. The concept of region has most often been used to delineate geographical areas: the prairies from the mountains; the coastal areas from inland regions; certainly the North from everywhere else. Canadian political economy looks at these spatial considerations in the context of capitalist development and the role of the state in "the political creation of regions" (Brodie 1989, 156).

Maritimers with long political memories, and those aided by a new generation of Maritime historians, view the Canadian Confederation with scepticism (Buckner 1990). From their perspective, the political act of confederation helped wealthy investors create a nation *a mari usque ad mare*—from sea to sea—by removing impediments to the movement of people and resources from the Maritimes to Central Canada. Nor was the political expansion of the Canadian state into the West greeted with universal accord, certainly not by the Métis and their leader Louis Riel, acknowledged as a hero of his people by the Canadian Parliament a hundred years after his execution (Saint Onge 1985; Sprague 1980).

Close attention to the rise and fall of regional prosperity reveals that regional inequalities are expressions of relations of power and the prevailing distribution of resources both within and between regions. This means that there are no permanent winners and losers, but rather a shifting cast of advantaged and disadvantaged players, with a small minority better placed to protect their own interests. For much of the period since Confederation, Maritimers have had a lower per capita income than people living in Ontario (Matthews 1980, 45). Within Atlantic Canada, as elsewhere, women have a much lower average income than men, blacks than whites, Aboriginals than non-Aboriginals. To put it another way, we could say that living in a region that is "disadvantaged" is very advantageous for some, particularly for the small group of people who control much of the land and resources. There are very rich capitalists in Atlantic Canada, for example, and they may or may not reinvest their profits in the region.

Shifting and uneven rates of employment across the country provide stark evidence that wealth and poverty are not evenly distributed (see table 3-2). Explaining these shifting differentials of employment and income—differentials that influence health, mortality rates, educational attainment, career options—launches us again onto controversial theoretical terrain. Many argue that Confederation was masterminded by political and economic elites in Central Canada to expand their own opportunities at the expense of the Maritimes and then the West. In this interpretation, Confederation either led to, or coincided with, the dein-dustrialization of the Maritimes as capital was used to drain the natural resources from that region into world markets, with most of the profits accruing to the Central Canadian capitalists. Similarly the western provinces provided wheat for the East and, through protective tariffs, were forced to pay high prices for eastern manufactured goods that could have been purchased for less from the United States (Forbes 1979; Stevenson 1980).

Such interpretations must be historically specific. This flow of capital out of the Maritimes and the West was not geographically deter-mined; nor are these regional disparities frozen in time. People with capital make investment decisions that may or may not be supported by federal and provincial governments, and in general these decisions are not made with local, regional, or national loyalties in mind. As histori-ans Christopher Armstrong and H.V. Nelles conclude about the Canadian capitalists who invested in Latin America in the first decades of this century, "For the men who created these utility empires other nations were merely markets, for capital or promotions. Countries were not things to be used by or to be loyal to; they were things to use—and they were interchangeable" (1988, 277).

In most of the literature on regional disparity in Canada, women are invisible—whether the focus is upon federal–provincial conferences, tar-iffs and transportation policy, or social movements. The relatively recent feminist literature has taken up this challenge, and several broad consid-erations seem clear. First, women develop survival strategies for them-selves and their families that are thoroughly attentive to the changing conditions created by regional disparities. The belief that women are economically dependent upon men, and that men are obligated to sup-port wives and families does not sustain families where unemployment is high or employment seasonal, where men are thrown out of work because of mine and factory closures, or even where men may make a living wage. Pat Connelly and Martha MacDonald's (1986) research in Nova Scotia fishing communities reveals that women have worked per-manently in the fish plants (until the recent collapse of the fishing indus-try), made childcare arrangements, and encouraged their husbands to "help" with cooking and housework. Changing conditions and capital-ization of the fishing industry meant that men's wages could not be stretched to cover basic familial needs.

TABLE 3-2

Full-time and Full-year Employment Rates[a] by Region, 1983–93

	1983	1984	1985	1986	1987	1988	1989	1990	1991	1992	1993
All provinces											
Full-time	48.1	48.8	49.4	50.2	51.2	52.1	52.6	52.1	49.7	48.4	47.9
Full-year, full-time	38.6	39.1	41.1	41.6	42.1	43.6	44.6	42.8	41.2	40.4	40.0
Atlantic Canada											
Newfoundland											
Full-time	38.2	38.0	37.7	38.5	38.9	40.7	41.6	41.1	39.7	37.0	36.2
Full-year, full-time	24.6	26.3	26.1	25.5	26.7	28.8	29.4	28.6	25.9	25.7	26.7
Prince Edward Island											
Full-time	45.1	45.2	45.7	45.7	46.3	47.9	47.4	48.0	44.9	44.9	44.0
Full-year, full-time	28.6	31.2	31.9	33.0	30.5	33.3	34.0	33.7	31.6	32.7	33.0
Nova Scotia											
Full-time	42.2	43.7	42.9	43.5	44.1	46.1	46.3	46.8	44.8	42.9	42.0
Full-year, full-time	31.9	32.7	34.8	33.2	35.9	36.9	37.1	37.5	34.3	32.8	33.6
New Brunswick											
Full-time	39.7	39.8	40.8	41.5	43.0	43.8	44.2	44.8	43.3	43.5	43.3
Full-year, full-time	29.1	30.1	31.7	31.7	32.2	32.0	35.6	34.2	34.7	35.7	33.4
Central Canada											
Quebec											
Full-time	45.5	46.6	47.1	47.7	49.1	50.1	50.2	49.8	47.5	46.3	45.6
Full-year, full-time	35.9	35.7	38.0	39.0	39.3	40.0	42.2	40.1	38.9	38.1	37.6
Ontario											
Full-time	50.7	51.9	52.8	53.9	55.0	55.8	56.0	54.8	51.3	49.6	49.0
Full-year, full-time	41.8	43.7	45.5	44.8	47.0	48.9	48.8	45.9	43.6	43.2	41.6
Western Canada											
Manitoba											
Full-time	49.4	50.2	50.6	50.9	51.2	51.1	51.3	51.2	49.3	48.1	48.7
Full-year, full time	41.7	40.6	42.1	42.4	40.7	43.0	43.3	42.1	39.0	40.9	42.4
Saskatchewan											
Full-time	50.1	49.5	50.8	51.0	51.2	51.0	51.1	51.5	51.2	49.9	49.9
Full-year, full-time	40.5	40.6	42.5	41.7	41.6	40.3	42.3	42.7	41.9	41.0	40.8
Alberta											
Full-time	54.4	54.3	54.7	55.2	55.0	56.3	56.9	57.0	56.4	54.4	53.6
Full-year, full-time	43.3	42.0	45.6	44.2	44.1	46.0	47.4	47.6	46.2	43.8	44.2
British Columbia											
Full-time	45.2	44.8	45.3	46.5	47.5	48.4	50.8	50.5	49.1	48.8	48.8
Full-year, full-time	37.2	35.5	37.4	38.6	39.7	42.5	42.7	41.6	41.6	40.2	41.6

[a] Proportion of working-age population employed full time and full year.

Source: Statistics Canada, Cat. 75-001E (Autumn 1995), 29.

In her study of Nova Scotia's offshore fishery, Marion Binkley explains how the industrialization of the fishery eroded earlier gender complementarity within the household. "Historically, fishing families exercised a strict gender division of labour. Men caught and gutted the fish, while women and children processed the fish on shore" (1995, 50). While men still catch the fish, they now do so on company-owned and operated vessels, and women process the fish in industrialized plants. But the wives of offshore fishers were less likely to work in the plants than were the wives of fish plant employees because of the difficulty of providing care for children during their husbands' long absences. Offshore fishing is also dangerous work, and the division of labour includes an emotional division: "fishers trivialize the risks they take, their wives characterize their lives as being full of uncertainty and fear that their husbands may return maimed or not return at all" (ibid., 154). Such complete dependence of wives upon husbands aggravates tensions and expectations. As one fisher told an interviewer, "When I come up over the dock, she better have the car turned around, the driver's door open, the trunk open and be sitting on the passenger's side waiting for me. . . . My car not being there really spites me. . . . I just hate waiting to go home. I only have forty-eight hours" (quoted in ibid., 58).

With the collapse of the offshore fishery, tens of thousands of men and women have lost their livelihood at the same time that the federal government has been slashing assistance programs. Women and men stitch together survival strategies that draw upon social welfare, part-time and poorly remunerated work, work in the informal economy, exchanges of goods and services with friends and neighbours, and intensified household work to make ends meet, as Suzanne Mackenzie (1986) also found in Trail and Nelson, BC, and Kingston, Ontario.

In the decades since the 1930s, many farming families have sold their farms, overwhelmed by debt and the impossibility of competing with large agribusiness. In 1973 Canadians learned that farm wives could also lose their right to any share in their farms at the time of a marriage breakdown. Irene Murdoch's marriage ended in 1968 after a violent incident in which her husband broke her jaw. She took her case for a share of the family ranch to the Supreme Court of Canada and lost. The court argued that Murdoch's work—which included "haying, raking, swathing, mowing, driving trucks and tractors and teams, quietening horses, taking cattle back and forth to the reserve, dehorning, vaccinating, branding"—was only the work "of any ranch wife" (quoted in Prentice et al. 1988, 398). Such work did not give her a claim in partnership.[3] The assumption that women are economically dependent upon men, and in return provide "a labour of love," including sexual access, underwrites such a decision.

Regional inequalities have fuelled social movements that identify Central Canada as the enemy and have buttressed other movements that target the power of capitalists (who have been concentrated in Central Canada). The predecessor of the New Democratic Party, the Co-operative Commonwealth Federation (CCF), was founded by women and men from across Canada, but the greatest support for its program, the socialist Regina Manifesto, was from the Depression-racked Prairies. Women's participation in such movements, once as hidden as their work in the household, has been brought to light through autobiographies, feminist research, and a new generation of social historians who look behind official institutional histories (Finkel 1993; Sangster 1989).

From a feminist perspective, we might speculate that women are more affected and bound by regional differences and inequalities than men. Their primary responsibility for children and home has tied them more tightly into local conditions and encouraged them to make the best from what they find there (Conrad 1986). Men with capital to invest not only move to the centres of capital, but may travel the world to make the deals upon which profits depend. Young working-class men have been likely to "go down the road" looking for employment elsewhere; married men commute to seasonal and permanent employment in those locations where capital investment in natural resources and mines provides work (Bray 1991).

When women and children accompany husbands and fathers who have found jobs in new locations, it has often been to the resource towns built north of the main line of settlement across the country. Such towns have been built because capitalists and planners wanted to attract and keep a stable work force. The reasoning was that men accompanied by, and responsible for, women and children were more likely than single men to stay (Luxton 1980). Such towns have been described as "no place for a woman" (Kreps 1979). As Phyllis Bray, a wife in a resource town for ten years, demonstrated, company towns provided no paid employment for women. The towns were designed with little concern for women looking after young children in small detached houses through long, hard winters and with no resources to create a life for themselves. Yet women still raised families and started churches, libraries, volunteer groups, and more recently (and with much community opposition) resources like shelters for women escaping abusive husbands (Bray 1989; 1993). The towns that women developed became home for many of them, and when company closures destroy the possibility of making a living—as they have across the country—women have worked hard to attract new industry and to provide new ways of sustaining life (Mackenzie 1987).

Arguing that women are more tied to particular (regional) locations is not meant to obliterate the long history of female migration to Canada and across Canada, nor to overlook those women who broke with gendered expectations by migrating alone and taking up many of the activities believed to be the province of menfolk. But it is to say that there is no excuse for the invisibility of women in the regional literatures. Women have created regions, stretched the constraints posed by location, and been active in those movements that sought to redress poverty, devastation, unemployment, high infant and childhood mortality rates—indeed, the whole spectrum of conditions that are exacerbated by regional inequalities.

Just as Marxists and neo-Marxists have tried to specify and demonstrate that the state is deeply implicated in protecting capital and enhancing the interests of those who own and control capital, feminists have been exploring the ways in which the state may be seen to embody and produce patriarchal relations between men and women as an intrinsic part of its mandate. But before considering this question more specifically, we need to look at the broader feminist insight that, whatever the role of the state, the relations of domination and subordination between men and women are constituted in society more generally. In pursuing this idea, socialist feminists have drawn on the ideas of neo-Marxists on the relationship between the state and what has been called "civil society."

State and Society

Liberal pluralist theorists seldom speak of *the state* but rather of *government*. In their work they incorporate the study of the institutions—legislative, judiciary, and civil service—that ostensibly govern the society. Their interests include the study of federal, provincial, and municipal governments and their respective jurisdictions as defined by the British North America Act and the subsequent changes to that act. In this conception, the distinction between government and governed is quite straightforward, as is the process through which the governed select and change their government.

In the neo-Marxist conception, the state is not a set of institutions with discrete functions, but rather a dense network of relations that are informed by the same struggles over political meanings and goals that are occurring throughout society. These struggles are about everything from competition for support from different kinds of capital, to the form and substance of the welfare state, to the debates over curricula in the schools and universities. From this perspective, what falls outside the state—which does not mean that it is impervious to its influences—is called *civil society*: familial and household relationships, labour unions, churches, voluntary associations, and political parties. Whether and how a concern or demand within civil society over values, meanings, priorities, and precedence is taken up within the state is highly variable and complex. The history of how any concern moves from "private trouble" to "public issue" will not only depend on the numbers of people with the private trouble but also upon who they are. Do they belong to a powerful class, group, or sector? Are they seen as credible by those who are powerful? Do they articulate the concern in a language and form that resonate with others? Does it become incorporated within dominant forms of discourse? A feminist analysis reveals that the private troubles of women have had a rocky history in attempting to become part of the dialogues and debates through which state policies are reconsidered (Walker 1990).

If we conceptualize the relations between state and civil society as continuous and multifaceted, we can see that the power relations within civil society will provide some with more access than others to having their interests taken up by the state. So it is not just that women have been part of the "private" world, but that within the whole realm of civil society—family, church, labour unions, and political parties—they have, for the most part, been subordinate to men. Long before issues might become part of state dialogues, then, the concerns raised by women in their families, in the women's auxiliaries of churches and political parties, and within labour unions, have been effectively marginalized and silenced.

Consider the derisive laughter that greeted women during the movements for suffrage, during the hearings of the Royal Commission on the Status of Women, and even during a presentation to the House of Commons in 1982 on wife battery. This is not just (nervous) laughter at the actual content of women's demands, but also a reaction to any articulation of their demands in the public sphere. We might imagine Canadian society as a broad panoply of stage settings—women around breakfast tables with men and children, at church meetings, at party nomination meetings. Here in the varied and elaborate settings of civil society we can see the thousands of jokes that greet women's ideas, particularly when they constitute challenges to authority. Such ridicule, sometimes backed up by physical force, constrains women from taking even their own feelings and demands seriously. When enough women dared to be the objects of male humour, all the small private jokes broke through into public ridicule and laughter in the House of Commons, in the heart, we might say, of the state. We knew that something had changed when those laughing men themselves became the target of scorn and public censure.

Here we may see why the liberal pluralist notion that governments should play a limited role in society has been challenged by many feminists. In particular, such a conception of government is predicated upon the division of society into private and public life, with liberal theorists arguing that governments should only intervene in public life. Radical and socialist feminists, in particular, have challenged this understanding of state and society. First, they argue that the interconnections between public and private life are dense and thorough. Second, they maintain that the state not only intrudes in the so-called private sphere but that it helps create its boundaries and the relations that inform family and household. Third, they insist that the theory that the state should not intrude in private life has provided a rationale for sustaining the economic dependence of women upon men, and has provided a virtual licence for the more powerful members of households to physically and emotionally abuse the less powerful.

It is not difficult to find support for these claims. Feminists in Canada, for example, have waged a twenty-five-year struggle for the right of a woman to choose to terminate a pregnancy. That the state had laws that not only prohibited abortion but also forbade contraception makes a mockery of the liberal notion that the division between public and private life is clear and that the state does not intervene in private life. During the same years, however, feminists have waged just as vociferous a campaign to insist that the rape of a married woman by her husband was indeed rape and should be against the law, and that the battering of women by their intimates should be prosecuted, as are assaults by strangers. Here the rationale of the law had to be challenged: a man's home, feminists argued, should not be his castle.

The state's role in legitimating marriage provides shifting sets of advantages and disadvantages for men and women, the married and the unmarried, and for heterosexuals, lesbians, and gays; this history alone defies any analysis that claims the absence of the state from so-called private life. What feminists have argued, then, is that not only is the state patriarchal but so is the liberal conception of the relationship between government and governed, based, as it is, on a presumed natural division between public and private life.

By looking at Canadian society in terms of the relations between state and civil society, we can see why feminists direct their attention to both the hierarchical relations within civil society and the structure, relations, personnel, and discourses of the state. Unless the subordination of women within civil society is challenged, it is unthinkable that sufficient numbers of women would be in a position to engage in the public discourse that leads to transformation of the relations, policies, and legislation of the state. Yet this is not a one-way street. To the extent that state policies enhance the possibility of women's economic independence, they help women challenge their unequal place in their personal lives as well.

A Patriarchal State?

THE ARGUMENT THAT THE CANADIAN STATE is a patriarchal state has been made from a number of feminist perspectives. Taken together, the case is persuasive. The Canadian state was negotiated by men (the "Fathers of Confederation"). The existence of the participating colonies was predicated upon, but did not acknowledge, the invisible labour of women in households and on farms (Errington 1996). Since Confederation, the vast majority of those with formal power in all aspects of state relations—from members of Parliament to primary school principals—have been men. The legislation of the state—from family law to criminal law—has been gendered in ways that disadvantage women politically, socially, and economically. Not only have those with influence been predominantly male, but they respond to the world in ways that protect the interests of men throughout the society, and ruling-class men in particular. Finally, the society in which the state is located is informed in all its relations by male–female hierarchies.

To describe the Canadian state as patriarchal, however, is not to identify a monolithic or unchanging structure or set of relations. The complex relations between state and civil society have been uncovered by long periods of feminist activism. When women disrupt the relations of civil society and challenge their subordinate locations in that realm, those disruptions are felt within the relations of the state. The reaction of governments and state bureaucracies has been to re-establish their legitimacy with the population by appointing women, sometimes even feminists, to higher office and by undertaking policy review and legislative changes. Writing from her experience as director of the Women's Program at the Department of Secretary of State during the 1970s, Susan Findlay concludes that "when the state is more vulnerable to women's demands, feminists [within the state] can play a more active role in the development of state proposals to promote women's equality . . . by taking advantage of the state's need for legitimation" (1987, 48). It is clear, however, that in Canada the process of incremental reform is neither linear nor even. As Findlay says, "the reforms that emerge from these periods are not necessarily permanent" (ibid., 48). How transitory such gains may be became glaringly apparent from the late 1980s when federal and provincial governments responded to financial deficits by cutting back social programs that are particularly necessary to women. Any lingering doubts about the permanence of feminist gains were removed by the election in Alberta of Ralph Klein's Social Credit government and in Ontario of Mike Harris's Conservatives.

While the slashing of social programs has been justified on economic grounds, even feminist reforms that did not cost money have often had unintended negative consequences. Reforms to family law that were intended to place women on an equal footing with men at the time of marital dissolution, have been designed and implemented in ways that disadvantage some women even more than in the earlier legislation. Mary Morton (1988) has argued that this is because the new legislation has been predicated on the fallacious assumption that men and women are equal *now*. When judges treat divorcing couples as a pair of equals, dividing marital property but giving women no right to a share of their husbands' future earnings, they ignore the overwhelming evidence that women who have spent years looking after their children are in no position to maintain the marital standard of living (Chunn 1995, 196–99). Divorced men—usually the non-custodial parent—are, by contrast, more likely to be better off financially after divorce.

There are similar problems in the Charter of Rights and Freedoms with two sex equality provisions—sections 15 and 28—which came into effect in 1982 after considerable feminist lobbying. A study of 591 equality decisions handed down by lower courts during the next three years revealed that only fifty-two of these decisions involved sex equality claims. Only nine of these were brought by women, mainly in the context of civil litigation, and five of these cases were won. Men won almost three times as many of the remainder. In half of these cases, men initiated equality challenges to defend themselves against sex offence provisions of the Criminal Code. Brodsky and Day argue that most often the targets in cases brought by men "are legislative protections and benefits that women have acquired in the last ten or twenty years as a result of intensive lobbying efforts" (1989, 58–59). Eleven years after the Charter came into effect, the Supreme Court of Canada had not yet issued any decision based on either of the sex equality provisions (Baines 1993, 266). Some feminist legal scholars have tried to untangle these outcomes. Why have feminist struggles for equality been subverted in these ways? Equality, they now argue, has been predicated within liberal theory on notions of sameness. But women and men are not the same, either biologically or sociologically. In particular, women's monopoly on childbearing and their subsequent responsibility for those children do not figure in liberal understandings of equality.

Contrary to liberal pluralist notions, however, the state is heavily implicated not only in the process of controlling production and capital accumulation, but also in shaping the conditions in which women have and do not have children. This influence can be direct—laws about birth control, abortion, taxation, mothers' allowance, social welfare—and indirect, by enhancing the possibilities for some women and not others to have and raise children. Again we should remember that the state does not produce patriarchal legislation within a vacuum but rather in the context of its complex interrelationships with civil society. In the case of abortion, for example, we see very clearly that the struggle is not just within civil society or between civil society and the state. Rather the state has been one of the sites of struggle as politicians, legislators, and civil servants become involved in writing legislation, formulating policy, and directing (or not directing) funds to pay for abortions.

From the early 1970s, feminists argued that if equality of opportunity was to have any meaning for women, all members of society had to take responsibility for childcare. That meant tax-supported twenty-four-hour childcare centres. A feminist peace poster of the mid-1970s challenged the state's funding priorities: "What if there was child care for every child and the military had to have bake sales to buy their bombers." Feminists argued that a state with unlimited resources for the military and for war and few if any resources for childcare earned the designation patriarchal. Such an argument has been bolstered by the struggles of lesbians for custody of their children, and by the challenges of gays and lesbians to their exclusion from the military.

Making the claim that the Canadian state is patriarchal does not eliminate the need for an historically specific analysis that attends both to changes over time and differences across space. In the next chapter, the focus is upon how the patriarchal assumptions, policies, and laws of the Canadian state are manifested and experienced by the Aboriginal peoples, by Quebec francophones, and by those disadvantaged by racism. In those discussions, a further debate about the Canadian state is raised: What are the historical and contemporary grounds for arguing that this state is not only patriarchal but racist? From this vantage point, we may look at the ways in which patriarchal, racist, and class interests are intertwined in different social and political locations.

Notes

1. In British North America, some women of property appear to have voted in some elections, particularly in Lower Canada. There were debates about the legality of women's suffrage and, in the end, specific legislation was required to ban women from voting (Prentice et al. 1988, 98–101; Riddell 1928).

2. See also DuBois (1978). She argues that it was women's involvement in the suffrage movement as historical and collective agents, "far more than the eventual enfranchisement of women, that created the basis for new social relations between men and women" (201).

3. The lump-sum maintenance payment that Murdoch was finally granted in 1973
    was not on the grounds of the economic partnership of the marriage but rather on
    the grounds that women were entitled to support during marriage and appropriate
    maintenance after break-up in return for domestic duties and sexual availability
    during the marriage. The Murdoch case helped fuel the feminist struggle, which
    resulted in legislation in most provinces recognizing that domestic and other eco-
    nomic activities, usually done by women, made it possible for wage earners to
    acquire money and property (Prentice et al. 1988, 398–99).

Challenging the State: Self-determination, Nationalism, and Anti-racism

ON THE FRONT-PAGE of the *Globe and Mail* on 16 October 1988, there was a story headlined "New map diminishes Canada."

Canada's sprawling place in world cartography is cut dramatically in a new world map issued by the National Geographic Society. And at the unveiling of the new map yesterday, society officials were only slightly apologetic that it shows a distinctly wizened true north strong and free. The problem, they said, is that Canadians have been living a geographical lie. The sweeping expanse of pink on most maps that has reassured generations of Canadians about their place in the world gives the country about 2 and 1/2 times the credit it is due. The new National Geographic map uses a projection designed to remedy much of the distortion that is inevitable when a sphere is portrayed on a flat piece of paper. . . . Instead of being 158 per cent larger than it would be on a globe of the same scale . . . , Canada shrinks to 21 per cent larger.

Map making, as the inventor of the new projection, Arthur Robinson, commented, is "pretty much an artistic process rather than a scientific process." Maps are representations, symbols, just as words are symbols, and as such they communicate and distort simultaneously.

The Aboriginal peoples living on that land represented by the "sweeping expanse of pink" point to another distortion inherent in the depiction of "Canada." In public protests and negotiations, many Aboriginal people have made it clear that they do not acknowledge the legitimacy of the Canadian state. This state, they argue, was formed by conquest, broken promises, and expansion by force and trickery. European laws instituted a regime of private property that excluded the original inhabitants from access to the land and use of its resources.

Since the mid-1960s, a growing number of people of French descent in Quebec have also provoked a renewed challenge to the legitimacy of the Canadian state for failing to accommodate the aspirations of the French nation in North America. In the second of two referenda on the question of independence from Canada, held on 30 October 1995, the vote in Quebec between those favouring secession and those against ended in a dead heat, with the "no" side unable to claim more than a truce. To complicate this picture, the Cree of Quebec acknowledged that the Québécois had a right to secede from Confederation but no right to the vast proportion of the land occupied by Aboriginal peoples. The Cree asserted that they would continue to negotiate with the government of Canada for self-determination, regardless of the outcome of the referendum.

This chapter continues the discussion of feminist challenges to the Canadian state by looking specifically at the Aboriginal struggle for self-determination, the Québécois quest for independence, and the continuing struggles by those disadvantaged by racism to transform the policies and practices of the Canadian state. There are three main themes to the discussions that follow from the introductions in the previous chapter. First, the formation of the Canadian state was based on and is sustained by fundamental inequalities. These inequalities are not incidental features of a society that in all other respects is fair-minded and just. Second, all of these structured inequalities are informed by patriarchal assumptions and laws, but we can only understand how this is so through specific historical and sociological analysis. Third, the patriarchal state has different ramifications for women of different social classes, in different civil societies, and for those who are advantaged or disadvantaged through racist assumptions and practices.

Colonization and Dispossession: The Canadian State and the Aboriginal Peoples

THE ABORIGINAL PEOPLES OF CANADA[1] lived in the territory that is Canada for thousands of years before the arrival of the French or the English. Their claims that the Canadian state does not represent them and that, by deception and force, they were deprived of the use of the land on which they had lived have been made eloquently and often in the law courts, through the media, in political protests of many kinds, and in forums like the International Court of Justice (Abele and Stasiulis 1989; Tennant 1990). A stunning array of evidence—from census data on life span, health, and infant and maternal mortality to ethnographic and anthropological studies that detail how a way of life was destroyed—has been brought to bear on the case that there is a third world within Canada's borders.

In mounting their challenge to the legitimacy of the Canadian state, Aboriginal peoples have faced overwhelming obstacles. They share a history of dispossession of land, disenfranchisement, ill health, and poverty. In 1990, for example, nearly 33 percent of Aboriginal women and 28 percent of Aboriginal men had incomes below Statistics Canada's low income cut-off, compared to 17 percent of non-Aboriginal women and 14 percent of non-Aboriginal men (see table 4-1). Many have argued that Canada's Native peoples share a history of cultural genocide (Wotherspoon and Satzewich 1993, 28). They are not one people, but many, each with a long history before European contact and a particular history of contact with Europeans. Without a common language, culture, and—most importantly—territory, Aboriginal political struggles with the Canadian state have generally been isolated and fragmented, spread out over thousands of miles. At the same time, the ongoing struggle at the local level for individual and community survival has been monumental and exhausting.

Yet from these diverse locations, a shared Aboriginal response has been in the making for at least the past two decades. The increasingly unified Native demand to have their territory returned and for sovereignty over that territory was forced dramatically onto the Canadian political agenda in the summer of 1990 with the roadblocks at

TABLE 4-1

Incidence of Low Income[a] Among Aboriginal and Non-Aboriginal
People, by Age, 1990

| | Aboriginal people[b] | | Non-Aboriginal people | |
	Women	Men	Women	Men
Persons aged	%		%	
Under 18	35.1	33.7	17.0	16.9
18–24	41.2	30.9	22.4	17.5
35–44	28.5	20.7	14.6	11.8
45–54	24.6	21.0	11.7	9.7
55–64	33.1	26.5	17.1	13.8
65 and over	31.3	22.4	22.9	13.7
Total	32.7	27.9	16.9	13.8

[a]   Includes respondents with incomes below Statistics Canada's low income cut-offs.
[b]   Includes respondents with Indian registration who do not have Aboriginal origins.

Source: Statistics Canada, Census of Canada.

Kanesatake and Kahnawake and with Elijah Harper's vote in the
Manitoba legislature against the Meech Lake Accord. Harper's vote was
heralded by Aboriginal leaders throughout Canada. Clearly Aboriginal
peoples are finding ways of demonstrating that excluding them from
negotiations that affect their lives and the viability of their communities
will have crucial repercussions for the political future of the country.

We can examine the precontact histories of Aboriginal peoples and
the history of the Aboriginal–European encounter by asking some feminist questions. First, what was the precontact history of gender relations
in the diverse Aboriginal societies? There were great differences across
these societies in the relations between men and women, the status of
women, the sexual division of labour, and the roles of men and women
in decision making. Yet most of the anthropological evidence, including
the earliest oral histories provided by elders, depicts societies organized
on relatively communitarian and egalitarian lines. In the hunting and
gathering and agricultural economies of Eastern and Central Canada,
women appear to have had "relative autonomy in sexual life and mar-

riage; influence in politics or group decision making; and participation in the religious or ceremonial lives of their people" (Prentice et al. 1988, 31). Among some northwestern and western peoples, on the other hand, women seem to have been relatively powerless (ibid.; Mitchell and Franklin 1984). Noted North American anthropologist Bruce Trigger asserts that "in North American Indian societies, decision making depended upon a slow process of achieving consensus" (1991, 1214). There is evidence that, in many of these societies, women were by no means excluded from that process (Van Kirk 1987).

A second question is, what was the impact of the arrival, settling, and consolidation of power of Europeans upon the relations of power between the sexes within European and Native societies? Again, this is a question that reaches back to the first contact and continues today. Several points, briefly put, will help frame the discussion. Roman Catholic missionaries came to the New World in the seventeenth century to christianize the "heathens." Their belief that the unconverted faced eternal damnation in a fiery hell helps to explain why some missionaries were willing to face martyrdom in pursuit of saving souls. Successful conversion, the missionaries came to believe, had to involve a transformation of the Aboriginal way of life and a reconfiguring of Native relationships. In their work with the Huron and Montagnais, for example, the missionaries were struck by women's freedom and autonomy, especially in regards to sexual practices and marital relationships. The missionaries urged men to bring their wives under control and to practise sexual monogamy to ensure that their wives bore only their children. In anthropologist Karen Anderson's assessment, in no more than three decades "many women had . . . been subdued, rendered docile and obedient" (1991, 4).

Two centuries later, the policy of collecting Indians on reservations began in earnest. Marlene Brant Castellano has summarized the devastating effects of this policy, particularly on Indian men in the migratory groups "whose education from infancy was directed to preparing them to assume the roles of hunter, warrior, [and] visionary." Ojibwa women, under conditions of deepening hardship, retained much of their traditional role caring for children, processing and preparing food and other necessities, and adding "colour and beauty to the daily round of subsistence work through the creation of handicrafts" (1989, 48). Clearly there is no single answer to the question of the impact on Aboriginal men and women of the arrival and settlement of Europeans.

An extensive anthropological literature reveals that hunter and gatherer societies are likely to have more egalitarian relations between the sexes than are sedentary agricultural societies (including the feudal societies that predated capitalism in Western Europe and England) or capitalist societies (Gough 1973). As power becomes more centralized and as state structures replace household structures as locations for decision making, men gain the advantage and women are increasingly excluded. Certainly there was some centralized decision making in some Aboriginal societies, and women seemed to have played a less direct role than men in such decisions. But this centralization pales in comparison to postcontact history when power over people and resources was wrested away from Native communities and replaced by the interventions of white male administrators from the Department of Indian Affairs.

In this process, women were more excluded and disadvantaged than men because the laws and policies that structured access to resources were thoroughly informed by the patriarchal relations of the white conquerors. In general, the white Western patriarchal notion that men look after women means that when Western, developed nations "come to the aid" of undeveloped nations, the resources—from job-training programs to discretion over distribution of material resources—are channelled through male leaders and targeted for men (Fiske 1991; Hale 1988; McFarland 1988; Mosse 1993). With Aboriginal men coming to hold most of the leadership roles in postcolonial organizations, the negotiations that have taken place between the First Nations and the representatives of the Canadian state could be described as racist sessions of a boys' club.

In the past thirty years, Native women have begun organizing against the ways in which the patriarchal practices of white society have affected their status within their own society (Silman 1987). This has meant challenging not only the Canadian state but also male Indian leadership. These women argue that many male Indian leaders identify their community's interests with their own interests. Women are excluded from decision making, have fewer resources than men, and have become subordinate to men in ways unimaginable in precontact days. The inequality between Indian men and women was specifically written into law by the Canadian state during the 1880s with the Indian Act. This specifically patriarchal aspect of the Indian Act was also an enabling measure for a racist policy.

The Indian Act was a racist piece of legislation in a very precise meaning of the word racist. First, the category Indian was created, and the people of disparate societies who lived in the provinces and territories of Canada were so labelled. In creating a category Indian, another category, non-Indian, had to be created. The decision about who is in what category becomes entirely arbitrary, since the creation of the categories themselves was an arbitrary act. The underlying assumption for this argument is that there is no meaningful biological category called race that has consequences for reproductive or political life; there is, rather, one race—that is, the human race. What divides people are social practices, including laws that create such categories. Such laws can be called racist because they assume that people can be divided into such categories in ways that matter. Racism then serves to divide people both by categorizing them and by consolidating the hierarchical arrangements that originally motivated the categorizations.

The Indian Act clearly served to divide people. It divided people arbitrarily into racial categories—Indian and non-Indian—and then mandated different treatment, different obligations and responsibilities, and differential access to resources to each group. In so doing, arbitrary differences between people were encoded into law, while all differences between those placed in each category were made invisible. So it was that many people who considered themselves members of Aboriginal societies and whose parents, brothers, sisters, and cousins may have been categorized as Aboriginal were deemed non-Indian. The means for implementing this racist categorization was propelled by a thoroughly patriarchal idea: that societal membership of women and children is determined and legitimated by their husbands and fathers.

The Indian Act incorporated the Western patriarchal law that children are the children of their mother's husband.[2] A non-Indian woman who married an Indian man became an Indian, as did her children. An Indian woman who married a non-Indian man became a non-Indian, as did her children. The law was made retroactive, and the business of registering Indians was based on an attempt to determine whether a person's father, not mother, was an Indian. Given that the law was made more than two hundred years after the first contact (including sexual contact) between Europeans and Aboriginals, the attempt to figure out who was and who was not Indian would be the subject of satire if it had not had such far-reaching and tragic consequences.[3] A non-Indian could include a person with two Aboriginal parents as well as all those with no Aboriginal ancestors.

The Indian Act proved useful for the Canadian state. The categorizations that it created and perpetuated pitted members of Aboriginal societies against each other: men against women, sisters against sisters, those who had married Indians against those who had married non-Indians. In the last two decades, some Aboriginal women have struggled successfully against the racism and patriarchalism of the Indian Act, in particular section 12(1)(b). Their struggle was motivated by the poverty and destitution of their societies, their exclusion from decision making within those societies, their analysis that male leaders, husbands, and fathers were misusing their power and resources, and, most dramatically, by the forced evictions from Indian reservations of women, along with their children, who had married non-Indians.

Martin Cannon has analyzed this exclusion as discrimination at the intersection of race and gender (1995, 38). This specific discrimination was accomplished by treating sex and race as separate categories, rather than as inseparable dimensions of power, identity, and ascription that inform the relationships among individuals. This categorization made possible and sustained legislation and social policy based on an original fiction: that women—and only women—were divisible. They could be *either* Indian (by marrying an Indian) or women (by marrying a non-Indian), but not both. Indian women's struggle for reinclusion was a struggle against discrimination that made them unequal to Native men, who did not lose status when they married out, and to non-Native women, who gained Indian status by marrying an Indian. In another sense, we could say that it was a struggle for recognition as Indian women.

Just as the Indian Act divided and categorized people, so has the resistance by those seeking to sustain the exclusion of women who married out. In the 1970s, status Indian organizations such as the National Indian Brotherhood feared that any tampering with the Indian Act would aid the Canadian government's attempts to eradicate the special citizenship rights accorded to Indians by the act. More recently, the struggle by Indian women has been resisted in the name of collective rights. In a brief to the Standing Committee on Indian Women and the Indian Act, the Assembly of First Nations (AFN) argued that "as Indian people, we cannot afford to deal with individual rights overriding collective rights" (quoted in Cannon 1995, 98). First Nations leadership uses this argument, for example, to block attempts by Aboriginal women to use the Charter of Rights (and thus the Canadian state) to settle what the AFN perceives as internal disputes.

The assumption implicit in the position of the AFN is that Indian women struggle for equality as women, while the status Indian groups struggle for the collective rights of Indian people. But it must be remembered that Indian women were first separated from the collective by the Indian Act. This forcible separation has made possible their treatment as individual women whose struggles are now seen to threaten the collective. What the AFN fails to recognize is that the Assembly itself is an outcome of imposed systems of Indian Act governance. The AFN mobilized against the Charter in the name of culture and tradition that predated colonialism. Yet it was their history as a colonized people that produced not only the partitioned and subordinate status of Indian women but also political organizations like the AFN itself, which were no more part of traditional culture or politics than was the discriminatory treatment of women (ibid., 103).

In contrast to the position of the AFN, the Native Women's Association of Canada (NWAC) has supported the application of the Charter to the First Nations. NWAC representatives argue that Native culture and tradition have been transformed by the history of colonialism, a history that lodged official power in the hands of the mainly male leaders of postcolonial Native organizations. Thus, without the Charter, Native women would be unable to resist the discriminatory actions of band councils, or any future form of self-government (Stacey-Moore 1993; see also Cannon 1995, 92–93).

Some Aboriginal women state categorically that they share neither NWAC's position nor what they perceive as a feminist preoccupation with equality. For such women, equality promises something different from—and less than—the kinds of relations between men and women in their precontact societies. Skonaganleh:ra, a Mohawk woman, explains: "I don't want equality. I want to go back to where women, in aboriginal communities, were complete, where they were beautiful, where they were treated as more than equal—where man was helper and woman was the centre of that environment, that community" (Osennontion and Skonaganleh:ra 1989, 15). Certainly the concept of equality does not have easy applicability in those societies with no concept of individual economic rights. Some insist that Aboriginal societies were animated by a "communitarian" notion of responsibility rather than egalitarianism (Prentice et al. 1988, 40; see also Turpel 1993, 180). But history is a resource that can be mobilized to serve various contemporary positions. John Borrows argues that "while colonialism may be at the root of our learned disrespect for women, we can not blame colonialism for our informed actions today" (1994, 46). Indeed, "status and gendered hierarchies, along with patriarchal prerogative, have been institutionalized and internalized" within Native communities (Cannon 1995, 105).

Aboriginal women's struggle for full participation in their own communities and within Canada and Quebec, for the sharing of decision making, and for access to resources for themselves and their children is complex and multifaceted. Their struggle for self-determination for their communities has had to include the struggle for full recognition *within* their communities.

This analysis of the history and contemporary circumstances of the Aboriginal peoples reveals their rationale for challenging the legitimacy of the Canadian state. The colonization of this country by Europeans and the subsequent formation and expansion of the Canadian state wreaked havoc, by accident and design, on the peoples who had lived here for hundreds of years. The call of Aboriginal peoples for self-determination today is based not only on the legal claim to land never relinquished, but also upon the evidence of the past century that the Canadian state does not represent their interests as collectivities or individuals. For women of Aboriginal societies, the struggle for self-determination is painfully complicated by the splits in their own communities between men and women. Many Aboriginal women insist that this struggle will not be successful unless they first restore the position and status that they enjoyed before their communities were decimated by the advent of the Europeans and before their men were persuaded by the privileges of male domination. As Sandra Lovelace Sappier said, "We could get Indian self-government but we have to work together and be equal" (quoted in Silman 1987, 245).

The formation of the Canadian state was negotiated as if there were no Aboriginal peoples in the country. Their struggle for self-determination stems in large measure from their invisibility in the resulting confederation. But the Canadian Confederation also consolidated another systemic inequality between peoples—the French and the

English—that produced another and, to date, more politically successful challenge to the legitimacy of the Canadian state.

Quebec and Canada: "Deux nations"

THE QUÉBÉCOIS CHALLENGE to the legitimacy of the Canadian state rests upon the existence of a conquered people with a common language and shared culture living in a particular territory. But the remarkable success of this challenge owes a great deal to the constitutional map drawing that provided them with a state of their own—the province of Quebec—within Canada. Although there are many conflicting and complex inter-pretations of this history, my intention is to provide a basis for understanding the relations between English and French in Canada as a relationship between nations. Such an interpretation contributes to an understanding of nationalism in Quebec and underpins the social movements for sovereignty-association or for a separate state.

By the Treaty of Paris in 1763, New France was ceded to Britain. Because most members of the elite in New France had strong ties with France based on patronage from the Crown, trading alliances, and famil-ial networks, they left the ceded territory and returned to France. Approximately 60 000 people of French origin, most of them living within the modified feudal structure of the seigneurial system, were left in the colony. Men, women, and children lived and worked within family-based households, dependent upon each other's labour. The priests and nuns of the Catholic Church ran the hospitals and schools, but their numbers were sparse and, as with most European peasant populations, the church's influence on the daily life of the people was minimal. After Quebec was ceded to Britain, British traders and settlers moved to Montreal and, with their capital and contacts, soon dominated in trade and business (Guindon 1988; Hamilton 1988).

English economic domination was parallelled by attempts to ensure political domination. This was attempted by redrawing political bound-aries three times—in 1791, 1840, and 1867. The Constitutional Act of 1791 created the division between Upper and Lower Canada, which gave the English, then the minority in the colony, control within Upper Canada. In the late 1830s, rebellions against the aristocratic elites domi-nating politics roused much of the population in Lower Canada against

English rule and their domination of the economy. The resolution of the rebellions of 1837–38 was to render the French a minority by creating a joint legislature of the Canadas, Canada East and Canada West. By this time, the United Empire Loyalists and their descendants had swelled the English to majority status within Canada. Thirty years later, the Canadian Confederation ensured that the French would remain a minority in the new country. Nevertheless, the French were powerful enough to oppose the unitary state favoured by their English counterparts, thus securing a federal-provincial system. Given that this meant Quebec would henceforth be one province among several English provinces, there was much hostility in Quebec for the new confederation.

Confederation created a federal state and (eventually) ten provinces and carefully delineated the division of powers between them. Provincial prerogatives over crucial areas such as education and social welfare mean that the assumptions and laws that deal with the relations between men and women vary from province to province. These differences are particularly notable between Quebec, where the French Civil Code prevails, and the other provinces, which follow British common law. The British North America Act continued the process through which Quebec became the (only) geopolitical location for the French nation in Canada and at the same time ensured its subordinate status.

For one hundred years after Confederation, the Catholic Church provided the institutional framework for the survival of "la langue, la foi, et la famille." The church was in the position to do this because of the remarkable mobilization campaign engineered by Bishop Bourget in the 1840s to bring church people, disaffected with postrevolutionary, "godless" French society, to the more hospitable New World. By the time of Confederation, the church had defeated almost all of its internal enemies who were seeking secular institutions. It had developed the entire infrastructure of schools, hospitals, and social welfare that persisted in Quebec until the Quiet Revolution of the 1960s (Fahmy-Eid and Laurin-Frenette 1986). These institutions provided work for men and women; by 1930, one in ten francophone adults was a priest or a nun.

Sociologist Hubert Guindon has argued that the underlying political contract of Confederation was between English-speaking capitalists and the Catholic Church of Quebec. This arrangement was facilitated by another provision of Confederation: the protection of Protestant institutions within Quebec. This provision effectively preserved English as the language of business and helped to ensure that English capitalists would own and manage the corporate structure with its links to the rest of Canada, the United States, and Britain. The French would run a small provincial government—small because so many of the functions that were handled by governments in the rest of the country were organized in Quebec by the church. French politicians and bureaucrats who wanted to work in the federal area had to work in English (Beattie 1975; Guindon 1988). The relationship between the provincial government and the Catholic Church in Quebec from the time of Confederation was, with dramatic exceptions, symbiotic. The men of the church and state shared the same faith, came from the same families, and were educated in the same schools. From the vantage point of a largely francophobic English Canada, this meant that Quebec society was reactionary, an economic backwater, and the people slavish followers of church dogma, superstitious and unwilling to accommodate modern ideas.

That women did not win provincial suffrage in Quebec until 1940, two decades after most of the other provinces, contributed to this belief. Yet a more nuanced reading is required if we are to explain the Quiet Revolution of the 1960s and the enormous success of the second wave of feminism in Quebec. Is there another reading of this history that helps to explain the massive acceptance of feminism in the 1970s in Quebec?

A popular idea, with origins in the 1920s, suggested that the French defeat on the Plains of Abraham had been avenged by women who were willing to devote themselves to bearing and raising large families. In this way, the English—who desired nothing more than the extinction of the French—were outwitted. This idea was encapsulated in the phrase *la revanche des berceaux* (the revenge of the cradle). Such an idea was powerful in Quebec, capturing both the nationalist anxiety about French-Catholic survival and male anxiety about women breaking out of their maternal role. This idea was invoked during the successful struggles not only against suffrage but against all of women's claims to civil and political equality in Quebec (Stoddart 1973; 1981; Trofimenkoff 1977).

But were women the docile baby makers and saint-like mothers that politicians and bishops venerated and English Canadians scorned? And if so, how was it possible that women in Quebec abandoned this role with such apparent ease? First, it is important to realize that the veneration of mothers by the Catholic Church in Quebec was not simply rhetoric adopted to keep women in their place. As early as 1866, Abbé

Lafleche wrote that the raising of children was the work of the mother and the priest. How different this is from Protestant formulations, which stress that the father is the head of the household. It is true that the mother was to obey her priest, but given that this was not a daily consultation (as it might be with a husband on the premises), in theory, at least, this arrangement left her with a good deal of discretion within the home. Furthermore, there is ethnographic evidence to support the church's claim that the mother was the centre of the family and that her influence over the daily life of her children was paramount. I would speculate also that because the wife/husband relationship was treated as a secular rather than a holy relationship by the Catholic Church until well into the 1940s, Quebec women's subordination to their husbands lacked much of the ideological and psychological resonance of that of their Protestant sisters. When the power of the church collapsed in the 1960s, women accepted the idea of equality between the sexes with astonishing rapidity and pragmatism.

A second challenge to the conventional history of women was launched by feminist historian Marie Lavigne (1979). In pathbreaking work, she showed that only a minority of women in Quebec had had very large families. Many women remained celibate—both in convents and in lay society—and many more had small families. Why then, Lavigne asks, did everyone believe that all women had huge families? Her answer has a simple resonance: because most people *came* from large families. There were many more people with several brothers and sisters than there were people with one or two, or none at all. Her research suggests that many women did not follow church teachings, and that many married women must have practised birth control despite the church's prohibition.

A third note of caution comes from historians who have researched the history of nuns in Quebec. For a number of reasons, feminists have tended to view nuns as obstacles to women's emancipation. First, it was assumed that nuns were simply servants of the church, with little opportunity or desire to take initiative or wield influence. Second, in Quebec, it was nuns who did much of the nursing, teaching, charity, club, and church work that in English Canada was being taken up by lay women. Thus, ambitious middle-class women in Quebec found less scope for activities outside the family or the convent than did their sisters in the rest of Canada.

Both of these ideas were challenged by feminist historian Marta Danylewycz (1987). She pointed to evidence that laywomen and nuns co-operated in many instances. In addition, she argued that traditional interpretations overlooked the range of opportunities open to nuns in a society where the entire infrastructure was organized by the church. Nuns ran hospitals, schools, orphanages, and charities. Indeed, it is now clear that many women entered convents not simply because their religious beliefs were strong but because the work open to a nun provided desirable alternatives to life as a wife and mother.

With the collapse of the church in Quebec, thousands of nuns and priests left their religious vocations to do similar work in newly secularized institutions. Young women no longer looked to the church for work but, like their aunts and older cousins, they did not automatically opt for marriage and motherhood either. Many women of all social classes continued to choose a single life, or to combine one or two children with paid labour. Women flocked into existing feminist organizations in massive numbers and also started new ones (Bégin 1992; De Sève 1992; Dumont 1992).

From the late 1960s, many women linked their feminist demands with nationalist aspirations. They argued that their goals of equality with men would mean little in a society informed by hierarchical relations between the English and the French. As long as the language of work—particularly managerial and professional work—was English, and as long as priorities regarding health care, immigration, and cultural life were determined in Ottawa, women and men in Quebec were destined to subordinate national status. Not surprisingly, the campaigns by feminists in the rest of the country for section 28 of the Charter of Rights and later against the Meech Lake Accord for the omission of a guarantee of sex equality were not joined by many Québécoises. While feminist nationalists understood the rationale for these campaigns, they argued that transforming the patriarchal relations of their society also meant emancipating Quebec from its subordinate national status and that the Canadian state did not represent them either as women or as Québécoises (Dumont 1995). This was a double challenge to the legitimacy of the Canadian state. At the same time, both history and contemporary politics indicate that struggles to ensure that feminist demands are an intrinsic part of the nationalist agenda require vigilance (Dumont 1995; Lamoureux 1987; Maroney 1992). Just as important, there has never been unanimity among feminists for the independence option. Indeed, at the largest conference of feminists in Quebec in 1992, the delegates refused to take a position on the constitutional referendum because they could not reach unanimity (Cauchon 1992). Non-white women, in particular, fear a nationalist agenda predicated upon notions of "real" Québécois—those with French ancestry, born and bred in Quebec (Hamilton 1995).

The 1995 referendum campaign proved disappointing to long-time feminist nationalists in Quebec for its lack of attention to women's emancipatory goals and its failure to address the diversity of the society. There was little acknowledgement from the leadership of the "yes" side that Quebec itself is a multicultural society, riddled with racism towards non-whites and immigrants. Nor did the sovereigntist leaders display much understanding of the aspirations of Aboriginal peoples for self-determination.

This process of deconstructing Canada and looking behind appearances has uncovered the systemic inequalities between Aboriginal peoples and the rest of the population, and between French and English. The struggles to dismantle these inequalities produced demands for self-determination and independence, respectively.

Central to the early development of the Canadian state was the dispossession of the Aboriginal peoples from their land and the subordination of the French nation to the English. Subsequently, in the period since Confederation, people from all over the world have immigrated to Canada. The history of immigration provides an opportunity to review John Porter's research to see if Canada remains a vertical mosaic with people from England and Scotland occupying the lion's share of elite positions as well as the more favourable positions throughout the stratification system.

Porter's research also revealed the presence of economic categories based on race. Although pre-Confederation Canada had only a short period of legalized slavery, black people who lived here from the eighteenth century, and whose numbers were swelled by United Empire Loyalists and by those escaping slavery on the underground railroad, were confronted by as exclusionary a regime as that existing in the segregated South of the United States. Their treatment, and the treatment accorded later generations of non-white immigrants, together with postcontact European–Aboriginal history, provides evidence that the Canadian state is a racist state.

The Vertical Mosaic: Ethnicity and Racism

PORTER'S ANALYSIS has been subjected to a number of important criticisms. *The Vertical Mosaic* did not address the particular situation of women but rather assumed that, for the most part, their location in the stratification system was a function of their fathers' and then husbands' position. Nonetheless, women's role as primary caretakers of children meant that their work as mothers and wives was shaped by the amount of income their husbands earned and were prepared to devote to family/household survival.

Like the liberal pluralist equality of opportunity perspective, Porter's analysis concentrated on individuals rather than on the structured networks of hierarchical relations in which their lives were embedded. Nonetheless, two important findings from Porter's research remain viable, even if explanations for the findings have shifted. First, in an otherwise unfavourable assessment of Porter's work, sociologist Robert Brym concludes that "ethnic inequalities at the elite level appear to be considerably greater than at the mass level" (Brym with Fox 1989, 112). This suggests that members of the elite have been able to reproduce ethnic privilege both by preparing their own children with the particular skills required, and by acting as gatekeepers to those not similarly positioned. Ann Duffy has noted the importance of the role of upper-class women in reproducing the elite (Duffy 1986).[4] In Bonnie Fox's words, "Maintaining power requires that money be transformed into 'social capital'—the kin and friendship networks, and the social events and institutions that maintain such relationships—and that the people largely responsible for this 'social capital' are women" (1989, 138–39).

While men of British descent—with the active help of their mothers and wives—continue to be overrepresented in the elite (Nakhaie 1996b),[5] there is considerable evidence that the rest of Canadian society is not as ethnically layered as it once was (Brym with Fox 1989, 112–13). All the available research uses data on the occupations of fathers and sons and indicates that the relationship between ethnicity and occupational status was weaker for sons than fathers (ibid., 111). Gender is a complicating factor in any analysis, and until recently sociologists have solved this problem by studying only men (Fox 1989).

Clearly, however, the social and economic mobility experienced by successive waves of immigrants owes much to the labour of women, as wives, mothers, household managers, and waged workers. Explaining the far lower rates of mobility for women involves looking at both the gendered hierarchies in Canadian society and the particular nature of patriarchal relations that men and women bring with them as part of their cultural and gendered identities, and at how the second is played out in the context of the first. Because women who migrate are treated by the laws structuring immigration as appendages of men, the state puts few, if any, resources at the disposal of women. The power of men in their households is thereby intensified, and the possibilities for women, overworked and often abused by male relatives and employers, are few (Burnet 1986; Gannagé 1986; Ng 1986).

The history of immigration to Canada is riddled with shifting assumptions about who is a desirable immigrant and who is not. These decisions usually reflect the requirements of capital and state for labour. Some peoples were deemed useful for certain kinds of labour that those already in the country refused to do, but they were not desirable as permanent citizens. A head tax on every Chinese immigrant made it virtually impossible for women to accompany the men who built the railroad. Later, when the need for such labour declined, a federal law was passed prohibiting Chinese immigration, which was repealed only in 1947. When the labour of women is needed—as with domestic labour—the conditions of entry change depending upon the class and racial biases of those seeking help and making policy. In 1919, the goal was to attract "the best class of household worker" rather than "unqualified women from British mill and factory, who in addition to their lack of training for domestic service, bring with them only too often, serious mental and moral disabilities. . . [and who] end up, alas! too frequently, in our jails, hospitals, and asylums" (quoted in Barber 1985, 114).

Although there have been successive policy changes regarding foreign domestic workers, Rina Cohen argues that the latest version—the Live-in Caregivers' Program (LCP), enacted in April 1992—is "the most intrusive program created by the state's immigration authorities" (1994,

86). If we want to understand why there has been "a gradual regression in both citizenship and labour rights for foreign domestics throughout the twentieth century," we must look at changes in the racial composition of domestic labourers (ibid.).

Under Canada's present immigration law, there are three broad classes of immigrants: family class, refugees, and independent immigrants.[6] Although about half of all people who immigrate to Canada each year are women, the largest proportion arrive as family-class immigrants, sponsored primarily by close relatives already in the country. About 85 percent of the world's refugees are women and children, but men accounted for nearly half of those admitted to Canada as refugees between 1981 and 1991.[7] Less than half the women admitted as refugees were the principal applicants, compared with 91 percent of the men. There are many reasons for this: the United Nations convention on refugees does not include gender as grounds for persecution; women are less likely to meet admission criteria based on education, employment, and social opportunities because they are subordinated in their countries of origin; refugee services do not usually select women and children for permanent resettlement because they are perceived as only temporarily separated from fathers and husbands (Boyd 1994, 9).

All of these factors mean that women face insurmountable obstacles in meeting the criteria for admission for themselves and their children. In response to mounting pressure from refugee advocates, the Canadian Immigration and Refugee Board released guidelines in 1993 to assist its members in assessing claims based on gender persecution, and the following year about 195 women gained refugee status under these guidelines (Rinehart 1995, B6).[8] While Canada has been applauded for this initiative, a House of Commons committee reviewing the policy urged that more steps be taken to ensure that immigration officers recognize "the particular vulnerabilities inherent in the female condition" (Thompson 1995, A3). These "vulnerabilities" were partially recognized in the United Nations Women at Risk program initiated in the 1980s.[9] The particular risk the UN had in mind was male violence, including sexual assault from fellow refugees and local bandits (*Globe and Mail* 1995).[10] Nancy Worsfold, executive director of the Canadian Council for Refugees, faulted the Canadian program for failing to keep its promise to identify women and children in danger abroad and resettle them in Canada. Indeed, "the paperwork for the program is so slow that the UN

High Commission for Refugees hesitates to refer women to the Canadian program because the program itself can put women in the [refugee] camps in danger" (*Winnipeg Free Press* 1995).

Canada's immigration policies can also place at risk those women who are admitted as immigrants and refugees. Women who are sponsored by husbands are unable to leave abusive relationships without losing their immigrant status (Thompson 1995, A3).[11] As dependants, women have been denied access to (admittedly inadequate) resettlement programs, including language training.[12] Running through immigration and refugee policies at both the international and national levels are patriarchal assumptions that women will be protected and supported by male family members. Yet, the "particular vulnerabilities" of women are nothing less than the consequences of male domination and privilege, consequences that follow women from their country of origin through flight as refugees and, for the "fortunate" few, to their new home in Canada. The most recent criteria governing immigration are even more disposed to favour those with capital, formal education, and particular skills.[13] This means that women will be even less likely to gain admission to Canada unless they are attached to affluent men.

One way of approaching the entire history of who is welcome in Canada, and under what circumstances, is by examining the changing dominant understandings of who belongs here and who is "other." This categorization can be described as racist (always cross-cut by gendered and sexist assumptions), in the sense that racism creates the shifting categories of hierarchically arranged races. We examined the ways in which racist assumptions informed the making of the Indian Act. Throughout much of this century, the failure of the French to conform to English norms was explained by deep-seated cultural, psychological, and even biological differences. Former Prime Minister John Diefenbaker once referred to the "three great Canadian races—the English, the French and Everyone Else." The non-English-speaking immigrants who came to Canada in great numbers in the early decades of the century—Ukrainians, Italians, Mennonites—were perceived in many quarters as "dangerous foreigners" who even with time could scarcely be assimilated, let alone accommodated within an English-speaking Dominion (Avery 1979). Jews trying to escape Nazi Germany were turned away by Prime Minister Mackenzie King who saw them as members of another species (Abella 1982).

During the last decades of the twentieth century, the idea of race tends to be reserved to distinguish superficial physical differences, notably skin pigmentation. Whiteness now includes, by common usage, all shades of pale and many people of darker hues, once not seen as white. Yet race clearly still matters. Consider Robert Brym's conclusion to his discussion of Porter's work on ethnicity and stratification: "a substantial body of research demonstrates that, with important exceptions—consisting mainly of racial minorities—ethnicity does not strongly influence status or income attainment" (Brym with Fox 1989, 113). Here "racial minorities" appears as a self-evident category, a kind of subset of ethnicity. I am arguing that racial minorities are neither: who gets included in the category racial minority is historically specific, and race is not a subset of ethnicity. Racism is more properly identified as a system of power relations that rationalizes and normalizes differential treatment at the institutional and personal level. We have already examined how this has worked historically to create hierarchies of power and resources between the descendants of Europeans and Aboriginals. The other glaring and continuing example of institutionalized racism in Canada resides in the historical and contemporary treatment of those now identified as African Canadian. That the racial hierarchy between white and black is not about ethnicity—which could be described as residing in shared culture and language—may easily be seen. The black population of Canada is part of the African diaspora that was initiated by European slave traders three centuries ago and includes immigrants and refugees from various African countries, and indeed from throughout the world, who have been arriving ever since.

Black people have been in Canada for centuries, and English or French is the first language for most (Brand 1991). Yet they are disproportionately represented in low-paying jobs and face a tangled web of practices that exclude them from promotion, housing, and decent treatment on the street. They cannot be described as "exceptions to the general rule" (Brym with Fox 1989, 110) whereby succeeding waves of different ethnic groups achieve proportionate distribution in the stratification system: they do not constitute an ethnic group.

The social relations of racism have pervaded the country's history from its inception, creating sustained and shifting categories of "otherness"—those defined for all practical purposes as outside the Canadian polity. As Abele and Stasiulus conclude, "The picture of racism that emerges is that of an immensely supple, variable, and seemingly intractable 'common sense,' socially and politically constructed within a range of important locations—education, social services, private corporations, trade unions, and the mass media" (1989, 266).

The process of racialization rationalizes the creation and sustaining of social and economic inequalities. But it is a mistake to think that racializing the other is dependent upon these hierarchies. The history of anti-Semitism in Europe, for example, was nourished by envy for the perceived political and economic success of some Jewish people and the political opportunity presented for scapegoating such a people for the ills of the society. Political philosopher Hannah Arendt provides a complex analysis of the process through which what she called social anti-Semitism became racism during the first half of the twentieth century:

> It was Hitler who . . . knew how to use the hierarchical principle of racism, how to exploit the anti-semitic assertion of the existence of a "worst" people in order properly to organize the "best" and all the conquered and oppressed in between, how to generalize [their] superiority complex . . . so that each people, with the necessary exception of the Jews, could look down upon one that was even worse off than itself. (1951, 121)[14]

Nikki Gershbain and Aviva Rubin write that "although at this moment in Canada the light-skin of many Jews grants us a relative degree of privilege, when this no longer serves the purposes of the state, our access to it may simply be revoked" (1994, 58). The complexity of the history of Jews in Western civilization provides important theoretical understandings about racism and graphic illustration of my major point that race is socially and historically constructed. "Racism," asserts Arendt, "may indeed carry out the doom of the Western world and, for that matter, the whole of human civilization. . . . For no matter what learned scientists may say, race is, politically speaking, not the beginning of humanity but its end, not the origin of peoples but their decay, not the natural birth of man but his unnatural death" (1951, 37).

The systemic and shifting inequalities between Aboriginal and non-Aboriginal peoples, between English Canada and French Quebec, and between those privileged and victimized by racism have motivated demands for more equal methods of distribution of resources, more equitable representation in the forums of power, and even for secession from Canada. Women have challenged the Canadian state to intervene and transform the gender hierarchies that inform the relations of state and economy and civil society at the same time as they have participated in movements for self-determination, sovereignty, and regional equity, and for an end to the racist practices rooted in the history of the country.

Taken together, we can argue that the promise of equal opportunity for all is more honoured in the breach than in the observance. People live their lives within the intertwined networks of capitalist, national, gendered, and racist relations. Individuals may achieve social and economic mobility. Overall, the contemporary political/economic system provides high rewards for a very few, moderate rewards for a middle range of managers and professionals, decent wages for a (declining) industrial working class, low wages for many (including most women in the expanding service sector), unemployment and underemployment for a growing number, and bare subsistence payments for those unable to enter the work force because of age, disability, or responsibility for child-care or the care of dependent adults. This means that significant changes to people's lives can only come through transformed economic and political relations.

The Canadian State and the International Economy

A RECURRING THEME IN THIS BOOK has been the enormous power of investors with capital to create and destroy towns and communities, shift regional boundaries and inequalities, and make environments less hospitable to all forms of life. A central argument in Canadian politics since Confederation has been whether to facilitate or control the free movement of capital. From the building of the railroad and creation of the National Policy through the Auto Pact, the nationalization and privatization of Petro-Canada, and the negotiation of the Free Trade Agreement, Canadians have debated and ruled on this question. Concurrently, there has been debate about the kind of society we want to build. In response to social movements and left-wing political parties, Canadian governments have implemented social programs ranging from medicare to unemployment insurance. But none of those programs, taken singly or as a package, is immune from the decisions of future political actors who would dismantle them, in the interests of making Canadian workers more "competitive." Women have been in the fore-front of the struggle for what has been called a "social wage"—those pro-grams that accrue to people by virtue of permanent residency in the country. The economic dependence of women upon men has made them peculiarly aware of their individual vulnerability, and many women have fought for state programs that would make their lives more secure (Andrew 1984; Brodie 1995).

In the current political climate, the biggest question is whether fed-eral and provincial states can, in sociologist Patricia Marchak's words, "somehow legitimate, . . . make believable and worth defending, a national political structure which is dominated by an international eco-nomic system" (1980, 95). In the years since Marchak wrote this, such a task has become far more daunting. In the Canadian context, the "new world order" means losing jobs to the third world. How people respond as their friends and neighbours are thrown out of work will matter a good deal in this context. If those still with jobs simply cling to their privilege, the current movement of capital will simply erode whatever national interest and outlook remains. On the other hand, declining eco-nomic opportunities can also fuel new social movements, with people determined that the Canadian state push the limits of its political power vis-à-vis the international bourgeoisie rather than acceding to its impera-tives. Women were represented strongly in the movement against the Free Trade Agreement as workers, artists, writers, housewives, and mothers.[15]

The opposition of the National Action Committee on the Status of Women to the Free Trade Agreement was based on an economic argu-ment that "many workers in the manufacturing and service sectors risked losing their jobs, with broader claims regarding societal costs that would follow from a weakening of Canadian labour and social legislation" (Bashevkin 1989, 367; Burstyn and Rebick 1988).[16] This social legis-lation—so free traders argued—would have to be eroded so that Canadians would not have unfair advantages compared to Americans. If Canadians continued to have better provisions for health, welfare, and education, as well as better job protection than Americans, they could afford to accept lower wages, thereby disadvantaging their southern neighbours. Moreover, as Marjorie Cohen predicted, "the result of bring-ing our tax structure more in line with that of the United States may mean reduced revenues for government and unless there is a willingness to increase the federal deficit, there will have to be cuts in spending in the public sector" (1987, 75). In the years since the passage of the Free Trade Agreement, such predictions have relentlessly come to pass, in ways that have surpassed the worst fears of its opponents.

It is worth noting that in the election on free trade, big business broke with its custom of dividing its election largesse between Liberals and Conservatives to fund the campaign of the latter to the tune of some $56 million (Fillmore 1989). In the outcome of the election, money spoke.

Conclusion

IF CANADA IS TO SURVIVE, national policies that legitimize its power must be pursued. But those national policies must include rather than thwart the aspirations of the Aboriginal peoples for self-government, the people of Quebec for sovereignty, and the visible minorities for full citizenship. Across all these divisions run the jagged and shifting hierarchies between men and women. Women have been part of general social movements and have created, more than once, their own autonomous movements. Whether feminists can unite around common interests for equality, and whether they use whatever power they have to work together to erode rather than buttress the inequalities of nation, ethnicity, region, and gender are open questions. But upon such considerations the future of this part of the globe surely depends.

In the next chapter we look at the whole area of work, which is informed by all of the hierarchies that have been discussed so far. Work-related issues rank high on feminist agendas throughout this century and have involved challenges to the state to change laws, remake public policy, and open private and public institutions to women.

Notes

1. Shifting terminology results from the process whereby those living on this land prior to the arrival of the Europeans were named *Indian* by the newcomers, and the response of the first occupants—over time—to name themselves. Wotherspoon and Satzewich provide the following summary: "Aboriginal peoples refer collectively to

status Indians, non-status Indian, Metis and Inuit people in Canada. . . . First Nations tends to refer to groups of status Indian origin: groups who are the first occupants of the lands that now make up Canada. Status, or registered Indian people are those who are defined as Indians by virtue of the Indian Act" (1993, xv).

2. Prior to contact, Aboriginal societies had determined the membership in their tribes by a variety of principles of descent, marriage, residence, and adoption. Most tribes followed a bilateral method, tracing descent through both the mother's and father's lineage. Most of the rest of the tribes were matrilineal, with patrilineal descent much less common (Weaver 1993, 95).

3. In her research on the fur trade in the early Canadian West, Sylvia Van Kirk has examined "the remarkably wide extent of intermarriage between incoming traders and Indian women, especially among the Cree, the Ojibwa and the Chipewyan." These relationships—known as marriage *à la façon du pays*—were key to the generally harmonious relationships between Indians and Europeans in the Canadian West until the early nineteenth century. It was primarily Anglican missionaries, arriving in 1820 under the auspices of the Hudson's Bay Company, who began roundly denouncing such unions as "immoral and debased" (1986, 64). Van Kirk concludes that "this attack upon fur trade custom had a detrimental effect upon the position of native women" and together with the arrival of British women served to augment racial prejudice and class distinctions (ibid., 64).

4. For an excellent historical treatment of how upper-class women contribute to the reproduction of class, see Katherine McKenna's biography of Anne Murray Powell (1994).

5. I am grateful to my colleague Reza Nakhaie for providing me with a copy of this paper prior to its publication and with his unpublished paper (1996a).

6. The family class includes people sponsored by close relatives living in Canada. Refugees may be either convention refugees or members of designated classes. Convention refugees include persons who are unable or unwilling to return to their home country because of fear of persecution for reasons of race, religion, nationality, public opinion, or membership in a particular social group. Independent immigrants include all those other persons applying on their own initiative. This group includes assisted relatives and other independent immigrants, such as skilled workers, entrepreneurs, investors, and self-employed persons.

7. Children under age fifteen represent about half the population in flight, but account for only one-quarter of those admitted (Boyd 1994, 8). The fate of children is overwhelmingly linked to their mothers. At the same time, women are excluded from launching successful claims as refugees and immigrants because they have children. Monica Boyd observes that 59 percent of men admitted to Canada between 1981 and 1991 as UN convention refugees and 45 percent admitted as members of designated at-risk groups were never married. What this figure conceals, of course, is that these men ostensibly have no children for whom whey are responsible.

8. Women who face forced genital mutilation or persecution for refusal to wear the veil have been granted refugee status under the guidelines (Rinehart 1995, B6).

9. Canada only admitted 391 persons (including women and their children) under this program between 1988 and 1991 (Boyd 1994, 11).

10. This was part of a statement issued by the UN High Commissioner for Refugees on 1 March 1995. Sadako Ogata said that sexual violence is widespread in camps around the world. Guidelines to help secure the safety of women and girls include putting latrines close to shelters and distributing food directly, rather than through men who may use food to extort sex. A report from Amnesty International, released the same day, said that women are the "invisible" victims of human rights abuses, subject to rape in wars and to sexual and other abuses as refugees. Amnesty media director Anita Tiessen said, "Women are raped in custody. They're flogged for violating dress codes. They risk being stoned to death for so-called sexual offenses or they find themselves jailed because of family connections" (*Globe and Mail,* 1995, A10).

11. This was noted in a House of Commons Committee Report entitled *Refugees, Immigration and Gender* (Thompson 1995, A3).

12. The Canadian government's recent decision to cut back on English-language training increases resettlement problems for all immigrants and refugees from non-English-speaking countries. While this is usually seen as a problem only for employment, Macthoura Nou, a Cambodian refugee, recounts how the doctors did not understand when she tried to tell them about the respiratory problems of her infant son. "I just tell him that my baby cry and stop breathing. [The doctor] told me, 'Don't worry, your baby won't die from crying.' He did not understand me and my baby died." Nou now helps other Cambodian women get English-language training in Winnipeg (Lett 1995, B3).

13. Tom Denton of the Citizenship Council of Manitoba called the federal government decision to cut down on family-class immigrants "racist." In addition, he pointed out that the new "landing tax" for each immigrant (reminiscent of the Chinese head tax) is out of the range of most who come from the Third World (Carr 1994, A6). Needless to say, women, the poorest of the poor, would find the tax yet another "unbreakable" barrier in achieving resettlement in Canada (Boyd 1994, 10).

14. Hannah Arendt's analysis in *The Origins of Totalitarianism* is too complex to consider here and needs to be read in its entirety. But consider this observation: "It is a truism that has not been made truer by repetition that antisemitism is only a form of envy. But in relation to Jewish chosenness it is true enough. Whenever peoples have been separated from action and achievements, when these natural ties with the common world have broken or do not exist for one reason or another, they have been inclined to turn upon themselves in their naked natural givenness and to claim divinity and a mission to redeem the whole world. When this happens in Western civilization, such peoples will invariably find the age-old claim of the Jews in their way. This is what the spokesmen of pan-movements [in Europe in the nineteenth and twentieth centuries] sensed, and this is why they remained so untroubled by the realistic question of whether the Jewish problem in terms of numbers and power was important enough to make hatred of Jews the mainstay of their ideology. As their own national pride was independent of all achievements, so their hatred of the Jews had emancipated itself from all specific Jewish deeds and misdeeds" (1951, 121). Arendt observes that "the pan-movements preached the divine origin of their own people as against the Jewish-Christian faith in the divine origin of Man" (ibid., 112).

15. A poll conducted in October 1988 showed a significant gender gap in support of the Free Trade Agreement. Fifty-three percent of the men polled favoured the agreement compared to only 33 percent of women. Eleven percent of the men and 18 percent of the women were undecided (Bashevin 1989, 369).

16. NAC's position was based on the analysis of economist Marjorie Cohen (1987).

Feminism and Work

A N IRONIC CHARGE AGAINST FEMINISTS has been circulating for some years now. Feminists, some say, have denigrated the work that women do in the home; they have belittled the contribution of wives and mothers to children and to society more generally. Feminists have encouraged women to become like men. The quintessential feminist-inspired woman is pictured abandoning her children and husband on a daily basis, picking up her leather briefcase and heading out to the corporate world dressed in a professional suit (Pierson 1995, 1). Resting on her conscience, say her detractors, should be the overwhelming problems besetting modern society: the collapse of the family, rampant juvenile delinquency and crime, the degeneration of morals.

Feminists deal with these charges in different ways—confronting them, ignoring them, ridiculing them—but, like crazy glue, the charges have a kind of stickability. They surely contribute to the oft-repeated sentence, "I am not a feminist but. . . ." They not only feed active hostility to feminism but create confusion and distress among many who long to see the relations between the sexes transformed.

In this chapter I consider feminist perspectives on work, on women and work, on women and children, on women, work, and children. My method will be both historical and theoretical. First, I note the main issues that feminists have raised over the past century about women, work, and children. Second, I discuss the main theoretical questions that contemporary feminists have asked about these same issues.

In this process, feminists—particularly feminist historians—have revisited the past and raised new questions and produced new interpretations on women and work. Feminists from different theoretical perspectives—liberal, Marxist, radical, cultural, lesbian, anti-racist, poststructural—have looked at these issues through their different lenses, and this will also guide the discussion.

What I believe will become clear in the course of this discussion is just how immensely complex feminist considerations of women and work have been. For this is a huge topic that encompasses—from some perspectives at least—almost all of social life. In this chapter, I hope not so much to put the charges against feminists to rest, but rather to show how and where they misrepresent the focus of much feminist discussion and also how it is that the charges can still stick.

First Wave Feminists

FROM THE LATE NINETEENTH CENTURY until the end of World War I, feminists took up the question of women and work in several ways. First, and perhaps best known, were the struggles women undertook for admission to higher education and entrance into the professions. Equally important, for many decades, were responses feminists developed to problems facing women who worked for wages: the conditions and hours of work, wage levels, and safety travelling to and from work. Third were the problems of sexual morality that, many observers argued, faced working women, especially young women. A fourth set of concerns was how women would care for their children when they were at work. Finally, many first wave feminists insisted that women's special nature and interests suited them for particular kinds of volunteer work in the broader society. Let us look more closely at these five issues, the context in which they were formulated, and some contemporary feminist reflections upon them.

Admission and Accessibility

Many of the women who fought for the right to attend university and enter the professions were no more willing than many young women today to call themselves feminist. They wanted to get on with their lives;

many of them experienced a "calling" to a particular profession—the ministry, medicine, teaching, or law. During the early decades of the century, when two-thirds of the population living in Canada were regular church goers, young women often framed their aspirations for themselves and their society in religious terms. Whether these women adopted the label feminist or not, their struggles allied them with those whose avowed political purpose was to create equality between men and women in the public sphere.

Even when women tried to legitimate their goals in religious rather than secular terms, they still often faced astringent opposition (Brouwer 1990). In the Fédération Nationale Saint-Jean-Baptiste (FNSJB), founded in 1907, Catholic feminists in Quebec tried to negotiate a path that the church would recognize as legitimate. Given that the church not only opposed suffrage, but officially opposed women's access to the professions and higher education as well, this was ultimately a doomed struggle (Lavigne, Pinard, and Stoddart 1979, 86). In 1909, for example, the Archbishop of Montreal censored an article on compulsory education written by journalist Françoise (Robertine Barry) for the Fédération. Barry wrote to FNSJB president Marie Gérin-Lajoie protesting the acceptance of such censorship:

> I recognize that, for the Federation to triumph, you need the force of the clergy, all-powerful in our country. Sacrifice your burnt offerings to them. I only hope that they will not ask you for yet greater sacrifices such as . . . giving up women's suffrage. In the meantime, I pity you, because in sacrificing me you go against the sense of integrity, loyalty, and justice which I have always admired in you, since, as you avowed yourself, you saw nothing reprehensible in what I wrote. (quoted in ibid., 79–80)

God, it seems, had not intended women to become professionals, an argument made in more specific, but still blunt and vociferous terms, by Pope John Paul as late as 1994 to exclude women from the priesthood of the Catholic Church.

Closely allied with the religious argument were various biological arguments that many male doctors used to insist that their field (and most others) should be restricted to those of their own sex. In 1892 *The Canadian Practitioner* printed a report of a lecture given by Sir James Crichton-Browne, MD, to the Medical Society of London in which he "traced out several bodily differences between the sexes . . . [in particular] . . . differences in the brain." The doctor cited evidence that "the specific gravity of the grey matter in every lobe of the brain in the female was lower," and the consequences of this for female "victims of higher education" were horrendous: tuberculosis, chorea, mental malfunction, and "gastric disorder now so common that it might receive a distinctive appellation and be called anorexia scholastica" (257–59).

Such attitudes were not universal. Two years earlier, the editors of *The Canada Medical Record* had defended women's place in medical school after women at the Women's Medical College in Kingston had met with a "cold shoulder" from male students:

> We cannot view with any satisfaction the tendency of the women of this age to shirk their manifest and divine destiny; but, in spite of all this and the many physical disabilities under which the female doctor must labor, there will be female doctors. As long as women labor under the delusion that it is an easy way to earn a living, it would be unjust and ungenerous for us to throw any obstacles in their path. We may as well welcome them to our ranks, and let the fittest survive the struggle. (119)

Canada's first female doctors graduated in the United Kingdom and the United States, having been refused entrance to universities in this country. By the last decades of the nineteenth century, several Canadian medical schools were accepting women, to mixed receptions from faculty and students (Prentice et al. 1988; Strong-Boag 1979). Only in 1918 did McGill University accept its first female medical students. Jessie Boyd Scriver of the class of 1922 recalls the university's opposition:

> We knew that repeatedly through the years, McGill had refused to consider admitting women to the Faculty of Medicine. It will be remembered that in 1888 Grace Ritchie appealed unsuccessfully for the admission of women to Medicine and that our renowned Maude Abbott was also denied entrance to the Faculty—but both received their medical degrees from Bishop's University in the early 1880s. (Years later [1910] when Dr. Abbott was recognized as a world-wide authority on congenital cardiac abnormalities, McGill bestowed on her an M.D. degree *honoris causa*.) (1984, 5)

Like students at other universities, Scriver and her classmates found most faculty and students helpful, or at least tolerant. But some male students suggested that they drop out of school rather than face a dissecting class "which would be very distasteful to young ladies of our upbringing" (1984, 6). Women were not supposed to know how bodies worked, or even what they looked like.[1]

Women and Waged Work

It is always easier to see the hypocrisies of another age. But it is hard to imagine how those people opposed to the entrance of women into the professions conducted their campaigns for so long and with such righteous indignation when all around them women were working for appallingly low wages and long hours in factories, sweatshops, and in middle- and upper-class homes. Middle-class feminists took up some of the causes of their working-class sisters, but in ways that revealed their class biases (Klein and Roberts 1974, 214–18; Strong-Boag 1976). Working-class men sometimes defended working women in the union movement, but in ways that betrayed their patriarchal assumptions. Working-class women took up their own cause in private and sometimes in public venues. It is not surprising then that there were different and often competing understandings of what the problems were, and what the solutions might be.

Responses to the plight of women in the work force were debated in both suffrage and labour organizations. One such response was the idea of protective legislation. Generally speaking, suffragists were more concerned about the ways in which such legislation would be used to further exclude women from gainful employment, while trade unionists "viewed any protection against sweated conditions, no matter how it was won, as a desperately needed reform" (Ramkhalawansingh 1974, 301). Male unionists demanded a "family wage" for working men, which would enable men to be the sole supporter of their families. Working women—when we hear their voices—demanded equal wages and access to work. They participated in work stoppages as strikers or members of the families of strikers (Klein and Roberts 1974; Sangster 1979; White 1993). The Ontario Commission on Unemployment of 1916 seemed surprised to find that "generally speaking women wage-earners are not convinced that the principle of higher pay to men as bread-winners works out justly" (cited in Ramkhalawansingh 1974, 269). We will deal with these concerns in turn, but it is worth while noting that all these responses were formulated in a society that had not yet come to terms with the full consequences of industrial capitalism. Nostalgia for an idealized rural life, where men and women worked side by side in the clean country air for themselves and their children, fuelled the discussions about the outrages of waged work for women.

Public concern about the conditions of work for women led most provinces to hold Commissions of Inquiry into women's wages, hours of labour, and working conditions in industrial occupations. The resulting protective legislation took several forms: exclusion of women from those occupations defined as most dangerous to their health or reproductive potential; a limit to the hours that women and children could work; and laws setting minimum wages for women working in the new industries. In addition, the federal government amended the Criminal Code in 1920 to provide penalties for male employers who tried to take sexual advantage of "previously chaste" female employees under twenty-one (Burt 1993, 217–18). Middle-class social reformers, including some feminists, argued that these new laws addressed the worst abuses of the capitalist order.

The list of worst abuses, as formulated by these reformers, did not generally include the pitiful wages for the large numbers of women who worked as domestics (Errington 1993; Leslie 1974). Neither did they include unequal wages for men and women, wages that were insufficient for women to support their children. Rather, the underlying concern was "protecting women's reproductive functions and . . . keeping young working girls pure for marriage" (Burt 1993, 218). As the Nova Scotia Commission put it, "If we are to have a healthy virile race, it is of primary importance to preserve the homes and conserve the health, morals and efficiency" of women (quoted in ibid., 217). Single girls should remain virgins and support themselves when necessary. But most were to marry and stay home, supported by their husbands. As the Minimum Wage Board in Ontario declared, the minimum wage should be "the least sum upon which a working woman can be expected to support herself" (quoted in Ramkhalawansingh 1974, 299; see also Burt 1993, 217–19; McCallum 1986, 126; Prentice et al. 1988, 126). Even this view was not widely shared. For example, employers stressed in the Report of Labour Conditions in British Columbia that "women were not expected to have to live on their salaries and, therefore, women's wages had nothing to do with any notion of a living wage" (Creese 1988, 125). Such a notion was long-lived: as Ruth Pierson notes in her study of unemployment insurance debates during the Depression, "It was principally as non-mothers that women and their labour-market interests qualfied for the attention of trade union spokesmen, socialists, and eventually liberals" (1990, 83).

Men, on the other hand, were said to need what came to be called a family wage, and this was one of the major grounds on which the labour movement demanded higher wages for its members. In precapitalist society, a wage was most often a supplement to the support people gleaned for themselves from the land (Clark 1982 [1919]). The idea that individuals would actually have to support themselves with a wage was a long time coming, and wages very often didn't (and still don't) reflect that reality. As life on the land gave way to wage labour, men and women—married and single alike—sought waged work, although married women were more likely to take intermittent, part-time jobs. Since anything less than employment for all adult members left many working-class households destitute, this meant that there were many desperately poor families (Bradbury 1993). The demand for a family wage was intended to ensure that only one adult in the family had to work for wages. Not surprisingly, that one adult was assumed to be the father/husband (Pierson 1990).

When the voices of women working for wages are heard, it is usually to demand higher wages and better working conditions for themselves. If the voices of working women in the written records are few, they had other ways of clarifying their preferences for some work over others. In overwhelming numbers they voted with their feet, deserting positions as servants in the homes of others and opting for work elsewhere. Work as a servant in a nineteenth-century household was physically arduous, with hours often limited only by the number in a day and a night. Servants were constantly on call. Their behaviour on and off the job (seldom off—many advertisements indicated that a free Sunday afternoon was all that might be expected) was monitored by their employers who used the presence and behaviour of their servants to mark their own status and respectability. With no possibility of a social or domestic life of their own, servants were often on the move (Errington 1996; Leslie 1974).

Middle-class reformers loudly lamented the dearth of servants, complaining that they had trouble finding a "good woman" to assist in their households. They insisted that domestic work was much more suitable an employment for women than any of the alternatives (Barber 1985). Domestic work was what women did naturally (how interesting, then, that the complaints about the work habits of domestic servants went on endlessly). Such work was safe, appropriate, and provided good apprenticeships for later lives as wives and mothers. It is no small wonder that protective legislation was never instituted with regard to domestic service. From our vantage point, middle-class feminists appear caught in a conflict of interest. Ostensibly concerned about working conditions for women, they seldom turned the spotlight on the working environments in their own homes. Rather, they joined in recruitment efforts abroad to find replacements for recalcitrant Canadian "girls." Great Britain was the preferred recruiting ground for English-Canadian households that could afford servants. Not only would British women share language and culture but, in time, they would take their own place as wives and mothers in the expanding Canadian nation (thereby, of course, keeping the "servant problem" alive) (Bacchi 1983, 95–96).

Those who struggled for the family wage shared the assumption that work for women should be a stopgap measure until marriage and motherhood. The growing union movement developed aspects of Marxist analysis and rhetoric indicting capitalist employers who, for a pittance, would squeeze every last ounce of labour power from every member of the family. The struggle of union members meshed with some of the concerns of middle-class reformers that family life in working-class sections of the burgeoning cities was all but impossible. With fathers, mothers, and older children all in the factories for long hours, younger children and babies went undernourished and neglected. Children reared in such households lacked not only physical care but moral guidance, and threatened to swell Canada's delinquent and criminal populations. The family wage was meant to remedy all this. Providing a working man with a decent wage enabled him to support his wife and children. With a mother at home to care for her children, the runaway social problems that endangered the very social fabric of the new nation would be brought under control. The key to well brought-up children and future good citizens was a wife/mother in the home.

Certainly working-class women had much to gain from decent wages for their husbands and the fathers of their children. But like protective legislation, the family wage was also intended to keep them out of the paid work force, certainly out of those occupations that commanded better wages. Furthermore, the family wage remained an elusive goal for most male income earners, and an illegitimate demand for women, even those who were the sole supporters of their children.

Women, Work, and Sexuality

Waged work for women threatened the physical and moral well-being of their children: working-class unionists and middle-class reformers could agree upon this. But they also shared another perception: waged work put women themselves in the way of moral dangers. How was the sexual purity of women to be preserved once they entered the dangerous and tempting fray of the working world? Again, nostalgia for what was believed to be the wholesome rural life pervaded discussion and solutions. Middle-class reformers claimed that domestic service offered a negotiated way through the thicket. Such service provided wages for women in environments that were supposedly morally safe.

The testimony of working women provides a different story. As Karen Dubinsky (1993) has noted in her study of turn-of-the-century Northern Ontario, "rural live-in domestic servants found themselves in a position of extreme vulnerability" and were subject to a range of abuse from employers, including sexual assault, life-threatening violence, and an array of daily, small humiliations. Clearly domestic service was not excluded from public discussion about women's safety and morality because such work actually provided safe havens. Although we may understand why families and households did not come under scrutiny from those in influential positions in the union and reform movements, we may still ask why many such people mounted vitriolic attacks on alternative and morally less dangerous workplaces.

Perhaps it was because women who worked in factories had more freedom than those in domestic service to engage in their own liaisons, create their own fun, and decide how to spend their discretionary time (Barber 1985, 105). For many in the middle class, unattached young women working for wages became a symbol of a society in potential decay. Women, it seemed, could not be trusted to preserve their own sexual purity, nor could the men about them be trusted to provide pristine guardianship. Whether naive, weak-minded, or lascivious, women needed others to tell them what to do. Paradoxically, while many proclaimed that women's natural proclivities were for wiving and mothering, they remained anxious that women, especially young women, left to their own devices, might choose otherwise. The concern that vulnerable young women would engage in sexual intimacies or, worse, in prostitution informed the debates, laws, and regulations about their engagement in waged work. Carolyn Strange has noted, for example, that the *Report* of the 1889 Royal Commission on the Relations of Labour and Capital only discussed women workers in sections of the text devoted to the moral implications of urban industrialization (1995, 33–34; see also Valverde 1991, 20). Many middle-class feminists, far from being the upholders either of women's natural virtue or of their right to their own sexual lives, shared these concerns (Strange 1995, 22–23). Unsupervised women— both those with, and in need of, a livelihood—would meet unsuitable men, might even marry them.

Canada's immigration policies have long represented an unholy amalgam of pragmatic needs for labour and explicitly racist practices. As we noted earlier, political and economic leaders were willing, on occasion, to admit those who didn't qualify as "white" to fill particular labour shortages, but they did not admit their families. Such policies, as it turned out, had unintended consequences. Racist employment and immigration practices did not prevent men and women from forming relationships across shifting "racial" lines. "White" working women were presented as vulnerable to a shifting parade of "foreign," racialized men from Italy, China, East India, or, in the case of middle-class women, any man from the working class. Carol Bacchi has written about the racist attitudes of English-Canadian suffragists, concerned that pure white women would fall for the empty promises of untrustworthy, non-British men. Once again, domestic service was presented as protection from mixed gender and racial working environments, and from the dangerous freedom waged work presented for women during their leisure hours.

Mothers, Children, and Waged Work

In Canada's preindustrial and precapitalist settings, women cared for children, raised crops and tended animals, made clothes and soap, and preserved food, all at home (Errington 1996). During the nineteenth and early twentieth centuries, the physical separation of home and work, the separation of most men and women from the land, and the growing dependence on wages produced a crisis for women that continues one hundred years later. Almost everyone, including most first wave feminists, who left any sort of record of these times seemed to agree that women's special mission was to care for children, husband, and home. Some feminists countered this prevailing ideology when they struggled for women's access to education and the professions. But most of them seemed to concur that women who chose careers must also choose singledom. The radicalism in this view was the insistence that remaining unmarried to pursue a career was not unnatural.

There were various efforts by social reformers to provide childcare for very poor women. The East End Day Nursery in Toronto and the Jost Mission in Halifax not only provided care for children but acted as employment bureaus for women, though often for the most menial and poorly paid jobs. A report in *Saturday Night* commended the arrangement whereby women could leave their children at a creche during the day: "These nurslings of poverty cannot be expected to behave like little ladies and gentlemen and we cannot blame private families for objecting to their washerwoman or seamstress bringing their offspring along" (quoted in Klein and Roberts 1974, 211; Simmons 1991).

Activist Flora Macdonald Denison was a vocal critic of such creches and the society that forced women to use them. She repeatedly pointed out that all women did not have men to depend upon: "The women who were worst off were those mothers who had to be out in a labour force that did not recognize their right to be there and that therefore provided them with little or no support or protection" (Gorham 1979, 65). She became a radical critic of the privatized family, arguing for more communal and democratic arrangements.

Women, Community, and Society

Whether out of pragmatism or sincerity, most feminists argued that women should be in the wider world because that world desperately needed the special skills and predispositions that they had carefully honed for generations in the home. Just as certain kinds of waged work were more suitable for women, so were particular venues in the social and political sector. The world needed cleaning up, and women were cleaners par excellence. Capitalism needed a human face and nurturing hands and heart. Women should provide them. Men needed taming;

they required persuasion to abandon boyish wickedness and become men. Certainly husbands and fathers needed the law to ensure that they shared their hard-won wages with their wives and children and treated them kindly in the process.

There were many women's groups at the turn of the century that concerned themselves with "social housekeeping." The Woman's Christian Temperance Union (WCTU), founded in the late nineteenth century, was the largest and most effective nationally organized women's reform association of its time. It fought for prohibition of the sale and consumption of alcohol, which temperance advocates identified as a primary curse of family life: "it turns men into demons, and makes women an easy target of lust" (quoted in Mitchinson 1979, 154). As this quote makes clear, the culprits were men and the victims women and children. During the course of its long struggle, the WCTU supported other social reforms, including suffrage. Far from rejecting dominant views of women, members argued "that what made them different from men and what made them the centre of domestic life necessitated their involvement in temporal society" (Mitchinson 1979, 166; see also Cook 1995; Valverde 1991, 58–61).

The WCTU was a Protestant organization, and temperance was never as significant an issue in Catholic Quebec. Still, the Fédération Nationale Saint-Jean-Baptiste (FNSJB) espoused the platform of the Anti-Alcohol League in 1910, believing that women had "a unique capacity for moral regeneration" (Lavigne, Pinard, and Stoddart 1979, 77). In Montreal, where the infant mortality rate was one of the highest in North America, the FNSJB distributed milk to poor families and set up programs to aid mothers during and after childbirth. It also campaigned against prostitution. After the First World War, the FNSJB increasingly succumbed to the conservative influence of Catholic social doctrine, even withdrawing from the suffrage movement. Nonetheless, the organization continued to work with other lay women and nuns to help parents care for their children. The orphanages run by nuns accepted not only children with no parents or those of single mothers, but very often the children of those too poor to feed and care for their young (Bradbury 1993, 209).

This examination of feminist responses to women and work in the late nineteenth and early twentieth centuries provides little ammunition for those who argue that feminists have devalued the work that women traditionally do. Yet many first wave feminists did seek to expand women's terrain to include higher education, professional work, social reform, and community and social service. While most feminists agreed with dominant views that women were especially suited to caring for others, they argued that such caring needed to be exercised not only within the home but in the larger society.

Second Wave Feminists

FIRST WAVE FEMINISTS tended to focus upon legal barriers to entry to professions and to share dominant societal views about the greater suitability of domestic employments for working-class women. Today, feminists from virtually all perspectives share an assumption that access to education, training, and all forms of paid work should not be denied because of gender. Such a simple-sounding goal has proved elusive, and a good deal of feminist theorizing and research has helped explain why that has been so. In the past few decades, the emphasis has been on elucidating and undermining systemic barriers, and revealing and transforming discourses on work that are explicitly and subtly gendered, sexualized, and racialized. Liberal feminists continue to focus upon the barriers to equality of opportunity in the workplace, although they have had to shift the boundaries of liberalism considerably in their quest. Socialist feminists focus on the intersection of capitalist and patriarchal relations in shaping women's super-exploitation in paid work, their primary responsibility for domestic labour, and the resulting double day of labour. Lesbian feminists have led the way in confronting the heterosexist practices that exclude them completely from some lines of work, as well as the images of femininity that subtly and not so subtly shape women's working lives. Feminists using the techniques of poststructural analysis have revisited the categories into which work has been divided to reveal how apparently neutral categories are infused with gendered language and assumptions.

So much had changed as a result of the victories won by first wave feminists and by the entry of so many women into the paid labour force. The formal barriers to higher education were down, and by the late

1960s women made up over one-third of undergraduate student populations. At the graduate level, there had been a gradual increase in female
enrolment since 1955. Nonetheless, when the Royal Commission on the
Status of Women issued its report in 1970, the figure had still not
equalled the 1920 high when 25 percent of graduate students were
women (see figure 5-1). Two world wars had revealed that women could
do virtually every job, although support for them to do so in peacetime
was slight. Women's relative strength in the labour market had grown as
first single women, then married women with no children or with grown
children, and finally during the 1970s the majority of women with young
children began working for pay. Overwhelmingly, however, they were
doing "women's work" for low wages and in poor working conditions.

How, then, have the issues about women, work, and children been
formulated in the past two decades? I am going to deal with these issues
under the same categories as in the first part of this chapter: admission

FIGURE 5-1
Enrolment of Women at Undergraduate and Postgraduate Levels as
a Percentage of Total Enrolment
(Full-Time Regular Session)

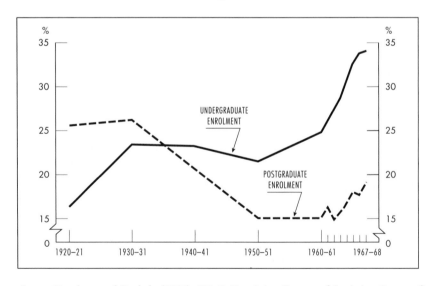

Source: Urquhart and Buckely (1965), 601–2; Dominion Bureau of Statistics, *Survey of
Higher Education,* Cat. no 81–204, 1961–62, 1962–63, 1963–64, 1965–66,
1966–67, 1967–68.

and entrance, women and waged work, work and sexuality, work and children, and women and society. The categories themselves have to undergo quite a metamorphosis in order to accommodate the discussion. This in itself serves as some kind of barometer for the continuities and changes in the lives of women during the twentieth century.

During the following discussion, try to keep in mind the question posed at the beginning of this chapter: just when and how did feminists come to be charged with devaluing the work women do in the home? How the quintessential feminist, as portrayed in the media, became the career woman so vilified by anti-feminists is a mystery that requires investigation (Dubinsky 1985).

Admission and Entrance

Early second wave feminists were a rather ungrateful lot, although their ingratitude was primarily a function of ignorance. Like others, they knew little of the struggles of their predecessors for entrance into university and the professions. But even when they did, many tended to perceive those struggles as narrowly middle-class, even elitist. Socialist and radical feminists spurned political mobilizations around these issues, even when many of them individually took an academic and professional route. Their long-term agenda was revolutionary, nothing short of the replacement of capitalist patriarchy with feminist socialism. Their immediate focus was upon working-class women both because they were the majority and because it seemed that they had more to gain and less to lose from revolutionary change than their middle-class counterparts.

Socialist feminist interest in the wages and conditions of working-class women coincided with that of many more mainstream feminists. One of the common goals of the struggle was to break down the gendered segregation in the non-professional sectors of the labour force. Such an interest resonated with women across the country, no longer willing to be confined to low-paying job ghettos.

In the period since women won admission to universities and to the professions, the huge area of white-collar jobs had opened up. Women made up the majority of office employees in the corporate and state sectors. Such jobs had once been done by men, and had been better paid and had more prestige than blue-collar jobs. But once such positions were dominated by women, wages in the white-collar ghettos were surpassed by the wages of the best male blue-collar jobs. Women all over the country began looking outside these sectors for work. *Nontraditional* became the label for those jobs from which women had been excluded and to which they now—individually, and collectively as part of feminist campaigns—demanded entry.

Protective legislation, the family wage, explicit policies of craft and industrial unions, and sugar-coated and blatant misogyny had kept women out of many jobs in all but the wartime decades of the twentieth century. In the early 1970s, many feminists began to focus on women's exclusion from these jobs. It was abundantly clear that many women needed to make more money: women who were supporting themselves and often their children too, whether out of choice, the desertion of their husbands, or their decision to leave an abusive marriage; women married to men who did not make the much-vaunted family wage; and women who were finding the courage and support to live openly as lesbians, and hence without the desire or expectation of male financial support. No longer was it just the exceptional woman who wanted waged work. Many women turned a critical eye on their economic dependence on men and determined that they—or at least their daughters—would be self-supporting. In this quest, they broadened their horizons and began looking at every kind of paid work.

If a primary rationale for women's exclusion from higher education and professions had been the unsuitability of their bodies for intellectual work, the argument that women did not belong in the better-paid jobs of the working class rested also on the inadequacy of their bodies, this time their physical weakness. When this argument wore thin, challenged by women capable of the most arduous physical work (Sugiman 1994) and by the fact that many of these jobs patently did not require great physical strength, secondary defences were produced. Men in dangerous occupations—primarily in war but also in mines and mills—needed to trust their comrades, the argument went. The presence of women interrupted male bonding. Moreover, what self-respecting man would be willing to look to a woman for protection? Male bonding, as some of the women first hired for jobs in such environments discovered, had a lot to do with objectifying and disparaging women (Gray 1987; Sugiman 1994). Some women described their experience with metaphors drawn from combat; others spoke of adjusting, becoming "one of the boys."

The idea that work should not be defined by gender has been taken up by women in the workplace and, notably, within and through their unions. Their success is visible in many areas of public policy and the law, employment practices and attitudes (Maroney 1987; Sugiman 1994). Pamela Sugiman has documented the major role played by a core group of women in the United Auto Workers in the late 1960s to break down sex-segregated workplaces. "Their struggle was momentous. They played a key role in amending the Human Rights Code in the province of Ontario [to include sex as a prohibited ground of discrimination] which in turn, eliminated all sex-based language from union contracts" (1994, 167). Decades later, the struggle to integrate nontraditional jobs continues. Those shop floors and mines that have not been shut down due to restructuring of the Canadian economy still have a predominantly male work force. When women are hired, they are also first fired.

Employment equity legislation has been the legal instrument devised for ensuring that women, visible minorities, Aboriginal peoples, and persons with disabilities are hired in those occupational categories—nontraditional, professional, and managerial—where they have been underrepresented. Those employers covered by such legislation are required to show how they plan to achieve equity goals. The guiding principle is that each occupational category should have numbers from each of the target groups that are proportionate to their numbers in the qualified population. Proponents of such legislation rested their case on the evidence that members of target groups face systemic discrimination in the work force, and that, left to their own devices, employers would not pursue equity goals.

But the very conscious and unconscious prejudices that exclude these groups (and we must note that three of the target groups are made up of women and men) come into play when people try to enforce such legislation. While some people use employment equity legislation in their struggle for inclusion, others, often in the name of individual rights, oppose any attempt to regulate employment practices.

The legislation designed to rectify women's systemic underrepresentation in the work force has been used to denigrate women who do get jobs: "You only have this job because you are a woman" has become a familiar line. In the universities, the question has been posed in terms of equity versus excellence. We are happy to hire women, many say, but more importantly we must always hire the best candidate. Such a statement carries with it several assumptions: "we" always know who the best candidate is; "we" ourselves are free from any prejudice against the designated groups; there is a yardstick that will objectively measure "best";

and, most fundamentally, "best" is an objective quality (Moghissi 1994). When a member of a designated group or groups is hired in a field dominated by white, able-bodied men—complete with all the credentials that confirm competence—s/he faces an ongoing charge, spoken and unspoken: "You only have the job because of your ascribed characteristics." Such assumptions create "chilly climates." Few would dispute that this is a step up from "frozen out," but in its numerous manifestations it can erode confidence in one's own competence and make life miserable and uncomfortable and careers impossible to pursue (Monture-Okanee 1995; Young and Majury 1995). Assumptions that candidates from targeted groups could not really be qualified have fuelled a backlash against women in previously male-dominated fields, especially those that have traditionally been better paid and associated with higher social status. Although Ontario's employment equity legislation called for employers to determine their own measures and goals to remove discrimination on the basis of sex, race, and disability and to make reasonable progress towards achieving this goal, the Conservative election strategy portrayed the legislation as a quota system. Some observers regarded such a stance as election-year manipulation: "If we call it quotas—and promise to get rid of it—they will vote for us" (quoted in Burr 1995). The Conservatives did call it quotas; they did win; and they did get rid of the legislation.

While women can no longer legally be excluded from work if they are or are perceived to be heterosexual, lesbians and gays still face legally sanctioned discrimination in some jurisdictions. Section 15 of the Canadian Charter of Rights and Freedoms does not include sexual orientation as one of the prohibited grounds of discrimination, but its wording is open-ended: "Every individual is equal before and under the law and has the right to the equal protection and benefit of the law without discrimination and, in particular, without discrimination based on race, national or ethnic origin, colour, religion, sex, age or mental or physical disability." On matters related to employment and services, most courts have interpreted the grounds broadly to include sexual orientation. But as James Robertson has noted, "the difficulty with relying solely on the Charter is that it applies only to governmental action . . . [and the process]. . . is costly, time-consuming and entails an adversarial approach" (1995, 3). As a result, lesbian and gay activists have been pushing for inclusion of sexual orientation in human rights legislation because this arena provides the possibility of swifter administrative action and broader remedies. In 1995, human rights acts and codes in all jurisdictions except the Northwest Territories, Prince Edward Island, Newfoundland, and Alberta included sexual orientation as a prohibited ground of discrimination. The struggle for inclusion is ongoing: Alberta has appealed a 1994 ruling by the Alberta Court of Queen's Bench that found that provincial human rights legislation contravened the Charter by failing to include sexual orientation (ibid.).

When the Ontario Court of Appeal ruled that the Canadian Human Rights Act was discriminatory because it did not protect gay men and lesbians from discrimination based on their sexual orientation, the federal government indicated in August 1992 that this ruling would be applied throughout Canada. Two months later, the Canadian Armed Forces admitted—after making an out-of-court settlement with former Air Force lieutenant Michelle Douglas—that its policy against hiring or promoting homosexuals was unconstitutional and announced the end of this restriction (Bindman 1992; Robertson 1995). Twenty-eight-year-old Douglas, who had joined the military in 1986 after having graduated at the top of her basic training class, had been stripped of her "top secret" security clearance and released from the military in 1989 because of "admitted homosexual activity" (Bindman 1990; 1992). She welcomed the settlement in these terms: "This is not only a great day for me, but it's a win for all gays and lesbians in Canada and in the Canadian Armed Forces" (quoted in Bindman 1992).

Another example of long public struggle by gays and lesbians is for ordination as ministers and priests. In 1988, the United Church of Canada finally granted lesbians and gays the formal right to be called to the ministry. The decision provided stark evidence of the degree of homophobia in society. Five years later, the first congregation publicly accepted a gay man as minister (Todd 1993). Whole congregations withdrew from the church rather than accept the majority ruling; newspaper reports were filled with the most virulently hateful quotations and letters from those intent on continuing the exclusive practices. Yet in the context of Canadian society, the United Church has been at the forefront in terms of the ordination of women as well as gays and lesbians.

Women and Waged Work

At first, the move to desegregate the labour force and ensure that women had access to better-paying jobs seemed straightforward enough. But some cross-cultural observers were quick to notice a problem created by the assumption that men's jobs paid more because they demanded more skill, more experience, more training. Such critics argued that the move to open nontraditional jobs to women was underwritten by the same assumption that rationalized unequal pay scales in the first place: that the work men did deserved higher pay. What if work traditionally done by women was badly paid not because it demanded fewer skills, but because women did it? Suppose it was the sex of the job incumbents that endowed the work with low or high status and corresponding pay, rather than the other way round? As Graham Lowe discovered in his studies on the transformation of clerical work throughout the twentieth century, previous researchers have missed "the rather obvious point that the increasing recruitment of women as low-priced administrative functionaries largely accounted for declining average clerical salaries" (1987, 163).

The Labour of Love Renamed

This line of thought dovetailed with the analysis feminists were beginning to produce on activities women did in the home: mothering, housework, cooking—all the "never done," invisible, and unpaid work. The deeply engrained belief that women's activities in the home were natural, demanding no special skills outside of genetic endowments, and that the work that they did for wages was simply an extension of this kind of gendered inheritance, helped explain the low wages and value accorded to that which women did. Clearly a full-scale reassessment and renaming of everything women did was required. In a society where only paid work was valued, it became crucial to begin by naming women's activities.[2] Thus, the "labour of love"—from childcare through housework, cooking, feeding and caring for husbands, and to sex itself—was finally recognized as work, *domestic labour*, as socialist feminists termed it.

But if this was work, and it was undervalued and unpaid, what should be done? The popular 1970s feminist children's record "Free to Be" by Marlo Thomas expressed the views of many: "If there's housework to do, do it *together*." As recent research into household division of labour indicates, this proved rather more difficult than the upbeat lyrics of the song made it sound. Women were easy to convince; they had more difficulty persuading their partners. Struggles in individual households over the division of labour picked up steam through the 1970s, and most evidence suggests that they continue. That women married to men who financially supported the household would do the lion's share of housework had seemed almost axiomatic. But as many studies show, this unequal division persists even when women are employed full-time (Haddad and Lam 1988; Nakhaie 1996a).

Not all feminists shared the view that domestic labour and childcare should be a joint responsibility. Some radical feminists argued that men—at least in their present incarnation—were not to be trusted around children. They argued for women-only households and communities where children could be raised in safety. Socialist feminists argued that sharing work in the household, however admirable, was not a sufficient solution. Domestic labour should be socialized: co-operative households and communes, communal kitchens and childcare provisions were all needed to ensure that labour was social and not privatized, recognized and not invisible. They engaged in hefty debates about the relationship between domestic labour and capitalism. Was such labour productive in the sense that it produced surplus value and hence profits? Was capitalism itself dependent upon the unpaid household labour of women? Many argued that women could not be liberated in a capitalist society.

Some feminists argued that women should be paid wages for housework, an idea that germinated with some women who remained, or wished to remain, home with their children. Most feminists were, to say the least, leery of this plan. Would it not simply confirm the gendered division of labour in its present hierarchical and oppressive structure? Social "wages" of any sort—for example, family allowance or mothers' allowance—have been notoriously low, Would not wages for housework simply sustain, even strengthen, the status quo where the alternatives for most women were to be economically dependent on men or very poor (or both)?

In the excitement of the huge insight that women worked in the home, worked hard at tasks crucial for the well-being of their husbands, children, and society, and for capitalism in particular, some rather disparate activities appeared to get lumped together. Children did mean work, but that wasn't all they meant. Many felt that the pleasures of having children were eclipsed in the new discourse. Similarly, sex for many might indeed function as an exchange for housework and personal care, but the appeal of such an analysis for most young people was less than overwhelming. I would argue that feminists, even in the heyday of the exciting new insights, never reduced intimate and nurturing relationships to work. Rather, they exposed the ideological mystifications that enveloped any consideration of women's contributions to men and children. But they have been interpreted as having so reduced these relationships, and we might want to keep this in mind in trying to understand the resonance of the charges against feminists.

Feminists were countering what some called the rhetoric of the pedestal, and many men and women resented this. Women's contributions were very valuable, conservative critics of feminism argued, far too valuable to be debased by the designation work. Women were born being able to do things that required patience, dexterity, and docility, whether that activity was changing a diaper, typing, caring for others as teachers, nurses, and mothers, or working long hours in a sweatshop, and they didn't really need monetary reward. Indeed, monetary reward would almost be insulting, an argument that was made when teachers and nurses began to organize for better salaries. Women did most of these activities out of love, and that came naturally too.

Unlike most first wave feminists, feminists in the 1970s challenged such assumptions and arguments. All the activities that women did—both in the economy and in the home—constituted work. That women did this work for little or no money wasn't because these activities did not require skill and training, or because women didn't need or want to be paid properly. Women did this work because they were oppressed in the household and exploited in the economy. The beneficiaries, whether as husbands or capitalists, were men.

As we noted, feminist solutions were both short- and long-term, reformist and revolutionary, and heated debates raged on the issue. For the purposes of the discussion about those areas of paid work from which women had been excluded, however, a consensus emerged. Certainly the labour force should be desegregated; certainly women and men should have access to all kinds of employment. But all this would be only a short-term solution unless all the kinds of work women were doing were seen as work and re-evaluated alongside men's jobs. Herein lay the core rationale behind pay equity legislation.

Like employment equity, pay equity legislation represents a contemporary outcome of feminist historical, sociological, and legal research into the relations of power that have shaped salaries and conditions of work throughout the labour force. It reflects, as well, the political mobilization needed to translate these interpretations into legislation. The notion that skill itself was socially and historically constructed in space and time was breathtaking. This analysis went beyond exposing the obstacles to equality of opportunity by calling into question the legitimacy of the opportunity ladders themselves. Pay equity legislation helped to erode the commonplace notion that people are paid what they deserve. Under this legislation, jobs done primarily by women are compared—in terms of skill, effort, responsibility, and working conditions—with those jobs done primarily by men.

Overall, however, pay equity represents the tip of the critical iceberg. The critiques of women's work in capitalist society have come from many sources: anthropological, historical, and sociological analysis of women's work in different modes of production; Aboriginal women and men; and feminist critics of imperialism and racism. For the purposes of the discussion at hand, I draw on these literatures to address one overriding question: What do they tell us about hierarchies of work in Canadian society? Such critiques go beyond those offered as rationales for pay equity to consider the underlying historical, political, and cultural explanations for the exploitation of working-class women and for the gendered and racialized organization of work.

Hierarchies of Work: Women and Unions

Socialist feminists argued that women's lower wages relative to those of men resulted in large part from the disproportionately small numbers of women in unions, and on their subordinate place within them. Many became active in organizing initiatives as feminists and as workers. Their writing provides an excellent source of material on the challenges and obstacles faced by wage-earning women. During the 1970s, women organized unions in banks, offices, nursing, and teaching, as well as caucuses within virtually all of the existing industrial and public sector unions and provincial and federal labour organizations. These struggles confirmed and furthered feminist theorizing on the state (Briskin and McDermott 1993; Warskett 1988) and provided new evidence of the unwillingness of many male unionists and union leaders to alter their practices to include concerns raised by women. Feminist initiatives brought out the particular hardships women face when they want to organize, hardships occasioned by their domestic and maternal obligations. Such difficulties provided graphic illustration of the lengths to which many working women would go to win better pay and working conditions as well as leadership roles within unions.

That labour unions are underwritten by ideals of social and economic justice, that they have deployed a rhetoric about the dignity of work and all human beings, and that they are engaged in ongoing struggles with representatives of capital and the state all help explain why, at times, women have been more successful in their struggle for union recognition than they have been in either capitalist (private) enterprise or the institutions of the state. For women, this has proved something of a pyrrhic victory as labour unions have been denuded of numbers and power both by the movement of capital to more fertile ground in impoverished Third World countries and by the draconian steps of the state to reduce debt. Unions have been forced into defensive positions, and in the process many of the potential gains made by women were unrealized, especially in the public sectors where women predominate.

Aboriginal Women and Work

In their quest to understand women's oppression in capitalist society, feminist scholars, particularly during the past twenty-five years, cast a comparative eye on precapitalist society and non-Western societies. They asked big questions. Do all societies have a gendered division of labour? Is such a division always hierarchically organized? Is it possible to transform the patriarchal division of labour in capitalist society? Feminist anthropologists and many Aboriginal women have argued that women in precontact societies in the territory now organized by the Canadian state lived in egalitarian, or communitarian, relationships with men and indeed wielded much of the influence and power (Anderson 1988; Fiske 1991; Leacock 1986; Monture-Angus 1995; Turpel 1993). The white conquerors not only destroyed the economic base of Native society as they progressively removed Aboriginal peoples from the land, but they also engaged in political and ideological assault on the status of women. Mary Ellen Turpel explains:

> The traditional teachings by our Cree Elders instruct us that Cree women are at the centre of the Circle of Life. . . . It is women who give birth both in the physical and spiritual sense to the social, political and cultural life of the community. It is upon women that the focus of the community has historically been placed and it was, not surprisingly,

against women that a history of legislative discrimination was directed by the Canadian state. (1993, 180)

Women's and men's work alike was undercut and often eliminated as Native peoples were dispossessed from the land and separated from their livelihood. In this process, the work that women do in Aboriginal societies has come more and more to resemble the domestic labour that feminists identified as women's lot in capitalist society. Just as the idea of working-class women as full-time homemakers was a kind of cruel parody of this practice in more affluent households, so it is in Aboriginal communities. Under conditions of extreme poverty, ill health, and demoralization, Aboriginal women struggle to keep their communities together and to raise their children. When they move to cities to look for paid employment, they are considered primarily for jobs in poorly paid service occupations (Peters 1987). Many Aboriginal women have created jobs in friendship, social, and health centres to serve their urban communities. Those who have acquired the formal training and education that provide the credentials for better-paying work often remain open and passionate critics of the system that they enter and of the consequences of European conquest for women's lives, both on and off reserves (Horn 1991; Monture-Angus 1995; Turpel 1993). They point to evidence that, despite the unspeakable hardships, women have remained central to the organization of families and households (Peters 1987). They argue that non-Aboriginal feminists have been too universalistic in their analysis of women's childbearing and raising activities, and that such activities were not only accorded the highest value in precontact Native societies but, despite all that has happened, continued to be highly valued.[3] Such interpretations highlight the importance of providing historically specific analyses of the work that women do as mothers and members of households.

Racism, Immigration, and Work

The women descended from those who first lived on this land remain, for the most part, in the lowest-paid jobs. In addition, Aboriginal women do most of the unpaid domestic work in their households, and under the most poverty-stricken conditions that exist in this country. The historical legacy of racism as an integral aspect of the practices and rationale for capitalism and imperialism has also shaped work and working conditions for those who have immigrated here since contact. When people came, from where, and whether and when they have been racialized all contribute to the creation of work hierarchies and how people are distributed within them (Henry et al. 1995). Consider the population of Canada variously labelled and self-identified as negro, coloured, of colour, black, Afro-Caribbean, and African Canadian. Some are the descendants of those who arrived in British North America as United Empire Loyalists or fleeing slavery during the century between the American Revolution and the Civil War. Others arrived during the 1950s and 1960s to attend Canadian universities and stayed. Others—women only—have come as domestic servants under conditions closely akin to indentured labour. Only a racist society would categorize all these people together. Only a racist society would provide the conditions for strategies of resistance based on "racial" characteristics.

But to refuse an analysis of race would render invisible the gendered and racialized hierarchies of work in Canada. Such hierarchies have been created by legal and de facto discrimination, by carefully crafted immigration policies and practices, and by personal and institutional prejudice. Rosemary Brown, Director of the Ontario Human Rights Commission and former British Columbia MPP, records her astonishment at the racism that she encountered when she arrived from Jamaica to study at McGill in 1950. The university moved her to a single room in residence "because the College had been unable to find a roommate to share the double with me. . . . I was stunned!" (1989, 24). Finding work in Montreal that summer was a "nightmare." After graduating, she and her husband moved to Vancouver. Jobs were plentiful, but "the unwritten rule seemed to be that, aside from entertainment, the special jobs open to [blacks] were domestic work for women and portering on the trains for men." Brown was "determined to find the one person in the whole city of Vancouver who would look beyond the colour of my skin and would hire me solely on the basis of my competence as a typist and my Bachelor of Arts degree from McGill" (ibid., 46).

Sedef Arat-Koc provides a critical analysis of the racist immigration law whereby women from the Caribbean were granted entry into Canada for the sole purpose of relieving the shortage of live-in domestic servants in affluent Canadian households. Such a policy only attracts people because of the abysmal conditions of work in the Caribbean, a legacy of slavery, colonialism, and foreign ownership of resources. Live-in domestics have only minimal legal safeguards, and those few a result of concerted struggle. Few can scrape together the resources or have the time to prepare for different work. The catch-22 is that if they do find other work, they may find themselves ineligible to stay in the country. Yet domestic work is valuable and necessary. My sister, Susan Russell, like many people with physical disability or degenerative disease, would not be able to live at home if it were not for the dedicated and skilled work of live-in caregivers from the Philippines and the West Indies. What requires transformation is the conditions of work and the role of the state in creating second-class citizens.[4]

Like Aboriginal women, some African-Canadian women have criticized the explicit and implicit universalism of some feminist analyses of the family, women, and domestic labour. They have argued that the family has also provided a site of resistance to racism. Furthermore, they point out that most black women have always had to engage in (poorly) paid work: historically, the "luxury" of remaining home with children while a husband brought home a pay cheque has seldom been available to black women (Brand 1984; 1991).

Other feminist scholars have written about the working conditions of non-English-speaking women who immigrate to Canada as part of families that both the Canadian state and their husbands see as male-headed (Arnopoulos 1979; Gannagé 1986; Iacovetta 1992; 1995). The assumptions about such women are many, the consequences predictable.

Assumptions	*Consequences*
No need to speak English or French	No language courses made available
No need to be self-supporting	Must have male wage-earner in household; no training or education made available
Cultural traditions are patriarchal	Resources for abused women not culturally appropriate
Likely to be a burden to Canadian taxpayer	Women should not be admitted without male supporter
Only capable of unskilled or "women's" work	Disproportionately present in lowest paid and unorganized job sector

These assumptions provide the rationale for public policy that not only meets the immediate demands of employers but also works to ensure that immigrant women who do not speak English or French have little or no occupational mobility. In such ways, particular kinds of work become identified with certain racialized groups of women and particular ethnic groups. Even when women from certain designated countries arrive in Canada with specialized training—for example, as nurses—they are often denied employment on the grounds that they lack training in the Canadian system.

Women, Sexuality, and Work

Women's presence on terrain once conceded as male has revealed that first wave feminist warnings about the dangers of the workplace—which they conceived as problems for women's sexual morality—were prescient. The dangers, it turned out, were real enough, but the analysis and solutions have been radically reconceived. Working women coined a new term—*sexual harassment*—and it became part of everyday speech. Sexual harassment refers to unwanted behaviours that (primarily) men direct towards women who are their employees, co-workers, fellow students, or simply those with whom they share space, for a moment, on a city street. The term has been used to capture a range of behaviours from a sexist joke to a bum pat to a suggestion that a woman's job or promotion might be linked to her willingness to have sex with the boss. As the stories from working women proliferated, women stopped silently blaming themselves for unwanted sexual and sexist behaviour. Once such behaviours became grievable under harassment policies, the privileges and prerogatives of men in working environments were converted into misdemeanours and crimes.

Contemporary feminists shift the burden of responsibility for such workplace dangers from women to men. Thus, if the workplace or classroom is deemed morally dangerous for women, the call would not be to exclude them; rather, the onus would be on those who create the dangers to change their behaviours. For contemporary feminists, the problems reside in unequal power relations between men and women and among women. The dangers for women at work produce demands for new laws, new practices, and consciousness raising.

Such a shift in perspective was part of the larger feminist critique of the double standard of sexual behaviour. Here most contemporary feminists part company with their predecessors whose overwhelming concern was with women's respectability, defined largely in terms of their sexual behaviour. Most contemporary feminists believe that a woman's sexuality is hers alone to express, regulate, or enjoy. Sexual dangers may lurk at work, but so does the possibility of meeting friends and lovers, the sorts of opportunities that created hand-wringing among early-twentieth-century social reformers, including feminists.

Before we shake our heads at our old-fashioned predecessors, we might want to look at a topic with which they were greatly concerned and which, some argue, creates similar concerns today for the same reasons: the prostitution question. Perhaps this question elicits more division among feminists today than any other work-related issue. Is prostitution simply another form of work, as some women working as prostitutes have argued? Should feminists simply be concerned with ensuring standards of pay and safety as in other gainful employment? Is the present-day feminist refusal to grant prostitution legitimacy as a job category a continuation of the moralistic concerns of their first-wave predecessors (Bell 1987)? Or is prostitution a continuing legacy of a patriarchal society in which men are permitted to use (and abuse) women's bodies for pay? Philosopher Christine Overall answers "yes" to this last question in the conclusion of her incisive analysis of prostitution in a capitalist patriarchal society, arguing that patriarchy creates "both the male needs themselves and the ways in which women fill them, construct[s] the buying of sexual services as a benefit for men, and make[s] the reversibility of sex services implausible and sexual equality in the trade unattainable" (1992, 724).

Would emancipated women who have fair options ever choose prostitution as a career? Perhaps, some say, it is almost impossible to answer such a question in a society with such a long and dishonourable history of dealing with women's sexuality. It stretches credulity for most feminists to imagine a world where contracts between equals over the buying and selling of sexual services could have as much or as little meaning as buying and selling labour power for the purposes of building a house. Yet that response smacks of condescension to some women working as prostitutes in the here and now. They point out that, despite the evidence, presented earlier in this chapter, of the exploitation, oppression, and racism informing so many working practices in contemporary society, no one suggests that people should abstain from working until the millennium.

Nearly three decades of feminist discussion has revealed how women historically and in the present are divided into "good" and "bad," depending upon their sexual practices and often upon the nature of their relationships with men. With all the shifting definitions of good and bad that have occurred, woman as prostitute remains almost continually the quintessential bad woman. Feminists might agree that one of the goals of their struggle is to eliminate these dichotomous categories of good and evil. The question some ask is, can this be done while retaining prostitution as a marked category that can never be admitted into the sphere of legitimate work?

This discussion does not conclude that there is a right answer to these questions, but it does serve to illuminate the broader issues surrounding women, work, and sexuality. Discourses of sexuality, feminists have argued, still shape ideas about women and their suitability for different kinds of work. Women have grieved against employers who have fired them or refused them employment or promotion for being too old, too young, too sexy looking, or too straight-laced. The woman dressed for success, as magazines and advertisements caution, has had to change her wardrobe several times in the past decades, depending on where she works. Should she wear a suit tailored like a man's? How should she express her "femininity"? What length should her skirt be? Are pants acceptable? When? Do pantyhose fit anyone?

All the ads make one thing clear: women at work should dress to please men, the men who are their bosses, their co-workers, and their clients. Such are the heterosexist assumptions that pervade most work environments. From the 1970s, the women's movement and the movements for gay and lesbian liberation publicly confronted these assumptions and, in the process, revealed the deceptions that lesbians and gays have had to perpetrate to get and keep jobs. Some have argued from the historical evidence that, in the first decades of the century, women who lived with other women were free from harassment or discrimination because no one thought of them as sexual beings (Faderman 1981). But in the era of sexual liberation, supposedly inaugurated in the 1960s, the willingness to tolerate such invisibility gave way to the desire for openness, on the one hand, and the assurance of unwelcome surveillance, on the other.

As co-workers get to know each other and talk about their personal lives, daily stresses, and ideas, many lesbians report that they are doubly cautious about revealing the names of their partners, let alone discussing their personal lives in any detail, for fear of ostracism, losing their jobs, and jeopardizing references for future jobs. Women who are not out to their colleagues pick up their homophobic comments, dropped casually in conversation, the bonding of "us" versus "them," and resolve to remain closeted. Or not. Either way, their daily work lives and long-term prospects remain informed by discourses of sexuality that divide the normal from the abnormal, and those who belong from those who don't.

This discourse still forms the basis of Canadian legislation on who qualifies as a spouse for whom. In this area, legislative discrimination against gays and lesbians remains absolute: "Canadian law continues to define 'spouse' uniformly in exclusively heterosexual terms" (Robertson 1995, 8). Because many laws use the term "spouse" to allocate rights, powers, benefits, and responsibilities to partners, lesbians and gays confront a deep thicket of exclusionary laws and practices. The relevance of these exclusions for working life helps explain the immense lobbying efforts by lesbians and gays to expand the definition of spouse (Blackburn 1995; Herman 1995). The failure of the Ontario legislature, in June 1994, to pass the Equality Rights Statute Amendment, which was designed to provide same-sex couples with the same rights and obligations as those of unmarried heterosexual couples resounded as a devastating defeat, and tangible indication of the depth of homophobia in society. The struggle reveals the permeability of the so-called private–public split. How people are treated in the workplace, even at the level of legislation, is shaped by their relationships and identities in their households and in their "free" time. Some relationships are called family, others are not, and on the basis of the biological sex of the participants. Two women who live together, share a bed, split finances, holiday together, and care for their children together do not constitute a family.

Mothers, Children, and Work

Essentially, children and work appear together in the feminist discourse of the past quarter century in two interrelated ways. First, as noted earlier, feminists insisted that, whatever else bearing and rearing children might be, in this society, the activities constituted work. Second, they drew attention, as had never been done before, to the fundamental incompatibility between reproductive labour and childcare, on the one hand, and paid work on the other, as well as to the profound consequences of this incompatibility.

At one level, it seems almost a truism that children mean work. Yet everyday expressions give away the extent to which this work still goes unacknowledged. "She's looking after the kids" does imply some responsibility, however casual. But we also hear, "she's at home with the kids" or "she's just at home with the kids," conjuring up the inherent passivity, innocuousness, and even triviality of time thus spent. As was suggested earlier, it is feminists to whom such views are often attributed. The irony is that it was feminists who first confronted such attitudes, arguing that childcare is indeed work, work that is integral to sustaining any society.

In their arguments to this effect, socialist feminists drew upon and elaborated a famous passage from Friedrich Engels' book *The Family, Private Property and the State*:

> According to the materialist conception, the determining factor in history is, in the last resort, the production and reproduction of immediate life. But this itself is of a twofold character. On the one hand, the production of the means of subsistence, of food, clothing and shelter and the tools requisite therefore; on the other, the production of human beings themselves, the propagation of the species. (1948 [1884], 5–6)

By only following up on production, Marxists had effectively eliminated from their analysis, strategies, and policies the work that most women do (Burstyn 1983). Mary O'Brien (1981) employed a Marxist materialist mode of analysis to argue that reproductive labour was not just labour *in name* (as in the expression "she's in labour") but also in reality and in its consequences. Harriet Rosenberg (1987) used the word *motherwork* to indicate the intrinsic connection between children and the creation of work.

At the same time as they countered popular notions that anyone—provided the anyone was of the female persuasion—could bring up children, feminists also had to engage and counter a parallel discourse about the needs of children. While it seemed that any woman worthy of the name should be able to mother, children required full-time home care by their mothers if they were to grow up to be good citizens and well-adjusted adults. In support of this view, post-World War II childcare experts drew upon the wartime observations of psychologist John

Bowlby. Bowlby reported that babies in orphanages who were left in their cribs all day did not develop normal attachments to other human beings. Those who were picked up for feedings did not demonstrate these symptoms of deprivation. Dr Spock, most famous of the childcare experts, warned mothers in his best-selling book, *Baby and Child Care*, that although the children of mothers who had to work usually turned out normally, some grew up "neglected and maladjusted" (1957, 563). Spock had to make a big leap from Bowlby's observations to the assertion that babies needed full-time mothering in the home. After feminists aimed their logical, practical, empirical, and critical objections at the assumptions inherent in such judgments, Spock's 1985 message was rather different. "Both parents have an equal right to a career if they want one, it seems to me, and an equal obligation to share in the care of their children, with or without the help of others" (37).

One of the major practical and political objections feminists made to the insistence that children needed full-time mothers in the home was that such a notion was predicated on the idea of the family wage, more especially on the economic dependence of mothers upon fathers. Such an assumption, many argued, was heterosexist, class-blind, overlooked the consequences of the absence of a male breadwinner in many households, and assumed all women's availability, suitability, and desire for life as a twenty-four-hour-a-day custodian and caregiver.

Here we may properly turn to the second overarching theme of the feminist discussions on children and work. Feminists argued that many women need and/or want to work for pay. But, as feminists began to reveal through historical and cross-cultural studies, by creating forums in which women could speak, and through mass political mobilizations, there was a fundamental incompatibility in Canada and other industrial capitalist societies between having children and working in the labour force. The problem was simple: at one point or another it faces every woman who is a mother and leaves the household to "go to" work. What to do with the children? Feminists led the way in transforming every woman's private trouble into a public policy issue.

Aboriginal women and feminist anthropologists have argued that childbearing and rearing were activities that were integrated with the productive activities of women and men in precontact societies. Similarly, feminist historians have argued that the majority of households in premodern societies permitted the integration of men's and women's productive and reproductive work. This integration, feminists have argued, is rent asunder whenever capitalist relations make their debut in a society. When men and women are "freed" from the land, in Marx's famous phrase, they are also separated from their previously productive households. When men and women are left owning only their labour power, which they must sell in the marketplace for a wage, the incompatibility between mothering and paid work enters the world stage. Today, some four hundred years after capitalism's inaugural ball in England, that situation may seem eternal, a fact of life.

Unlike their predecessors, women in the past few decades openly challenged this fact of life and the social, economic, and political practices that gave this "fact" its appearance and substance. If the organization of society could not take pregnancy and parenting into account, then workplaces and households alike required reorganizing. Feminists developed strategies that ranged from blueprints for new feminist socialist utopias, through lesbian communities, communes, housing co-operatives, and other forms of egalitarian spaces and households within capitalist patriarchal societies, to reforms intended to enhance equality of opportunity for women in the paid labour force.

The 1970 *Report of the Royal Commission on the Status of Women,* often described as the liberal feminist document *par excellence,* called for daycare and maternity leave. Yet, the extent to which children are held to be the responsibilities of their parents may be seen in the continuing controversies about the necessity and viability of state-supported daycare as well as in the continuing comparisons between parental care in the home and daycare. During World War II, when the state wanted women to work in industries related to and supportive of the war effort, objections to daycare were quickly overruled. As soon as the armistice was declared, the daycares were closed, not without protest from the women who used them. Historian Ruth Pierson has documented that women worked because they needed the money, and because they worked they needed daycare. The government of Canada portrayed women as working because of the war; once the war was over, they happily returned home to their natural destiny. Today "natural destiny" isn't "in" as a public statement, but neither, on the other hand, is daycare (Pal 1993).

In 1993, former Supreme Court Justice Bertha Wilson chaired a study for the Canadian Bar Association, which documented what she called the systemic biases against women in the profession of law. The suitability of future partners for law firms is determined within a legal culture that has been shaped by men, for men, and "is predicated on historical work patterns that assume that lawyers do not have significant family responsibilities" (quoted in Gibb-Clark and Fine 1993, A10).

First wave feminists, even the most utopian among them, never foresaw the day when a report with such findings would see the light of day (even in the 1990s it encountered more heat than light). Women who did become professionals tended not to marry or have children, and such a choice, painful as it might have been, seemed unavoidable.[5] Women who had to work for wages because they were in dire economic circumstances were seen as unfortunate. Special arrangements should be made for them, arrangements that whenever possible should enable them to remain at home.

Work norms in the law firms Wilson studied reflected the life situation of an ambitious, physically healthy man who could work all hours, including weekends. That schedule was (supposedly) facilitated by a wife at home, caring for him and for his children. The work norms assumed that there were no conflicts between parenting and work in the labour force. One woman, hired at a Canadian university in the late 1970s, asked about its maternity policy. "Our faculty don't get pregnant," was the reply from the personnel officer. Clearly, if women were hired, and this was still an unusual event, they were obliged to forego childbearing and rearing.

Feminists critiques of capitalist society draw attention to the absurdity of an economic system that makes no provision for the exigencies of human reproduction and childhood dependence. They confront the patriarchal relations and assumptions that leave women responsible for the care of their children without providing the resources or the opportunities to garner the necessities of life.

This analysis of women, work, and children would lead to the conclusion that women can either have children or they can support their children, but not both at the same time. Yet the majority of women today do both. Their strategies are various and are shaped by many factors broadly related to the economic resources they can deploy, the number of adults who play an active parenting role in their children's lives, and the age, health, and behaviours of their children. Some affluent families seek live-in caregivers to facilitate their working lives. Most of the time, the women they hire receive low wages for long hours of work. Because native-born Canadian women refuse such conditions, they hire women from Third World countries. Sedef Arat-Koc points out a consequence of these decisions: "As a relationship between female employers and workers, domestic service emphasizes, most clearly, the class, racial/ethnic and citizenship differences among women at the expense of their gender unity" (1989, 52). The wages and conditions of work of domestic workers reflect, more generally, the low value society places on the care of children. Daycare workers, most of them unorganized, earn low wages for exhausting and demanding work for which they often have formal training and much experience.

In light of the lack of daycare and after-school programs, many women seek employment that is as compatible as possible with their children's school schedules. For some, that is part-time work. Such a strategy provides less income, and usually means that a person will not be considered for on-the-job training or promotion. Jobs, not careers, usually result from part-time employment. As Duffy and Pupo argue in *Part-Time Paradox*, such work is "acceptable to women because it is frequently what is available to them and because there have been few structural accommodations to women's participation in the public sphere" (1992, 104). Some corporations describe part-time work for women who seek to combine careers with motherhood as the "mommy track." It goes without saying that this innovation—captured by Duffy and Pupo as "off the main track" (ibid., 116)—will not contribute to equality of opportunity with men unless there is an equally well-worn "daddy track."

In the absence of available and affordable daycare, most women working for wages choose the most acceptable options and then hope for the best. Hoping for the best under such circumstances increases the anxiety, stress, health problems, and fatigue inherent in the double day of labour. Nor do women receive accolades for carrying on. Rather, their options have been interpreted by middle-class social reformers and the media in ways that blame them for real or perceived negative consequences of their efforts to cope with the contradictions of mothering under capitalism. School drop-outs and students with high absentee records are often older children who have been kept home from school to look after preschool siblings whose mothers "neglect" them by working for wages. Latch-key children—inevitable figures in Canadian society for more than a century—are children whose mothers work for wages outside the home and who therefore have to look after themselves after school or when they are sick. Of course, fathers also leave the home to work for wages, but in their case they are not deemed neglectful for doing so. Rather they are considered inadequate fathers if they *don't* earn a family wage.

Women, Community, and Society

First wave feminists emphasized that women should be involved in the world beyond their households *because* of their special talents and concerns. Such reasoning has been hotly contested during the past decades. Feminists have tended to argue that women should be everywhere that they want to be. Transforming social institutions, attitudes, and practices so that this would be possible has, as we have seen in this chapter, engaged feminists from all perspectives.[6]

In this final section, I consider some of the work-related organizing that has been about creating (predominantly) women-only spaces— from women's centres and cultural sites and communities to an immense variety of small businesses. The varying perspectives of feminists have influenced where, how, and why they have organized, but the type of organization has also confirmed or challenged the assumptions of the participants. Some women who organized women-only spaces were motivated by a radical feminist or lesbian separatist analysis. But working in women's shelters and rape crisis centres and seeing the consequences of male violence for women's lives also provided the evidence, as some women report, for the correctness of such an analysis. One Vancouver woman wrote to her friends, describing her horrific experience leading support groups for women who had been battered: "I no longer think we live in only cold war conditions. It looks a lot more violent and hateful than that" (personal communication).

Today, virtually every city and town in the country includes organized spaces for women, although harsh government cutbacks have forced many closures. The movement for such centres started in the early 1970s. Feminists saw themselves not only creating space for women to meet and support each other, but also laying the ground for reform and revolution. Increasingly, such centres began responding to the needs of women who came, and feminists opened more specialized centres. There has been continuing pressure for these centres to become more like traditional, bureaucratic organizations. The sheer numbers of women who present themselves for support mean that struggling to help each woman can take the place of more long-term organizing goals. More importantly, given this overwhelming need, such centres have had to seek stable funding from the state. Although organizers struggle to maintain their decision-making autonomy, the pressure to rationalize the organization, produce a hierarchically organized staff that is "accountable," and keep countless records has taken its toll. From the outside, many centres now look like way-stations for the destitute run by a staff of poorly paid professionals. Some shelter workers claim that this has been the fate of these centres. However, this picture of co-optation scarcely does justice to the many ways in which women as paid workers and volunteers have negotiated their way through the administrative thickets without abandoning their ways of working or their goals. More serious have been the effects of government cutbacks. Many centres and services throughout the country have been forced to close, and those that remain open come to demand even longer hours from their workers in return for even lower wages.

The motivation for developing women-only work sites has run the range from the pragmatic to the revolutionary. Starting small businesses, for example, has been popular with women for different reasons: lack of employment elsewhere; the inclination to work according to non-hierarchical, collectivist principles; the desire not to have to work with men, which may include women providing safe spaces for themselves and others; the political motivation to provide feminist-inspired services for women facing and resisting abuse or poverty or seeking assistance in altering relationships, work, and life directions more generally; the desire to have more control over one's work life (Dickie 1993).

Some of the small businesses—from artisanal shops to book stores, credit unions, therapeutic services, and retail stores—have been inspired by those often referred to as cultural feminists. Cultural feminists seek to create a world—or as much of a world as possible—that is organized by women for women, along non-hierarchical lines. Particularly in large cities and towns, such establishments form a network to support alternative lifestyles, household arrangements, and politics. Often such networks include primarily lesbian feminists who have created spatial and social environments in which they may live openly with their partners, friends, acquaintances, and children (Nash 1995).

Conclusion

GIVEN THIS OVERVIEW of feminist questions and challenges to women and work, let us briefly consider the charge that feminists encourage women to turn their backs on children, on nurturing, on caring for others. Some of this resonates. Feminists have led many struggles for women's freedom to choose whether or not to have children. By redefining childcare—whether in the private household, daycare, or school—as work, feminists made it more possible to see having children as a choice, as indeed other forms of work are portrayed. The idea—let alone the reality—that women may choose whether to have children raises anxiety and hostility for different reasons. I cannot discount, as an important factor, the desire and interests of many in maintaining women's subordination and oppression both in households and in economic life more generally.

What about the charge that feminists have ushered in a world in which women are encouraged to model themselves on some version of the corporation man? As some women seek equality with men in the workplace, an equality that feminists espoused, many have chosen or felt forced to undertake the same gruelling work schedule that has been the route for many ambitious men. It is easy to blame the media for promoting images and views with which one is not in sympathy, but this does not mean that such blame is not warranted. For twenty years, the mainstream media followed the feminist story in terms of "the first woman who. . . ." More often than not "the first woman who" was a woman who had made it into the top ranks of a public or private corporation. Equally interesting to the media were stories about the woman who did and had everything: she had a successful job, fabulous kids, and devoted husband; she was an excellent housekeeper and cook; she ran the local branch of the Red Cross and was the kind of person everyone wanted for a neighbour. Of course, she was also "beautiful." "Ordinary" mortal women reading these stories were, at best, disbelieving, and, at worst, provided with another occasion to feel inadequate. Or they could just blame feminists for holding up such unworkable, unrealistic images.

But feminists provide a shifting target. In her *Globe and Mail* column, Margaret Wente charged feminists with failing to appreciate the gains made by some women in reaching the top. She took NDP leader Audrey McLaughlin and NAC to task for not cheering for a woman's success just because she was "white, privileged, ruthless, pragmatic, ambitious, unpleasant or (Goddess help us) profit-oriented" (1994, A2). Once, feminists were under attack for only being interested in the issues affecting white, middle-class women. Now that the face of organized feminism is identified by the media as NAC—which increasingly focuses upon poverty and racism, feminists are being attacked for the opposite sins that dogged them a decade ago.

The theme of this chapter has been that there isn't one feminist perspective on women and work, or even ten or twelve. Feminists from different perspectives, locations, and interests have developed analyses and strategies for immediate reform and sweeping revolutionary change. It is impossible to categorize neatly and put to rest the feminist position.

Feminists have offered explanations for the poorly valued, privatized, and unpaid nature of women's domestic labour, for their super-exploitation in capitalism, and for their uneven levels of exploitation depending on social class, country of origin, and their racialized characteristics. Debates among feminists continue and lead to different short- and long-term strategies, but feminist scholarship and politics have demonstrated that women's exploitation and oppression are the products of long-term historical processes that benefit the few at the cost of the many.

This chapter has provided an overview of many of the predominant discussions, debates, organizing initiatives, and issues that feminists have raised in the past century around women and work. There is no end to the story, of course. The current restructuring of the Canadian economy continues to erode the ranks of two sorts of workers: relatively well-paid men organized in industrial unions and the recently developed ranks of state-employed women in better paying jobs from nursing to social work to middle-level administrators.[7] Jamie Swift (1995) demonstrates that, increasingly, two kinds of jobs are being created: highly paid technical jobs and a far greater number of low-paid, casual, now-you-see-them, now-you-don't service jobs. The proliferation of jobs in the latter category helps to explain the continuing erosion in middle-class households, including those who only remain in these ranks because they have two full-time wage earners.

Given cutbacks in social services, daycare, and the social wage generally, and increasing numbers of low-paid jobs and sole-support mothers, there seems no reason to believe that the contradictions posed for women by the demands of childcare and care of aging parents and disabled family members, on one hand, and waged work, on the other, are abating. Many of the gains achieved through feminist organizing are already being turned back. Now it seems that many of those new good jobs for women are period pieces, there only during the days before the heavy cutbacks in state spending in every sphere. Autonomous organizations have been replaced by state services paying minimum wage to women who deal with the increasing casualties of an economic restructuring that provides more for the few and less for the many. Those who speak about a "post-feminist" world may be conjuring up a society in which there is no more organizing based on gender inequality, but putting a "post" before feminist will not eradicate the inequalities that feminist organizing continues to address (Brodie 1995).

In this chapter, we have examined women's paid and unpaid work, their interconnections, and the implications and consequences of the current distribution of work. Except for the very wealthy, the kind of paid work to which we have access shapes our standard of living, whether we live in comfort or poverty, and whether our children have access to education. The ways in which that work is organized shapes our influence and control over its conditions and our feelings about ourselves.

How we come to think about ourselves as gendered, what that means for our lives, and how we are presented to ourselves in literature, art, media, advertising, and political and legal discourse constitute the interrelated themes of the next chapter. These themes pervade all feminist-inspired organizing and writing. Chapter 6 looks at these issues of representation and subjectivity in the context of shifting definitions and discourses about gender, sexuality and sexual orientation, race, nationality, age, health, illness, and disability. Feminist questions and practices have helped bring these discourses to consciousness so that they might be critiqued and transformed. The geopolitical context remains Canada, but the topics of representation and subjectivity refer to culture, broadly defined, and these issues, perhaps more than those in the previous chapter, defy any national or geographical boundaries.

Notes

1. For interpretations of women's role in nursing, midwifery, and community and public health, see Dodd and Gorham (1994).

2. Wally Seccombe examines the ways in which some economists have moved to incorporate feminist insights into their models of the household. First, they began to conceive of unpaid work as integral to production as well as consumption. Second, they began to abandon the assumption that family households were always "income-pooling, work-sharing and joint consumption groups" and to grapple with the evidence that points to "persistent inequalities in labour burden, leisure, property ownership, pension provision and decision-making prerogative—all to the wife's detriment" (1986, 200–1).

3. I am grateful to Margaret Horn for first explaining this to me.

4. For an in-depth analysis of "the significance of citizenship status in mediating the entire matrix of relations pertaining to paid domestic labor on an international scale," see Bakan and Stasiulus (1995). They demonstrate the "pivotal role of private domestic placement agents in negotiating citizenship rights for migrant domestic workers and their employers" (304).

5. Agnes Macphail was the first woman seated in the House of Commons. She won her seat in 1920 and found that "most of the members made me painfully conscious of my sex." Prentice et al. note that Macphail "did not shrink from the responsibility that she had accepted, taking it so seriously that she rejected several marriage proposals, in order to continue her work. Sensitive over being a 'spinster' in an era when marriage was highly valued, Macphail took pains to announce the marriage offers publicly" (1988, 279–80).

6. Feminists have also worked to transform what social planners call the "built" environment. See Eichler (1995) and MacGregor (1994).

7. Historian Deborah Gorham notes that the growing number of women in medicine "may be as much an indication of the declining status of medicine as it is of the improved status of women." In particular, she examines the Ontario NDP government's "attack on newly qualifying family physicians" in 1993, "just when the gender balance in family medicine has shifted decisively in favor of women, and as the representation of individuals from racial and ethnic minorities has begun to increase" (1994, 196).

Representation and Subjectivity

THE LAST CHAPTER WAS ABOUT WORK. Work is a simple word; its meaning seems self-evident. Yet we saw that feminists expanded its definition to include the kind of activity women have done in the home, as well as community service and social action. Anthropologists report that the earliest form of the division of labour was based on sex. Historically, in Western societies, all forms of work have been deeply gendered; work is implicitly, and more often explicitly, perceived as "women's work" or "men's work" or at the least, more suitable to one sex than the other. More generally, not just work, but most forms of activity and behaviour are similarly gendered. I mean this in two inter-related ways. First, activities and behaviours, in every aspect of social life, are represented verbally and pictorially, as gendered. During World War II, government recruitment posters geared to attracting women were careful to depict conventional femininity. In case the point was lost, one poster showed a mother with a photograph of her daughters who had joined the service, with a caption that read "My girls are the real glamour girls" (Pierson 1986, 142–43). Second, women and men are likely to think of themselves in ways that make some kinds of work, activity, and behaviour more appropriate for them than others simply because of their sex. Old rationales for gendered employment ghettos—women's physical weakness, greater manual dexterity (good for typing), and raging hormones—are still summoned on occasion. Moreover, as Karen Messing (1987) has documented, keeping women away from equipment for the purposes of protecting their fertility and their foetuses provides new grounds for exclusion. She argues that this rationale is used selectively by employers for their convenience and ignores the effects of exposure for men's fertility.

What we do, how we see ourselves and are portrayed, and who we think we are are all interconnected. Feminists have explored each of these three aspects of social life, trying to figure out how they are related to each other and how, together, they shape relations of domination and subordination between the sexes. What motivates this analysis is a commitment to social change. But, strategically speaking, how do we go about changing society? Is it more important to expand women's and men's options for the sorts of work they choose? To change the ways in which they are represented? Or is social change well nigh impossible until women and men—that is we ourselves—are changed?

For analytical purposes, we could think of these three questions as reflecting three areas of social life: activity, representation, and subjectivity. The focus of the last chapter was on activity—in particular, work. In this chapter, the focus shifts to the last two parts of this trilogy. First, how are men and women represented in this culture? What are the dominant ways in which men and women are portrayed in the media, in law, in educational institutions and texts, in virtually any social location? Second, how and in what ways do human infants become men or women in social terms? What does it mean to be a man or woman in this culture? What are the connections between the ways in which people feel themselves to be men or women and come to behave as men or women, and the representations of men and women that they see in their social worlds?

My approach, once again, will be historical and theoretical. Such discussions immerse us in feminist debates about what is more important for women's liberation, how the various issues are connected, what sort of explanations are most useful for analyzing the relations between men and women, and which strategies are most likely to transform those relations. I am going to start with a dramatic feminist protest in the late 1960s and use the issues it raised to set the terms of the discussion in this chapter. That protest was about the sexual objectification of women, and this has been an enduring theme of feminist activism and scholarship ever since.

On 1 September 1968, the media reported that a group of women had disrupted the Miss America Beauty Pageant in Atlantic City. For many people, this protest, together with reports that some women had publicly burned their bras, not only marked the beginning of the women's movement but also became its lasting symbol. Bra-burning feminists: for many, the words were forever linked. The image amused, threatened, and outraged. Its meaning was pliable: on the one hand it was used to ridicule—*this* was what women were struggling for? How trivial! How absurd! But, if bra burning and beauty pageant protests were that trivial, why was so much sustained attention given to them? What did it mean when women protested against time-honoured beauty pageants and made the brassiere an optional garment? Why all the ridicule and why all the fuss?

First, the question of ridicule. Among the many and interrelated social movements of the last half of the twentieth century, the women's movement was surely alone in eliciting an early and predominant response of ridicule from the media. Women's protest, whatever it was about, made people chortle. Women could not be taken seriously even when they were rebelling. During the hearings of the Royal Commission on the Status of Women, Peter Newman noted that "most editors seemed to think there was something uproariously funny about the whole idea of women contemplating their navels" (1969, 23). Women's rebellion was ridiculous, and this ridicule helped legitimate continued subordination: this was an early insight that would be taken up more elaborately in later feminist cultural and poststructural analysis.

Second, if women's protests were so ridiculous, why so much attention? For the media, the protests provided great copy and good footage. But the level of interest betrays, I would argue, considerable anxiety. What did it mean to have women refusing the role of beauty queen? What did it mean when women insisted that they did not want to be represented as sexual objects? Taken together with feminist critiques of compulsory motherhood and demands for free abortion and access to contraception, feminists appeared to be pulling the rug out from under the whole social order. Protesting a beauty pageant was a protest against a system that judged men by their intellectual and physical achievements and women by their appearance. It was a protest against a single standard of beauty that measured women against each other and found almost all of them wanting.[1]

When we look back at the protests against beauty pageants, it is possible to tease out many of the substantive and theoretical issues that became important within feminist activism and scholarship. What were the forms, the extent, and the impact of sexual objectification on women's lives? What were the links between representing women as sexual objects and how women thought about themselves, how they treated others, and how they chose courses of study and work? More succinctly, what were the links between how women were portrayed and who women really were?

The insight that women are expected to present themselves, and be treated, as sexual objects contributed to an exploration of the ways in which women are represented in all aspects of social life. Feminists subjected advertisements, television programming, school textbooks, and pornography to searing critique and often mass protest. They went on to unmask how women were represented in family law, rape law, laws about contraception and abortion, and in the assumptions underwriting the development of reproductive technologies.

The issue of beauty and sexual objectification contributed to exploring issues around women and health. Feminists argued that the cultural standards of beauty demanded that women treat their bodies as enemies to be pummelled and starved into submission. Plastic surgery on parts of the body deemed too big or too small, constant dieting, and other "beauty" techniques that contribute to ill-health have been central feminist concerns.[2]

The question of sexual objectification became elaborated into more general reappraisals of sexuality. Defining women as sexual beings in their own right, criticizing the double standard of sexual behaviour, launching a full-scale critique of "compulsory heterosexuality," debating the meanings and consequences of pornography: all this captured the attention of feminists in many social and theoretical locations. Was sexuality a terrain of danger, pleasure, or both for women? What would it take for women to have the power to define and pursue their own desires?

The feminist analysis that presented women's oppression as intricately wrapped up with their sexual objectification was subsequently challenged, from many quarters, for its apparent claims to universality. All women were not treated as actual or potential sexual objects, and certainly not in the same ways. Racialized women, women with disability, older women, and lesbians, among others, wrote thoughtful and often stinging rebukes of the assumptions of what they came to call white, middle-class, ageist, and able-ist feminist assumptions.

Let us look back in more detail at the issue of sexual objectification and some of the related questions that this concept helped to mobilize and then at some of the critiques that have been offered of this analysis.

Women as Sexual Objects

UNTIL THE LATE 1960S, beauty contests were a regular feature on university campuses. My 1962 Carleton University Yearbook includes full-page pictures of Frosh Queen, Arts Queen, and Winter Weekend Queen. They received their titles by garnering the highest number of votes in a student plebiscite, after nomination by the specific dance committee. Pictures of all nominees flooded the campus in the days prior to the vote, and the winner was duly crowned at the dance. Only heterosexual couples attended the dance. "Girls" waited for an invitation—no invitation, no dance. Single men and women did not attend, nor did lesbians and gays. Indeed, there were no out lesbians or gays on campus. The dances were exquisitely heterosexual events; for women, attendance was a sign of their acceptability by at least one member of the opposite sex. Election as queen of the dance represented the epitome of more general appreciation.

Working women were also encouraged to participate in beauty contests. During the 1950s and 1960s, the Recreation Association (RA), catering exclusively to federal government employees, sponsored interdepartmental contests for Miss Civil Service. As the contest advertisement for 1952 pointed out, "Your Department has as much chance as the next one. All you need is a good-looking girl. From what we can see . . . there are a lot of good-looking girls in the Civil Service. And your Department has its quota" (quoted in Gentile 1995). Patrizia Gentile has argued that these beauty contests served at once to legitimate women's growing presence in the civil service and to reinforce almost perfect occupational segregation, hierarchically arranged.[3] The Civil Service Commission's method for keeping women down (and often out) was simple: women were hired as "'stenographers' and 'typewriters' while men became 'general clerks,' who, incidentally, climb the administrative ladder while 'typewriters' could not" (Archibald 1973, 15). There was a place for typewriters to compete, however, and that was at the "Night of the Stars." How well did they represent the "typical government girl"?

Winners were "preferably single with no children, heterosexual, well-groomed, tall, thin and 'beautiful' with shiny hair." Their height, weight, and measurements were published in *The RA News* (Gentile 1995, 29–30).

Looking back, it is easy to see why feminists attacked beauty contests.[4] That beauty contests were such an intrinsic aspect of university and working life indicated how pervasive was the system of judging women by their facial features and the shape of their bodies, rather than by academic accomplishments or even athletic prowess.[5] Women were to look at; men were to look. But of course women looked too—at each other and at themselves. Every day could be a re-enactment of the beauty contest, as women judged themselves harshly and surveyed other women as potential competitors. A beautiful woman with much male attention was assumed to have it all. Her penalty was often the hostility of other women. Such reaction wasn't supposed to matter. Women who saw their own opinions as mattering little, and their own physique as inadequate, assumed that they did not have the power to hurt a more beautiful and popular woman.

In the late 1960s, the beauty pageant appeared to feminist protestors as a straightforward case of men using women as sexual objects. The language varied, but feminists depicted the women who participated as falsely conscious or brainwashed. Deprived of their own desire, they strutted on stage to satisfy the voyeuristic pleasures of men. Underneath the eager-to-please exterior, feminists argued, lay the genuine woman, awaiting emancipation so that she might pursue her own projects and pleasures.

This interpretation may be described as part of the development of radical feminism. Men's power over women was blatant and easy to identify; feminists had to confront such power directly; men had to be prevented from continuing to wield this power over women. Once this happened, women would be free to exercise their own will and develop their own capacities and talents. Women would stop obeying men and begin to please themselves. Clearly this would involve an end to beauty pageants. But such contests were only a symbol of the problem: women dressed to please men; used cosmetics to please men; had sex with men in order to please men; and shaped their bodies in a myriad of ways to please men.

The radical feminist analysis was far-reaching in its critique, and many of the issues were taken up, disputed, and elaborated upon from other feminist positions. In *Sexual Politics*, an early text of second-wave feminism, Kate Millett cast the situation of women—the beautiful and the not-so-beautiful—into sharp relief:

> The continual surveillance in which she is held tends to perpetuate the infantilization of women even in situations such as those of higher education. The female is continually obliged to seek survival or advancement through the approval of males as those who hold power. She may do this either through appeasement or through the exchange of her sexuality for support and status. (1971, 54)

Millett succinctly captured the dilemma of women, thrown into competition with each other on the basis of their appearance. Treated as mindless, deprived of power, set against each other, women internalize the lack of esteem in which they are held and "despise both themselves and each other" (ibid., 55). Millett presents a more complicated picture than some radical feminist positions that suggested that lurking beneath women's outward capitulation to male power was their real self, a self capable of self-love, love for other women, and the capacity for realizing their own projects. In Millett's understanding, *misogyny*—the hatred of women—far from being a prerogative of men, is also lodged deep in women's own psyches.

Novelist Margaret Atwood has created female characters who may be seen in the light of Millett's conceptualization. Atwood's riveting portrayal of Cordelia and Elaine in *Cat's Eye* (1988) resonates with many female readers. Cordelia is everlastingly mean to her vulnerable friend Elaine, catching her off-guard, offering enough reward to sweep her back into her orbit whenever she demonstrates the will to escape:

> "There's dog poop on your shoe," Cordelia says.
> I look down. "It's only a rotten apple."
> "It's the same colour though, isn't it?" Cordelia says. (1988, 71)

With so much capacity to influence others, will Cordelia grow up to run a corporation, a university, or a family? No, by mid-life Elaine finds Cordelia living at the Dorothy Lyndwick Rest Home, "a discreet, private loony bin . . . the sort of place well-off people use for stowing away those members of their families who are not considered fit to run around in public" (ibid., 354). By then, Elaine has realized how she had internalized the contempt that Cordelia had projected: "There is the same shame, the sick feeling in my body, the same knowledge of my own wrongness, awkwardness, weakness; the same wish to be loved; the same loneliness; the same fear. But these are not my own emotions any more. They are Cordelia's; as they always were" (ibid., 419). Elaine and Cordelia were raised in the 1940s and 1950s, growing up to be women in a man's world. In their world of the relatively powerless, they jockeyed for position, humiliated others as a strategy for self-survival, and, at the limits, destroyed the other—emotionally and physically. All this was the stuff of ongoing daily interactions.

This is the complex conundrum that psychoanalytic feminists have addressed. What are the differences between growing up female and growing up male? How are the relations of domination and subordination lodged in the psyches of the next generation? This is not only the work of men subjecting women to their will, as the radical feminist position tends to suggest; this is also the work of girls and women, the Cordelias and the Elaines. In *The Bonds of Love*, Jessica Benjamin argues that this is *relational* work, that it takes two to tango. The powerful are equally dependent upon the powerless, although their inability to acknowledge this dependence leads to tyranny. Meanwhile, the powerless make a last-ditch attempt to save their egos by identification with the powerful (1988, 85–132). This is what conventional heterosexual romance and marriage has been about. Simone de Beauvoir reckoned that "when woman gives herself completely to her idol, she hopes that he will give her at once possession of herself and of the universe he represents" (1952, 717).

Cordelia's mother cannot affirm her daughter because she has not affirmed herself; she cannot take her daughter's projects seriously because her own life is about facilitating her husband's. Nine-year-old Elaine, from a more unconventional family, is getting the picture from her friends:

> Something is unfolding, being revealed to me. I see that there's a whole world of girls and their doings that has been unknown to me, and that I can be part of without making any effort at all. I don't have to keep up with anyone, run as fast, aim as well, make loud explosive noises, decode messages, die on cue. I don't have to think about whether I've done these things well, as well as a boy. All I have to do is sit on the floor and cut frying pans out of the Eaton's Catalogue with embroidery scissors, and say I've done it badly. Partly this is a relief. (Atwood 1988, 54)

Elaine is learning to be surveyed and found wanting; she is also learning that girls grow up to be women who are inordinately interested in domestic life. In her research on working-class high school students in Vancouver in 1977, sociologist Jane Gaskell confirmed the corollary: boys are not interested in things domestic. As one of her female respondents put it, "I just couldn't picture my husband doing it—cleaning, making beds, making supper. I guess it's picturing my brother and dad." Most of the boys in the study agreed with her: "If I marry my girlfriend, I'd help her out. I don't like doing it. If someone doesn't ask me, I won't do it"(1988, 154–55).[6]

In the 1950s, sociologist Talcott Parsons (1959) had noted that growing up female in America was a tricky business, though he stopped short of thinking that anything should be done about it. Girls had to present themselves as sexy in order to catch a man who would be willing to marry them. Once married, however, they were expected to shun the role of sexual object for a thoroughly domestic existence. Feminists pointed out that it was more complicated than this. Even beauty queens were to present themselves as sexual objects—to be gazed upon—not as sexual subjects with their own desires. Contestants were expected to be virgins; having already had a child, for example, was not just a disqualifier, it was a monumental blot on one's character.[7] So it was with all girls. Be sexy enough to keep boys interested, but never go "all the way." Girls who didn't get that message not only risked becoming pregnant (which was only the girl's fault), they could count on a reputation as "bad girl" and a lifetime sentence of singledom.

Feminists have linked the two symbols—woman as sexual object (always perilously close to whore) and woman as mother (hopefully as close to virgin as possible). Neither type is expected to feel or exhibit her own sexual desires. Although "the image of woman is associated with motherhood and fertility," Jessica Benjamin explains, "the mother is not articulated as a sexual subject, one who actively desires something for herself—quite the contrary. The mother is a desexualized figure" (1988, 88). Many students in my introductory class laugh nervously at the very notion that their fathers, or indeed any man, let alone woman, might have once (hopefully not *now*) seen their mothers as sexy. But sexy for women does not mean having sexual desire. As Benjamin continues, "the sexy woman—an image that intimidates women whether or not they strive to conform to it—is sexy, but as object, not as subject. She expresses not so much *her* desire as her pleasure in being desired." Benjamin confirmed through psychoanalytic analysis the discoveries of early second wave feminists that "neither the power of the mother nor that of the sexy woman can . . . be described as sexual subject" (ibid., 89).

Being a sexual subject is part and parcel of being a *subject*—that is, the author of one's own life script, one who directs energy into her own projects and not just into facilitating those of others. In her research with teenagers at a Toronto shopping mall in the 1980s, Elaine Batcher found that "whether it is an individual skill like breakdancing, or a group talent in football or basketball, boys are more likely to be found doing things, and girls found cheering them on" (1987, 154). The groups that Batcher observed "centre around boys who like power and girls who like boys" (ibid., 155). One of Gaskell's teenage male respondents expressed it this way: "there's a difference between raising kids and looking after them. The woman might spend more time with the kids, but the father has the authority" (1988, 161). Psychoanalytic feminism explores the links between sexual desire and desirability and these broader questions of autonomy and dependence. What is the relation between the sexual object and sexual subject? What are the processes through which cultural notions of proper femininity and masculinity are internalized and resisted in the course of psychosexual development?

For Benjamin, the enormous social, cultural, and psychic consequences of relations of domination and subordination between the sexes are rooted in the psychosocial construction of gender polarity: one is *either* masculine *or* feminine. This gender polarity goes far beyond individual expressions of masculinity and femininity because it pervades the structuring of both private and public worlds and their separation from each other. The public world is supposed to be governed by notions of *instrumental rationality*—that is, the emphasis is on the most technically efficient means of reaching goals. Whether in the realm of bureaucracy, public policy, or multinational corporations, the preoccupation with this narrow form of rationality marks the public world as a stereotypical expression of "masculinity."[8] All emotion, love, intimacy, caring, and nurturing are relegated to the private world of family and friendship, where they are marked as the special domain of women. Sociologists Reginald Bibby and Donald Posterski found these gendered differences reflected in their 1992 survey of Canadian teens. Girls placed greater importance on integrity and civility and a higher value on human relationships. *Globe and Mail* columnist Michael Valpy wrote that these findings "limn a society of dominant and subordinate constituencies—with feel-good, physically stronger, bellicose males on top. . . . They suggest that Canadians should think again about all the contemporary rhetoric of gender equality" (1992, 2).[9]

In her research on World War II, Ruth Pierson found that people perceived (appreciatively) that life in the army made men more masculine, but feared that military life threatened women's femininity (1986, 140). Similarly, women who reach beyond the glass ceiling in corporations or government bureaucracies report that they take great care in not presenting themselves as too feminine while at the same time steering clear of any behaviours that might be perceived as masculine. This is not an easy business. These women's clothes must give the message that their wearers should be taken seriously but that they carry no threat to male authority. Women's behaviour must negotiate the thicket between deference and assertiveness. *Globe and Mail* business reporter Kimberly Noble asks: "Ever tried confronting a guy who says something suggestive about your face or your legs or your breasts? The remark will pass unnoticed at a dinner party or in a roomful of people or on the street; if you get angry, however, you can ruin an evening, shock a crowd into embarrassed silence and be labelled as a bitter, aggressive ballbreaker who probably can't get dates" (1991, A18). Rick Salutin, a columnist for the same paper, marvelled

> at the hostility and ridicule [politician Sheila Copps] provokes from other politicians and the media. *Sun* columnist Doug Fisher on "her relentless bloodymindedness"; *Maclean's* Alan Fotheringham on "her rpms turned up too high"; The *Globe's* Jeffrey Simpson saying she's "never seen a microphone into which she could resist shrieking." Why shrieking? Would he use that word about a male MP? Would he even comment on the tendency? What's bugging them? (1993, C1)

It's a double bind: men must be protected from aggressive—strident, bitchy, shrill—women; but deferential women clearly don't merit success.

Decisions in the public world are supposed to be made without considerations of emotion, nurturance, or care. This tendency not only promotes the maintenance of male-only spaces—or, at the very least, male-only behaviours—in the lofty confines of major decision making, but also legitimates creating and sustaining a world that fails to take

account of the needs, desires, and dreams of most people. The consequences for the private world, as feminists have observed, are no less devastating. There, the knowledge that human beings are interdependent is
hidden from view by the relations of domination and subordination
between the sexes. As long as women provide for men without insisting
upon acknowledgment, men can have their cake and eat it: they can have
their needs met without having to acknowledge their dependence on those
who meet them. For their part, girls who grow up without receiving recognition for themselves as people whose own desires and projects matter
may identify with those who assume that they are—and should be—the
centre of their world. Such girls and women consciously or unconsciously
say, "I will strive for personhood by identifying with a man who assumes
that he is a person, and I will seek visibility (to myself) by furthering his
needs and wishes." Such asymmetry in relationships is both product and
cause of relations of domination and subordination.

Listen to conversations about boys, men, and love among girls and
women, and you can detect certain themes. There is often an assumption
that boys and men are unreliable: they pull you into involvements, and
then? Consider David Caravaggio in novelist Michael Ondaatje's *The
English Patient*: "He is a man in middle age who has never become accus-
tomed to families. All his life he has avoided permanent intimacy. Till
this war he has been a better lover than husband. He has been a man who
slips away, in the way lovers leave chaos, the way thieves leave reduced
houses" (1992, 116). Not that Ondaatje's female characters accept men's
behaviour without resistance. The English patient himself asks
Katherine Clifton, his colleague's wife:

> "What do you hate most?"
> "A lie. And you?"
> "Ownership," he says. "When you leave me, forget me."
> Her fist swings towards him and hits hard into the bone just below his
> eye. She dresses and leaves. (ibid, 152)

Shulamith Firestone, writing in 1970, argued that

> The very structure of culture itself is saturated with the gender polar-
> ity. . . . But while the male half is termed all of culture, there is a female
> "emotional" half: They [men] live it on the sly. . . . The question that
> remains for every male is, then, *how do I get someone to love me with-
> out her demanding an equal commitment in return?* (127, 137)

Feminist psychoanalytic approaches provide answers to this question by focusing on the *gendered* nature of psychosexual development and subjectivity. When women are nothing more than the objects of men's desire—that is, they are not recognized as full human beings in their own right—the way is cleared for their invisibility to others in their life, whether husbands, lovers, boyfriends, or children. If mothers are those who do for you, without thanks, acknowledgment, or any claim on reciprocity, if children learn how to be male or female from those who mother them, if boys grow up believing in their own autonomy and that any sign of dependence is a sign of weakness, then men will seek control at all costs because dependency causes such anxiety and threats to their (imagined) autonomy, and therefore their precarious sense of self.

Control may be wrought by means psychological, emotional, and physical. The 1994 Statistics Canada's survey, *Violence Against Women*, reported that "three-in-ten women currently or previously married in Canada have experienced at least one incident of physical or sexual violence at the hands of a marital partner" (Rodgers 1994, 1).[10] Over 20 percent of those abused by a marital partner reported that they were assaulted during pregnancy, and 40 percent of these women stated that the abuse began during their pregnancy (ibid., 12).

Since the early 1970s, with the growing realization of the extent of men's violence towards women, feminists have been in the business of developing explanations for these behaviours. All these explanations deal with power, men's power over women. Sometimes the exercise of this power is taken for granted, as in the phrase "men assault women because they can." This has undoubtedly been so. Men are often stronger; they have held control in households and in every area of society; until recently their behaviour was likely to go unnoticed except by the women subjected to their violence, and it was usually unpunished; male power and violence are represented as heroic and exciting in the media. But to say that men *can* use violence does not explain why so many men *do* use violence or, for that matter, why so many do not and, indeed, may not even be able to imagine themselves doing so. We might want to use an analogy here. All parents are stronger than their children. Many parents do use violence against their children, often or occasionally. But their ability to use violence is not sufficient explanation, for it begs the question, what about all the rest who could but do not?

There has been speculation that violence towards women increases with women's growing assertiveness. From this perspective, the feminist movement has been tagged as contributing to the increase in such violence (Phillips 1995). But, from a feminist psychoanalytic perspective, it is important to understand that the person seeking absolute control cannot bear to acknowledge that the other person is not just an extension of himself. The other person's separateness provides constant reminder of his dependence upon her. He may be the dominant partner, but he needs her, the less powerful, less valued person in the relationship (and in the culture more generally). Dominance is a strategy to avoid acknowledging vulnerability, and violence is one common technique in that never-ending struggle. Never-ending because, since internal vulnerability is the problem, control of the other can never be the solution. When a man murdered thirteen women at the Ecole Polytechnique on 6 December 1989, he then turned the gun on himself, as do many men after killing their partners. Eradicating the other is intricately related to eradicating oneself, whether physically, psychologically, or emotionally.

The evidence from the violence against women survey indicates that women may be at risk both when they resist and when they comply. Assault occurs when women leave partners—although it usually does not begin then (Rodgers 1994, 12)—and when they stay quiet and remain with abusive partners. Twenty-two percent of the respondents had never before told anyone that they had been assaulted—not police, doctor, clergy, friends, or family. Ten percent of these women had at some point feared for their life (ibid., 20). Yet the *Globe and Mail* could still provide space in its feature guest column on 10 November 1995 to air the views of a man who believed that the way to eradicate violence against women was for women to "stage a strategic retreat to the ostensible subservience of times past." David Phillips concluded that "as long as there is a rough parity between the sexes, violence and victimhood will be woman's lot" (A22).

I have been discussing the relations of domination and subordination as if they coincided with the relations between men and women. A good deal of feminist writing, including psychoanalytic writing, proceeds in this way. Language promotes unreflexive use of these categories. Common sense observations seem to support them, as does much research into male and female behaviour. What is important to remember, however, is that *in social terms* human beings become gendered *after* they are born. Not only are the classifications of biological sex "fundamentally social productions" (Findlay 1995, 46), but sociological gender has for a long time been recognized as a postnatal development by anthropologists, historians, and certainly by generations of feminists.

There are two considerations for feminists seeking to explain the development of gendered subjectivity. One explores how human beings become social beings who vie for domination or must tolerate subordination. The second focuses on the ways masculinity and femininity are themselves constructed and represented as discrete categories. The behaviour of women in boardrooms may be similar to the behaviour of men. But it may well be perceived differently because of the (perceived) sex of the biological body who is behaving. Similarly, seeking control in relationships may well be seen as masculine, but this doesn't mean that only (biological) men want to control. Research on relationships between men, and between women, whether of love or friendship, reveals that the power dynamics do not always tend towards reciprocity and symmetry. Some lesbians have written bitterly about their experiences of being turned away from shelters for battered women because their assailants were women (Elliot 1991).[11] We seem stuck with a vocabulary and a discourse that equates masculinity with activity and dominance, and femininity with passivity and subordination.

This is part of the conundrum that feminist poststructuralists have taken on energetically and insightfully. Their challenges to the discussions of sexual objectification, representation, and gender attend to the discourses through which assumptions about masculinity and femininity are created and transformed. Feminists working with poststructuralism and deconstruction have argued that the focus of attention should not be the gendered individual per se, but rather the ways in which specific historical discourses produce gender and gendered representations, both explicitly and implicitly. The reference here is not to a gendered individual, but rather to the ways in which representations of gender are part of a continuing production of language. The concept of *subjectivity* speaks to the ways in which individuals are constituted—in a myriad of continually shifting ways—through discourse. *Gendered subjectivity* refers to the ways in which masculinity and femininity are integral aspects of the production of subjectivity in any discourse.

Such interpretations do not distinguish between subjectivity and representation but rather see them, if you like, as *both* sides of the same coin. Gendered subjectivity is always a representation, never an actual reproduction or reflection. This is because language can never reproduce

an already existing reality, but is always engaged with producing interpretations. Those interpretations then become the object for (poststructural) analysis. Representation once referred mainly to visual
images—what women see reflected back at them in paintings, films, or
advertisements. The concept is now used to refer to visual, literary, doc-
umentary, and oral depictions. In poststructural analysis, the focus is
upon what the viewer or reader makes of those representations. The goal
is no longer to determine what the author or painter or advertising copy
writer intend to say. The focus is rather on the text or image itself and
the interpretations (or readings) of the observer, reader, or person in the
audience.

In poststructural approaches, close attention is paid to the meanings
and hidden meanings in the text or image. Representations produce
meaning only by suppressing other meanings. In her article on the
poetry and fiction of Michael Ondaatje, Lorraine York asks, "Why don't
we have a gender criticism of Ondaatje in the nineties?" (1994, 71). She
hypothesizes that "feminist critics shied away from Ondaatje because
they assumed that there wasn't much to write about" or that they would
end up simply cataloguing various "victim positions" of women that
appear in his work. While she insists that such indictments of male
authors have a place—she approvingly cites Kate Millett's *Sexual Politics*
(1971) for its "energizing, astringent effect on women readers and critics
who . . . [henceforth felt] that they had a right to a dissenting voice"—
York has a different aim. She seeks to reveal that Ondaatje shows increasing awareness of issues of gender, "especially as they relate to ownership:
the poet's ownership of the material, the patriarch's ownership of the
female, and the imperialist's ownership of the colonized" (1994, 75). In
other words, she demonstrates that gender and gender assumptions
infuse Ondaatje's politically complex texts, and not just in those places
where he is speaking specifically about victimized women or the "male
chaotic" (1994, 76).

Feminists using poststructuralism have shown how to read texts—
from foreign policy documents to corporate law to university lectures—
as gendered discourses. The old expression "appearances may be
deceiving" receives new meaning in the hands of poststructuralists. The
previous theoretical positions we have considered present gendered and
sexual identities as relatively fixed realities: fluid up to a point, socially
constructed in time and place, but nonetheless integral to a person's self,

personality, or character. Such theoretical formulations tend to confirm everyday understandings. We assume a correspondence between what we see and hear—that is, how people represent themselves—and who people really are in gendered and sexual terms. The poststructuralist position shifts the focus to the production of gender as a continuing outcome of discourse: hence the special interest in the text.

Critiques of Sexual Objectification

MANY WOMEN HAVE DISPUTED the link that feminists made between women's oppression and their representation as sexual objects for men's desire. Dominant standards of beauty—as represented in criteria for beauty contests, modelling, advertisements, or film—are rigid, with only a small fraction of women eligible. Nor have standards of beauty become more flexible since early feminist protests. Naomi Wolf reports that, in 1970, the average model weighed 8 percent less than the average American woman; twenty years later, she weighed 23 percent less (Wolf 1990, 184). If real women had measurements proportionate to the ubiquitous Barbie Doll—40–18–32—they would not have enough body fat to menstruate regularly. Older women continue to be represented as desexualized. Racialized women point out that they never met the standards of beauty of the dominant culture. Women with disability have raised the only apparently contradictory situation that they are more likely than able-bodied women to be the objects of sexual assault (Rodgers 1994, 6) yet are unlikely to be perceived as meeting the standards for sexual objects. There are many rich, nuanced, and historically and culturally specific analyses of traditional feminist views of sexual objectification, and we will look at some examples that deal with intersections between sexism and racism, able-ism, ageism, and sexual identities and desires.

Anti-racist Critiques

In 1979, Toronto writer Makeda Silvera took part in a protest with other black women against the Miss Black Ontario Pageant (1985, 69). The protest was ridiculed in the black community newspapers and, as she put it, "we were not given space in our newspapers to articulate our position on the issue." Such pageants were a response to the exclusion of black women from existing competitions. The 1960s slogan "black is beautiful" proved a powerful message of resistance to dominant cultural representations in which whiteness was a necessary, though not sufficient, condition of beauty. But in a patriarchal society, the slogan was parlayed into different meanings for men and women. Men would still gaze; women would be the object of the gaze. Adopting white sexist practices such as beauty competitions sidestepped the different ways in which racism shaped the lives of men and women, compounded the oppression of black women, and perpetuated heterosexism.

A black beauty contest did little to interrupt black–white hierarchies that made white women appear more desirable than black women to men generally. It also extended rather than challenged the treatment of black women as sexual objects that was rooted in its most brutal form in the political economy of slavery in North America. Such contests also had a different impact upon black men than upon white men. In the slavery and post-slavery days in the United States, black men were constructed as hypersexualized and were subjected to savage retribution for the mere charge that they had gazed upon a white woman. White men, on the other hand, raped white and, particularly, black women with legal and social impunity. The messages suggested, then, by a black beauty contest for the (gazing) black man appear complex and contradictory. Did such a contest suggest that black men might gaze on black women— but only black women—with impunity? Did the image of the gazing black man resonate with social constructions of hypersexualization, thus leaving white men—with their history of licensed assault—constructed as normally sexed?[12]

Black feminists have pointed out that black women had been portrayed as sexual objects, though not as beautiful sexual objects. At the same time, they were denied the other model of appropriate femininity open to white women, that of the good mother. The good mother was the mother who stayed home with her children, looked after by a good husband and father. Long before most white women sought waged work, black women worked, mainly as domestics in the homes of others, to support their families.[13] With black men in Canada generally relegated to jobs as porters and janitors (with a few in the entertainment industry), the family wage never reflected either reality or ideal for most black families (Brand 1984; 1991; Sadlier 1994). The experiences of black women—raising and supporting families, active in their communities, and struggling against discrimination—not only remained outside dominant representations, but also were not captured by feminist analysis. At the same time, writing by black women was rejected by white publishers (including feminist publishers) who were unable "to comprehend how the work resonates or illuminates the condition of women of colour" (Silvera 1985, 71).

Aboriginal women have a different critique of the feminist equation of women as sexual object with women's oppression. Beth Brant, an Indian lesbian writer, wants to dispel the prevailing idea "that Indian women are not sexual. . . . It really is a stereotype that we are not, that we just give birth to kids without a process, or that we're only interested in planting corn or something. This really angers me and I think that Indian lesbians are the ones who are going to be talking about sex" (1985, 59). Brant seeks to distinguish the stereotypes of the Indian woman "and all these things that we have been called as squaw" from "a truth that we are poor, that we often have to exist in substandard ways." The writings of Aboriginal women not only challenge dominant representations but also present a range of experiences, images, dreams, and desires that confirm the dilemmas inherent in any attempts to represent woman or Indian woman or Indian lesbian, as though one image would do for all who might be so categorized.

Beth Brant expresses the constraints and possibilities not only of images, but of the language in which she writes. The "language of our enemy," a language with

> new words that do not exist in our own language.
> RAPE, MURDER, TORTURE, SPEECHLESSNESS, INCEST.
> POVERTY, ADDICTION.
> These obscene words that do not appear in our language.

She asks, "If love could be made visible, would it be in the enemy's language?" And answers:

> It is the only weapon I hold: this pen, this tool, this knife, this language.
> The writer has to know how to tell. It is the weapon I know how to use.
> (1991, 16–17)

Dis/ability and Objectification

When I turn to look at the writing of "women with disability," I am struck by the impossibility, the distortion, even the deception involved in any attempt to represent them as though one image would do for all who might be so categorized. Not long ago, while facilitating a panel on women and diversity, I asked a panelist if she had seen a particular television program. "It's been a long time since I've seen any television program," she retorted sharply but with humour in her voice. Kristin is blind; for some public purposes, she calls herself a lesbian with a disability. She tires of raising the question of accessibility at all gatherings, feminist and otherwise, but feels compelled to do so when no one else does. As a result, she represents herself often, and may be perceived, as a "one-issue candidate." In any case, other people will categorize her as "woman with disability," along with women who—for reasons ranging from conditions attendant at birth through impairment suffered in accidents or from abuse to effects of chronic and progressive illnesses—may not be able to walk, talk, or read. If anything unites all these women, it is not their disabilities as such but rather both their treatment by a society that disadvantages them and their collective resistance to that treatment (Russell 1989).

Kristin's sharp retort to me, following my casual assumption about seeing, breaks with dominant representations of women with disability as "victim," as "needy," as "grateful," or even as "quiet and nice." My reaction—of embarrassment, some enjoyment that others were laughing at my expense, and admiration—resembled the "click" made famous in early issues of *Ms.* magazine to describe any moment when the penny dropped, when one had a consciousness-raising moment related to one's treatment as a woman. This time I was the one who had the click, certainly, and it resulted from this very public transformation in my perspective. My language had betrayed my assumption about what was natural and shared, and this assumption was shattered by Kristin's response.

Francine Odette has critiqued the feminist assumption that "identifies women's alienation from themselves and their bodies" with "the objectification of the female body" (1992, 42). Growing up with a physical disability may take one out of the running altogether as someone who elicits attention as an attractive person. The problem is not sexual objectification but exclusion from the possibility of the appreciative gaze. Recently, I saw a young woman with long blond hair who was modelling a sweater in an advertising brochure. She was sitting in a wheelchair. The presence of this image clearly resulted from the pressure for inclusion of those with disabilities in the range of images presented by TV programming, advertising, school textbooks, everywhere. This is surely a victory. In this culture, most girls spend considerable time on their appearance: they care about how they are perceived, whether they fit in, whether they look cool. As Odette notes, "for young girls with disabilities, the invisibility of our lives becomes reinforced by the fact that popular advertising suggests the 'normal' body is that which is desirable"(ibid., 42).

Feminists with disabilities critique the socially constructed notions not only of "the body beautiful" but also, in Odette's words "the notion of the 'body perfect'" (ibid., 42–43). Such challenges reveal the ways in which the lives, experiences, and fears of women with disabilities are similar to the lives of all women[14] and also how an attention to "differentness" extends the previous feminist cultural critiques. For example, although Odette raises an issue from the particular perspective of women with disabilities, the issue bears on the lives of all those who require medical consultations. While "the way in which women's bodies are portrayed as commodities in the media may not be a reality for many women labelled 'disabled,'... our bodies become objectified for the purposes of domination ... as part of the medical process" (ibid., 42). In hospitals, people's bodies are often used as a teaching tool as though they were detached from the thinking, feeling, meaning-creating human beings seeking control over what happens to them.

Age and Sexual Objectification

Second wave feminists who launched the critiques of sexual objectification and the unreachable standards that represented female beauty and sexiness were mostly in their twenties and thirties. They tended to share the presumptions of their peers expressed in the 1960s slogan "You can't trust anyone over thirty." Only members of a society seriously denying the process of aging could develop a slogan that propelled one into the arena of the bad guys for no better reason than the onset of one's thirty-first year on earth. But as second wave feminists inevitably crossed the line into their thirties, they began critiquing the partiality of their earlier formulations. In this process, growing old(er) was not only reclaimed as a universal human process, but the gendered consequences of aging became an important focus for feminist analysis and activism (Carpenter 1996).

In this process, one of the great taken-for-granted assumptions of cultural life was subjected to scrutiny and was rejected: namely, that women could be beautiful and sexy only when young, while men could gain in sexual power and attractiveness their whole life through. Canadians had a very public example of this truism: in 1971 Prime Minister Pierre Trudeau, aged fifty-one, married Margaret Sinclair, a woman twenty-nine years his junior. Everyone—including Sinclair's father, a one-time cabinet minister in Lester Pearson's government—expressed great pleasure upon this occasion. But what if a woman in public life—or any woman, for that matter—had married a man almost young enough to be her grandson? Such an act would evoke more than social ridicule; it would be almost against nature: a man marrying a woman *old enough to be his mother*? Indeed, as Judy LaMarsh reported in her autobiography, just travelling with a younger man on cabinet business, "although I was always careful never to travel with just one young man," became the subject of media scrutiny and was reflected in articles teeming with rumour and innuendo (1968, 304). That she was targetted for travelling with younger men during the same decade in which Trudeau contracted his marriage illustrates the gendered story of love, sex, and age in the 1960s and beyond. Why did the eye rolling and tongue clicking only happen when women were associated with men younger than themselves?

Feminists point to two related explanations. First, the mere suggestion of sexual encounters between older women and younger men may create a generalized anxiety because such relationships threaten the sexual hierarchy. The advantages of age may confound the advantages of sex. In relationships men were supposed to take the initiative, make the important decisions, certainly be the more experienced sexual partner. But when the woman was older, wouldn't *she* know more? Have more experience? Perhaps be less willing to be the subordinate partner? When a man is widowed or divorced, he has traditionally not only been free to remarry, but free to choose from among women who are younger, including the young and never married. But women, enjoined to marry only men older than themselves, have had fewer choices. No longer sexual objects, they are not acceptable as sexual subjects either. Wouldn't she dominate her partner? Would this not be against the laws of god and nature? The perspectives of older women reveal the dense nature of patriarchal relations, practices, and attitudes in all arenas of social life.

Second, women are positioned as sexual objects not sexual subjects, and then only when they are young and beautiful. Older women may be portrayed, but only as mothers, harridans, or caregivers. Relationships between older women and younger men raise the question: Can she be old(er) and sexy? Certainly the representations in popular culture provide one answer: a resounding no! The stereotypical explanation held that a younger man interested in an older woman was only after her money.

That older lesbian couples, in particular, escaped public scrutiny in so many communities in the days prior to women's liberation and beyond may be attributed in part to the assumptions discussed above. First, if women were sexual objects (for men's desire), not sexual subjects, then the question of sexuality remained publicly invisible when there was no man present. When Judy LaMarsh travelled with younger women, this was not news. Second, as women aged, any suggestion that they were sexual beings faded commensurately. Recently I asked my mother about Celine and Edith, friends she had in the 1950s:

> "What was the nature of their relationship?" I asked.
> "Well, they were friends."
> "Just friends?"
> "Yes."
> "Did they live together?"
> "Yes, for years and years."
> "How many bedrooms did they have?"
> "One."
> "How many beds?"
> "One."

My point here is not to draw conclusions from my number-of-beds-in-the-house research! There is much evidence that many married couples, for example, sleep in one bed without sharing an explicitly sexual life. But if my mother had known a man and a woman living in a similar arrangement, she might well have assumed that they were more than friends.[15]

Heterosexism and Sexual Objectification

The story of Celine and Edith draws our attention to one of the central critiques offered by lesbian activists and scholars to feminist analysis of the sexual objectification of women by men. Put simply, the dominant cultural stereotypes—however pervasive—that only young women are beautiful, that women are only sexual objects not sexual subjects, or that women care whether they attract male attention have served to hide more than they reveal. What they hid was the risky, often dangerous lives of women who loved women, of women who dressed to attract women, of women who—not to put too fine a point on it—couldn't have cared less if they attracted male attention except insofar as men might have been decoys for their interest in women. The National Film Board's *Forbidden Love* (Weissman and Fernie 1993) weaves together interviews with lesbians talking about their strategies for living and loving in the decades after World War II with a dramatization of a typical lesbian pulp novel of the period. One woman explained, with evident satisfaction, how dating gay men provided a front, diverting the attention of family and friends from her intimate life. Such creative acts of subterfuge reveal some of the limitations of reading the history of contemporary culture in terms of the sexual objectification of women by men.

Cultural stereotypes are steeped in heterosexist assumptions and, since the dawn of feminism's second wave, lesbians openly challenged much feminist writing for buying into those assumptions even as they aimed to transform them. The cultural stereotypes say little about who appears beautiful, desirable, or sexy to whom or why. Long-time peace activist Kay Macpherson revealed in her autobiography that "for a long time I clung to the conviction that a married woman who had a relationship with another woman wasn't really being 'unfaithful' to her husband" (1994, 148). The culture's heterosexism filtered out any understanding of sex and love that did not fit the preconceived categories. Women and men, lesbian, bisexual, and heterosexual, live lives that confound and oppose the stereotypes, and only by understanding this can we understand the origins of the social movements for sexual liberation of the last decades. These social movements not only provide locations from which to wage the right to live and love publicly, but they also occasion a profound questioning of the past. That human beings historically and cross-culturally engaged in a range of sexual practices, heterosexual and homosexual, is not at issue. But when and how do women and men forge identities, create communities, carve out space within hostile environments to find, attract, and live with those of their own sex?

Researchers have used such questions to reread the historical record: diaries, letters between friends, newspaper articles, advertisements, court records, and novels from the classics to pulp fiction. They conducted many interviews, and women have told their own stories (Chenier 1995; Ross 1995; Weissman and Fernie 1993) In this process, many divergent and overlapping paths for exploring "forbidden love," bestowing affection, creating space, and sharing time, households, and beds with other women have been made visible. A rich history of intimate female friendships and long-term coupling challenges conventional history. Lesbians carved out urban spaces such as bars and clubs where liaisons with those similarly minded could be wrought in comparative safety, and they developed a range of signs for ascertaining who might be interested in one's interest in them. All these practices challenged, whether openly or secretly, the dominant order.

Reinterpretations of lesbian histories, identities, and practices have not, of course, rendered irrelevant the cultural stereotypes that girls are judged not by their desire but by their desirability and that girls are interested in boys not girls. Coming-out stories are richly diverse and often funny, at least in retrospect. One woman writes about arriving at the Alberta farm of her Roman Catholic parents and making this announcement at the dinner table: "I've changed my name to Gillean Chase, the name I'll use when I'm published. I've converted to Judaism and I'm a lesbian" (Chase 1996, 62). Often there is relief, as with Joy McBride:

> Before my sister came out to me, I had never met anyone who was out. This isn't surprising, considering how hard I had worked to isolate myself socially. I had grown up with the theory that I was unlovable, and this stuck with me as an adult so strongly that it never occurred to me to think that I might instead be a lesbian—one who had been brought up in a world that hadn't taught me how to recognize or cherish myself. (1996, 183)

Surely no one, at least in contemporary culture, navigates the route from childhood through adolescence to adulthood without experiencing unrequited love; but those who have lived unremittingly as heterosexuals might stop to think how much more complicated this is when there are few, if any, ways of telling whether the object of your affections—or anyone else—even shares your desire for other women, let alone an interest in you. Some things have changed. In the 1950s, girls didn't dance with each other at school dances: we awaited invitations from boys and, when they weren't forthcoming, we remained "wallflowers," a status that brought neither prestige nor fun.

But young people growing up report that high school culture continues to normalize expressions of heterosexual affection, discussion, and ritual, while ostracizing and policing the same activities when performed by lesbians and gays. Indeed, activities like school dances, which were once the prerogative of high school students, are now normal events in primary school. Explicit and public priming for a heterosexual adulthood appears to start earlier and earlier. Becki Ross estimates that "nine-tenths of the 'lesbian population' continue to live in fear of disclosure and the attendant loss of family, friends, jobs and the custody of children" (1995, 9). Of course, it is not just children who come out to their parents. Parents also come out to their children, and sometimes they come out with each other:

> Sharing one's sexual identity with one's mother and sister is the norm if one is heterosexual. This is not the case if one is lesbian and living in St John's Newfoundland. As far as I know, we are truly unique. We [the writer, her mother, and sister] thus tend to be fairly conspicuous, as the three of us, with or without our respective lovers, enter the gay bar or the bimonthly women's dance. I have heard various kinds of comments, ranging from "Here comes the cute family" to "Do I have to get your mother's permission to dance with you?" (Yetman and Yetman 1996, 214)

Male/Female; Masculinity/Femininity

DISCUSSIONS IN THIS CHAPTER on representation of women and femininity presuppose, of course, a discourse on men and masculinity, and I want to deal with this more directly now. The assumption in early second wave feminism was that the problem of women's subordination was femininity (its attributes, dress, characteristics), restricted roles, and sexual objectification by men. The corollary was that women should give up feminine trappings—high-heeled shoes, make-up, skirts and dresses—for more sensible attire; they should abandon nurturing for self-actualization; they should train themselves for male-dominated professions and jobs; and they should refuse sexual objectification in favour of asserting their own sexual needs and desires. Although the explicit goal was not so much to become like men, but rather that women should share power and resources equally with men, there was a subtext that suggested that women, not men, had to change. But masculinity—its characteristics, attributes, aims, and hubris—was on the threshold of scrutiny from many quarters.

Radical and cultural feminists began to insist that the problem was not women's activities and characteristics but men's behaviour and psychology. Women should not strive to share the power that men wielded; rather, that power should be dismantled at the psychic and social level. Men have waged war; women have made peace. Men have been systematically violent; women and children have been their victims. Men are sexual predators; women are nurturing and affectionate. In short, women aren't the problem; men are. At a descriptive level, at the level of accumulated evidence, it's a hard case to refute. But satisfactory explanations for these gendered differences in power, behaviour, and experience are harder to come by, and not only because the generalizations can be shown not to apply to all men or all women.

The most obvious explanation—that the problem must be laid at the doorstep of biology—is rejected by almost all feminists and feminisms. Notice this response in the *New York Times Book Review* from radical feminists Catharine MacKinnon and Andrea Dworkin to the charge that they blame biology: "Biological determinism is the complete antithesis of everything either one of us has written and done for the last quarter-century. We have each explicitly and repeatedly denounced systems of inferiority and superiority based on biology" (1995, 47). If it's not biology, most feminists reason, it must be social. Something has to happen after birth to explain gender differences, to explain how ideas of masculinity and femininity appear most of the time as givens of social life. This understanding is captured in theories that explicate, in a variety of ways, two interrelated concepts—power and social construction. Relations of power inform, indeed saturate, the social relations between the sexes, socialization practices, and especially how such practices are received and internalized as children grow up.

Socialist feminists, especially those engaging with psychoanalytic formulations, launched a critique of the construction of masculinity, arguing that "normal" masculinity was constituted by denial of emotion and by subsequent aggression and violence, underpinned by deep psychic anxiety, self-hatred, and insecurity. In *Beyond Patriarchy*, Michael Kaufman (1987) discusses the masculine trilogy of violence against self, against other men, and against women. Boys growing up in this society must dis-identify with their mothers, their less powerful parent, in favour of identification with their fathers. The consequences are deep-seated, long-lasting, and extensive. Given that women are the only legitimate repository for nurturing, care, emotion, and attention to relationships, boys must repress their emotions, their love, and their feelings of dependence upon others in order not to be like their mothers. The vulnerability boys feel as small and dependent people goes underground; bravado and bullying take its place. But that vulnerability returns to be projected onto those perceived as vulnerable—girls and women. Hence the scorn, the repudiation, what psychoanalyst Ruth Brunswick called "the normal male contempt for women" (1948). The result, according to feminists, is not a good recipe for living in a social world, and it's certainly not been good news for women and children. The boy in the schoolyard who does not demonstrate success in this endeavour is called a sissy. A sissy is a boy who acts like a girl. Here we see early training for misogyny. If boys who act like girls are contemptible, what does this say about girls, the model for this contempt?

Many feminists challenge the view that masculinity is constituted through a set of social and linguistic practices that repeats and consolidates an apparently uncontested division between the sexes. They suggest that we could have a masculinity that was clearly linked with male bodies but did not share in this repudiation of femininity. This would amount to an analytical and objective distinction between sex and gender. Could such a distinction be sustained? Lately, some poststructuralists who have coined the term *queer theory* have been questioning the assumption that male and female bodies are givens, waiting to be filled, as it were, with socially constructed gendered and sexual identities. As Kathleen Pirrie Adams explains:

> By arguing that all gender identity involves the impersonation of an
> abstract (gender) ideal, and, by continually remarking on the artificial-

ity of the gender norms that organize and regulate sexuality, queer theory has shifted attention away from questions of who is (really) homosexual to questions about how homosexuality is realized and made visible socially, as well as how it runs throughout the culture as a whole—invisibly, inarticulately. (1993, 31)

For queer theorists, pride of analytic place shifts from the text to "notions such as performative identity, gender activism and gender performance" (ibid., 31). Performance draws attention to how we *do* gender as ongoing bodily and linguistic presentation. The concept of performance permits a convergence of the poststructuralist emphasis on discourse with a theorization of the body and therefore of sex and gender. From this perspective, sex and gender are understood as intertwined processes, produced as acts—"on site," as it were, through and with our bodies—and reiterated endlessly. The very reiteration of these acts—these *norms*, in sociological terms—masks their boundary-creating character. They appear with no history, no rationale; they are "what is." But we are the agents of these reiterations, and by these acts we participate in sustaining and shifting that which the culture permits and forbids.

Queer theory draws attention to these reiterations of gender and sexuality—to the social visibility of sexual differences—but sees them as an ongoing happening, always with the possibility of disruption. The disruptions may be more dramatic in some locations than others. Consider Adams' comments on the lesbian bar scene in Toronto:

> Who hasn't seen or been this: girl who arrives, returning weekly with a new sign (cropped, dread-locked, shaved or dyed hair, new boots, cut-offs, pierces, tattoo), leaving weekly with a new inspiration, a new friend, more certainty and more confusion. The bar is an arena of possibility, a public space in which sexual identity is sought and discarded, and so if we describe it simply in terms of what we do there—dance, talk, drink, have sex—we can lose sight of some aspects of what we are doing there. (1993, 30)

Judith Butler has been in the forefront in developing queer theory's reassessment of sexual and gendered identities. She questions what has usually been assumed in other theoretical (including scientific) perspectives, asking exactly what about the body and sex is given, already there?

She is not disputing that we have bodies, but rather she asks, just what can we say about those bodies that falls into the "already there" category? She argues that anything we might say about those bodies has already been taken up by socially constituted discourses on gender, sexuality, race, age, and so on. There is no pure discourse through which we can speak about the already given body.

Furthermore, our own sense of who we are—in psychoanalytic terms, our *ego*—is constituted (in part) through our projections of our bodies. But those projections are thoroughly informed by our participation in cultural (including linguistic) practices. The sense, therefore, that we have of being male or being female cannot be partitioned into biological and social compartments. It's not so much that the social infuses the biological, but that the biological can only be thought of and named through the social, namely through discourses, among others, on gender, race, sexuality, health and illness, religion and ethics, and physiology. These discourses, of course, infuse each other: only for the purposes of a list are they separable.

In Freudian discourse, for example, the significance attached to the presence or absence of a penis mobilizes a huge literature on gender, sex, relationships, neuroses, and psychoses. While some feminist appropriators of psychoanalysis have shifted the importance from the penis to the symbol of the penis—the phallus—there remains the connection between male bodies and power (either because of the presence of the penis or the connection between penis and phallus). But what sustains this connection? Butler argues that it is sustained through reiteration of linguistic practices, practices that, because of the reiteration, become *sedimented*, or materialized. But the sedimentation is an illusion to the extent that what sustains it is in fact the reiterations. The reiteration depends on people engaging in repetitious acts; however, the repetitions are never simply repetitions. Everything that has *not* been acknowledged in previous repetitions can always make an appearance in the next; that which is desired but unacknowledged always remains, in whatever partial or distorted sense, as possibility. In this sense, then, the connection between penis and phallus is not signed, sealed, and delivered for eternity, but neither will the connection be severed all at once.

Judith Butler seeks to destabilize the connection. For, as long as the connection between penis and phallus is not questioned, all the questions about power and gendered identities will take their cue from the *assumed* differences between men and women. This is Butler's critique of psychoanalysis in both its Freudian and Lacanian versions. Both versions assume that entry into the symbolic order—the social world—is predicated upon already existing, biological, prediscursive differences between the sexes. These theories organize the prediscursive differences hierarchically, with masculine principles constructed as the entry point into the symbolic order. Butler asks why acceptance into this world of meanings should be contingent upon collusion with masculine principles and a dichotomy between masculine and feminine. After all, this hierarchical dichotomy is simply the ongoing product of endless reiterations, including those produced by psychoanalytic theory. Why should the phallus (power) and the penis be assumed to be prediscursively connected and therefore left unquestioned? To put it another way: castration anxiety (the prototypical male problem) and penis envy (the defining characteristic of femininity) would lose their privileged status in psychic and social terms once the connection between power and penis became just one of many (optional) possibilities.

If this sounds unbearably abstract, think for a moment about the underlying messages behind the following oft-heard statements: "All she needs is a man"; "All she needs is a good fuck" (with the implication that only a person with a penis could provide this); "She's a lesbian because she had a bad experience with a man"; "He's gay because he had a suffocating mother"; "Lesbians/feminists hate men"; "He's a wimp, he must be gay"; or "Bisexuals can't commit." One of my (male) students told the following joke: "Why do so many men give their penis a name? Because they don't like to take orders from a stranger." Many feminists have used the word *phallocentric* to describe society or even civilization itself. The connection is to men via the assumed link between power and penis. Butler questions this connection theoretically and socially. In so doing, it becomes increasingly difficult to take the differences between male and female bodies as given. Accounting for, and deposing, male power becomes implicated with challenges to the privileged status accorded to sex/gender differences.

Feminists have been aware of this for a long time. In offering critiques to the first words said upon the arrival of a newborn—"It's a boy!" or "It's a girl!" rather than "It's healthy!" or "It's small!"—feminists have suggested that there was something problematic about the intense interest in this one aspect of the child. Moreover, it has recently become clear that when babies are born with genitalia that are not categorizable by appearance, the doctors *decide* whether the baby is boy or girl. It seems that a precondition for entrance into a human community is having a body that may be deemed male or female, even though some bodies don't present themselves that way (Findlay 1995).

What is so important about insisting upon this distinction between male and female? In social terms, what is riding on it? Butler argues that this distinction makes possible the discourse and practices that privilege heterosexuality. The founding principle for heterosexuality is the distinction between male and female. But what if the founding principle depends upon reiteration? What if the reiteration brings the founding principle into play—and keeps it in play—rather than the reverse? The enormous range of practices that sustains heterosexuality as normal, preferred, and unremarkable requires and mobilizes another set of practices that are banished, punished, and in other ways declared "outside." The "outside" is, of course, also "inside." What we repress remains; therefore reiterating our desires is never simple reiteration. Indeed, vehement reiteration of desire may indicate the instability of those desires. The old expression "The lady doth protest too much" captures the insight that statements, including statements of desire and aversion, cannot be taken at face value. Consider, for example, the following common statements: "I could *never* love a woman"; "I can't *imagine* being gay"; "I feel sick if a man approaches me in a bar." Virulent expressions of homophobia can be understood as anxiety-creating desires that are articulated as revulsion and projected onto others. Such statements provide evidence that we need to question "both gender binarism and the inside-outside logic that makes homosexual identity seem like heterosexuality's opposite" (Adams 1993, 31).

Homophobic assumptions—that gay men are effeminate and lesbians are mannish, for example—reify both masculinity and femininity as well as the categories straight and homosexual. At the experiential level, it is easy enough to counter such generalizations. But often these generalizations are refuted in ways that redraw the boundaries between acceptable and not acceptable. Consider the (defensive) remark "Of course gays don't 'have to be' wimps" (read they could be as macho as any (straight) man). Or "many lesbians are feminine and even wear make-up and high-heeled shoes" (just like straight women). In these cases, the proof of the normality of (some) gays and lesbians is seen to reside in their conformity to the very gendered roles that are elsewhere undergoing critique.

In such ordinary statements, we see how the categories male–female, masculine–feminine, gay–straight are all used to sustain each other, thereby constantly constraining, modifying, and confirming the sense of the possible and the impossible. From this perspective, conventional masculinity is produced through constant reiteration, and those reiterations aim to approximate some masculine ideal that does not exist prior to the reiterating process. But this ongoing attempt to approximate that ideal represents and produces psychic anxiety and social, political, and economic consequences. How can someone ever know if he is "being man enough?" Man enough for what, we want to ask? If we substitute woman for man in this phrase, we may be trying to demonstrate that woman can never measure up, or we may be parodying the original phrase to display its meaning and its vacuity. The phrase "being man enough" appears both full of meaning and empty at the same time.

Perhaps this is a useful way to apprehend the concepts of masculinity and femininity. There seems little question that they are charged with meaning, used and reused in multiple ways to reward and punish, exclude and include, valorize and undermine. But when we examine them closely, they seem to disappear before our eyes. Women speak of having to become like men to succeed in the corporation. For example, they may dress like men, suited up, briefcase in hand. But few of us think that masculinity actually resides in the clothes. Or do we? Consider the enormous interest, humour, and revulsion generated by those who most obviously flout convention—a man dressed as a woman and displaying feminine mannerisms, perhaps. A man cannot simply get up in the morning and decide to wear a skirt: immediately he is labelled a cross-dresser, with all that term entails. And his mannerisms: Why are such mannerisms seen as feminine, now that they are displayed by a male? But wait, is he a man? Or is he a woman dressed as a man? Is he a woman dressed as a man displaying feminine mannerisms? Is he a woman dressed as a man gazing at a woman dressed as a man who is "acting like" a woman?

At this point, you will probably have thrown up your hands. But consider this poem, written by Mikaela Hughes, when she was six or seven. Her best friend had just moved to Australia, and her cat had just died. At the same time, she had realized that her classmates had assumed that she was a boy.

> I seem to be a boy
> But really I'm a girl.
> I seem to be happy
> But really I am sad.
> I seem to not have a cat
> But really I have a cat that is dead. (1996, 146)

Why, then, all this categorization? What on earth does it mean in the end to ask, What is s/he "really?" *Exactly*, say the queer theorists. If you look only at the performance, the categories of sex and gender appear more as a chest of halloween clothes and props, a cultural resource for the mis/use of all. But Judith Butler is careful to point out that sex and gender are not garments to be put on in the morning; in the reiteration of acts, the specific materiality of the body is produced. We may feel ourselves to be male, female, masculine, feminine, gay, straight in the depths of our being. In her words, the "activity of this gendering cannot, strictly speaking, be a human act or expression, a willful appropriation, and it is certainly not a question of taking on a mask; it is the matrix through which all willing first becomes possible, its enabling cultural condition" (1993, 7).

Let us return to women who may try to appear like men in their bid to climb the corporate ladder. Dressing the part may be accompanied by attempts to appear unemotional at work. But does that mean that masculinity is coincident with failure to display emotion? These days, at least, there is a lot of attention paid to the idea that men can feel too. The "sensitive new-age guy" may not be a passing phenomenon. Or women may behave like men by taking on the corporate goals and culture. But does masculinity reside in the pursuit of profits and the instrumental use of others? Or women may sleep with women, like men (or at least like those men who sleep with women). But the limits for women's being like men seem to have been crossed in this last example. Indeed, women report that they often risk their jobs if they are known to share their intimate lives with women. Gay men in the corporation may well stay closeted. Loving other men—regardless of their other behaviours—may put them across the line of acceptance, promotion, or employment. Is this because they are, in this respect, like women—that is, like the women who love men, not like the women who love women as men (are supposed to) do? Here we see that, just as sexual boundary making draws upon and uses gender markers, so are the boundaries of masculinity and femininity maintained, in part, through sexual boundary making (Ingraham 1994).

Butler goes further in her theorizing, arguing that just as discourses on masculinity and femininity and discourses on sexuality enable each other in the ways we have seen, so too do they both depend upon and enable the continuous reiteration of other social inclusions and exclusions. In particular she points to the ways in which dominant ideas of normative masculinity incorporate and depend upon images of nonracialized men—that is, white men. In fact, we might ask, do we even have a discourse on masculinity (however full and empty we deem the category to be), or do we have discourses on masculinity intricately bound up with whiteness and racialization? If the latter, this would mean that reiterating one's identity as male depends not just upon the identity female but also upon the identities—the excluded identities—of colour, blackness, brownness, and all that those identities, in turn, are taken to mean.

Consider how often media accounts of the activities of the subgroup in the population identified as youth not only include the (assumed) sex of participants but also, their race—when they are not white. *White* usually requires no mention because it is seen to be normative, while "young" "black" "men" are presented as having an identity that distinguishes them from young white men, or old white men, or young black women. Much of their media image partakes of many aspects of normative masculinity: toughness, instrumentality, aggressiveness, refusing to take direction from others (known in other circles as "being one's own boss"). But somehow, in the process of being racialized, such characteristics take on menacing tones. "Boys will be boys," but these boys are threatening and are excluded from the more benign rendition of that cliché. Given all the data on date rape, wife battery, and child abuse, this can't be because there are no "white" "male" "youth" who are menacing anyone. On the contrary, Statistics Canada's 1994 survey found that "the highest rates of wife assault are among young men 18 to 24 years of age" (Rodgers 1994, 46). How is it that masculinity remains, at least in nonfeminist discourse, apparently untainted by such findings?

In a study of recent Canadian trial judgments, the researchers found some clues in the language of the judges (Coates, Bavelas, and Gibson 1994). They found that there is no consensus about the appropriate courtroom language to describe sexual assault in cases where the assailant is not a stranger to the victim. As a result, judges vacillate between using the language of "stranger" rape and the language of consensual sex. A man who entered a woman's bedroom while she was asleep and inserted his penis into her mouth was described in the trial judgment as having "offered" his penis (ibid., 189). Words that are common in discussing love making, like fondle, touch, and intercourse, were regularly used instead of the term sexual assault, the legal words for unwanted encounters. A man found guilty of sexual assault was described as having an "impeccable character" (ibid., 196), leading one to wonder just what he would have had to do to rule himself out of this category. Despite evidence such as this, an editorial in the *Globe and Mail* took the Canadian Panel on Violence Against Women to task for "an avalanche of recommendations, some vague, some silly, some worthy." In particular, the editors urged, "mandatory gender-sensitivity training for judges should be quickly rejected" (1993, D6).

Poststructuralism's focus on the text and queer theory's focus on performance permit an analysis of gendered subjectivity in all areas of human literary and artistic production from scientific documents through legislation to comic strips and television programs. The word games that maintain the boundaries between male and female, masculinity and femininity, need constant reinvention, but their reinvention relies on the fixed idea that men and women are different in ways that are known. But there is a trick here, to return to Judith Butler. The trick is that it is these reinventions (reiterations) that maintain the boundaries by presenting themselves as simple reflections of an underlying reality. For example, observers noted that Kim Campbell would "have to be aggressive to fight Liberal Leader Jean Chrétien, but when women become aggressive they are often labelled hysterical" (Smith 1993, A4). In an article arguing that "sharing the housework isn't a political gesture, it just makes sense," Ken Mark wrote that he recalled "Peter Gzowski's chat with a naval non-commissioned officer on the proper way to iron a shirt. These men are not wimps or sissies just because they know what is the business end of an iron" (1994, A24). Note how the category wimp and sissy is left untouched, presumably to be filled with some behaviour that *will* bring such opprobrium upon some men's heads. In another story entitled "Handywoman: Powerful new role model is plugged in," the reader is introduced to "icons of a new brand of feminism in the nineties—the handy yet feminine woman" (Williams 1994, A24). These reiterations create the exclusions and the inclusions, the hierarchical arrangements that feminists have variously called patriarchal relations, the sex/gender system, or the racialized sex-gendered system.

Poststructuralism's Feminist Critics

THE EMPHASIS IN THIS CHAPTER on psychoanalytic and poststructural-ist perspectives reflects my view that together they provide new and illu-minating insights for understanding subjectivity and representation. In our society, gender makes itself felt early and deeply in all human beings, and gendered understandings inform virtually every aspect of the social world in complex and interrelated ways. Psychoanalytic and poststruc-turalist perspectives have been the most attentive to this depth and per-vasiveness, but they need each other to provide satisfactory accounts of how gender is psychically lodged and linguistically sustained and resisted.

It is not the case, however, that they replace other feminist perspec-tives in providing explanations for gendered hierarchies. Their utility depends upon the kinds of questions one is seeking to answer. Psychoanalytic theories have not yet been developed in ways that explain how gender interacts with other social hierarchies—those of class, race, age, and so on—in the process of psychosexual maturation.[16] Moreover, as most proponents of the theories would concede, these approaches gen-erally make no sustained contribution towards understanding the gen-dered relations of political economy, including capitalism, imperialism, or racism, or towards strategies for the dismantling of these exploitative systems.[17] Strategies for social change at every level, however, need to include the insights of psychoanalysis, namely, that we are constituted as gendered human beings—as an aspect of deep psychosexual develop-ment—in the earliest days of infancy and childhood. To undo the equa-tion of masculinity with domination and femininity with subordination, therefore, not only requires more than one generation, but the willingness of adult men and women to revisit their own past with the hope of unlearning and changing basic patterns of self-perception and desire.

Poststructural approaches have also been challenged by many feminists, generally on two interrelated grounds. By focusing upon reading the texts or observing the performance, poststructuralism fails to distinguish between subjectivity as the constitution of a self (who we are), representations of that self (how we are portrayed), and activity (what we do). What this means, as some critics have argued, is that there isn't theoretical space for asking questions about *causal* relationships between gendered behaviours and attitudes, the depictions of men and women, and what men and women do. The absence of a causal analysis appears to leave feminists without strategic analyses for transforming oppressive and exploitative relationships. This political concern is related to a second problem that many feminists have with poststructuralism: that an understanding of subjectivity as an outcome of discourse—rather than as a site for the constitution of a *self*—fails to provide a full account of human agency and the potential of people to act individually or collectively to change the social world.

Neither explanation nor strategic thinking is the strong suit of poststructuralism, and most feminists show little interest in abandoning either. A poststructural approach continues to coexist, then—and I think necessarily—with older approaches and controversies about the interconnections between gendered subjects, gendered representation, and gendered activity.

Conclusion

AS WE DISCUSSED IN CHAPTER 1, different feminist perspectives provide different understandings of what is most important to changing patriarchal society. Let us take an example. A magazine editor accepts advertisements illustrating women who have dieted to produce the "perfect" body. A young girl reads the magazine and starves herself while another looks for alternative images of robust and cheerful women. How are the different responses to be explained? By the ads, by the presence or absence of alternative images, by variations in early childhood development, by what the reader sees women and men doing in her daily life?

Why do popular magazines routinely run such images? Because those who produce them share the dominant valuation in the culture? Because they help sell magazines? Because the advertisers realize profit from all the products designed to produce the body beautiful?

Such questions look for causal explanations. Liberal feminists have engaged in many, often successful, campaigns to pressure the popular media into providing alternative images of women and girls (Macpherson 1994, 149). Their belief in the saliency of education for changing laws and attitudes guides this kind of strategic thinking. What is clear—twenty-five years on from those first protests against beauty pageants—is that issues around sexual objectification resonate among subsequent generations of young women. Naomi Wolf's *The Beauty Myth* sold millions of copies; her speeches in the United States and Canada draw packed halls; and young women especially, whether self-described feminists or not, respond to her spirited critique of a culture that induces them to diet their way to oblivion. The protests against beauty pageants appear now as the first salvo in a long feminist challenge to a cultural economy that not only rewards and punishes women on the basis of their appearance but also induces them to spend lots of money on their appearance, to take unconscionable risks with their health, and to spend lives in a spiral of guilt-ridden dieting (Kirsch 1995, A3).[18]

Marxist feminists, by contrast, might begin with questions about profits and the dependence of capitalist relations upon the creation of needs. There are multimillion-dollar industries that depend upon women altering their body size through methods ranging from dieting to surgery. Such industries employ women in Canada, and abroad, at very low wages. From this perspective, therefore, an analysis that began with images of women and dieting would extend to the international political economy. But Marxist feminists would also highlight the continuing situation of women's economic dependence upon men, and how these relations of dependence help create the need for women to please men.

Radical feminists challenge the institutions of heterosexism, partly in order to loosen the hold that men have over women. Women have been coerced by man-made law and masculine violence—physical and representational—into heterosexual marriage, into degrading and oppressive work as models in pornography and as prostitutes, and into conforming with the entire heterosexist structuring of society. Why does the young girl looking at the magazine images feel that she should look like them? Does she believe that this will help attract male attention? Radical feminists insist that women must get out from under the power of men, and this involves action on many fronts. They have argued, for example, that men sexually violate women because they absorb violent pornography. Censoring such material, therefore, is justified on the grounds that it will diminish the violence that men wreak upon women.

Marxist feminists do not see censoring pornography as central to eliminating male violence, but focus rather on economic coercion in explaining many manifestations of gender. Women do low-paid gendered work because most of the time that is all that is available. From this perspective, women endure violence in the home because of their economic dependence on men, and men are more likely to act violently in the home when they are exploited at work (Luxton 1980). As the economic circumstances of so many people's lives worsen with cutbacks in social services and rising unemployment and underemployment, increasing numbers of women and children will be in growing jeopardy, including danger from physical violence.

The political discourse on the mid-1990s reinvents, with a vengeance, long-standing distinctions between those who are dependent on others and those who fend for themselves. In this rhetoric that provides the fuel for electoral success, increasing numbers of people find themselves with bodies that don't matter, written out of the social and political world. Psychoanalytic understandings of the false distinction between dependence and independence; poststructuralist and queer theory's readings of discourse and performativity; radical feminist insights into men's abuse of women's minds and bodies; liberal feminist insistence on the centrality of education and attitudes—all these, I would argue, contribute to an understanding of contemporary social life and suggest ways to destabilize the late twentieth century's version of the deserving and the undeserving. Finally, as I have indicated in other chapters, Marxist and anti-racist analyses of the contemporary global political economy draw attention to the immense power of those controlling capital to shape the lives of women, children, and men in different ways.

Notes

1. According to Prentice et al., the first public action of the newly formed Toronto Women's Liberation group was a protest against a winter bikini contest (1988, 353).

2. When Colleen Swanson, wife of Dow Corning's ethics advisor, experienced debilitating ill health, neither of them connected this with her recent breast implants,

implants produced and marketed by her husband's employer (Byrne 1995). Yet in a CBC radio interview, John Swanson reported that, in the 1970s, he had discounted warnings in *Ms.* magazine about the danger of silicone breast implants as feminist overreaction. An estimated 150 000 women in Canada had breast implants (*Winnipeg Free Press,* 1992a).

3. I am very grateful to Patrizia Gentile for providing me with a copy of her unpublished paper. She convincingly argues that "the beauty contest 'model' was appropriated by the federal service in order to enforce specific codes of femininity, masculinity and heterosexuality" (1995, 1). See also Kinsman 1995.

4. The Kingston Women's Liberation Movement held an elaborate protest against beauty queen contests at Queen's University in October 1969. Six members of the group entered the contest. When they were introduced, each in turn took the opportunity to address the audience (Adamson 1995, 262–63).

5. Beauty competitions could also be the occasion for reflections on competition itself. One of Canada's leading social activists, Joan Newman Kuyek, remembers her reaction to winning the beauty queen title at the University of Manitoba in 1962: "I saw the heartbreak in the faces of all the other contestants, and I realized what a horrible thing competition truly is. I was supposed to be happy at the expense of these other young women and I wondered, 'What kind of system is this?'" (Lowe 1995, 14).

6. Reginald Bibby and Donald C. Posterski's *Teen Trends: A Nation in Motion* (1992) cite a 1988 survey on male–female couples, aged 15–24, who live together. Forty-six percent of the respondents said the female partner did all the cooking, cleaning, and laundry, while only 4 percent said the male did most or all of these jobs.

7. In July 1957 a "weeping Miss USA" lost her title when organizers discovered that she was married and the mother of two children. Leona Gage told pageant officials that she and her cousin Barbara Gates had gambled every cent they had to finance her chance at fame and fortune (*Toronto Star* 1957, 1).

8. See Smith 1992.

9. See also Susan Russell's 1978 research in an Ottawa high school. She discovered that boys reported that their grades were improving even when they had deteriorated, while girls continually underestimated their performance (1987).

10. Statistics Canada has responded to John Fekete's allegations in his book *Moral Panic: Biopolitics Rising* that this was a "fake survey" and that Statistics Canada "traded science for voodoo" (Statistics Canada 1995a, 1). Statistics Canada responded that Fekete had made serious errors in his arguments, which led to misinterpretations of the nature and purpose of the survey and the survey results. They carefully refuted all eight of his allegations. In its response, Statistics Canada points out that "the Violence against Women Survey has been recognized by international experts as a major achievement and a significant contribution to the science in this area" (ibid., 7).

11. In a letter to *Ms.* magazine, Pam Elliot, co-ordinator of the Lesbian Battering Intervention Project in St Paul, Minnesota, wrote that she had been "besieged with requests nationwide for setting up support services on lesbian battering" (1991, 5).

12. In July 1994, a group of young Filipino-Canadian men and women protested in Winnipeg against the Maria Clara beauty contest held by the Knights of Rizal, a

Filipino cultural group. The protesters argued that Maria Clara, a fictional character in the work of Jose Rizal, was submissive, and that the contest encouraged young women to model themselves after her. They argued that "Filipina women have always been in the forefront of the struggle for national liberation and they should be celebrated without the kind of stereotyping that is so offensive to young women in Canada today" (Nett 1994, A7). My point is that beauty contests, like other cultural events, may carry with them a range of meanings about age, sex, gender, race, and nation.

13. See Maxine Tynes evocative poetry and stories about black women "in service" (1987, 11–12, 68–71), which capture the dignity of those who work for others, the complexity of the social relationships, and the resistance to discrimination, especially when it took the form of personal hypocrisy and rudeness (1990, 85–89).

14. Following her double mastectomy, the late Kathleen Martindale wrote: "I've got an invisible disability. I've become a quick-change artist in gyms and other places where there's no or little privacy. Most people cringe when they see my chest. They say I've been mutilated. In place of breasts with nipples I have a scar which extends from under my left armpit, goes jaggedly across my entire chest, and then ends up under what used to be my right armpit. My lover and I call it 'the zipper.' That's what it looks like, a long, red zipper" (1994, 12). Martindale also had to deal with the fact that there were no support groups for lesbian cancer patients even in Metropolitan Toronto.

15. In a memoir about her relationship with her sister, Karen, and their coming-out stories, Joy McBride writes that Karen "was involved in long-term relationships with women, though I very naively thought she and her 'roommates' just didn't have enough space or money for two beds. (Honestly)" (1996, 182).

16. There has, however, been some useful work in this area. For an elaboration on this development see Hamilton 1996.

17. But see, for example, the last chapter in Jessica Benjamin's *The Bonds of Love* (1988) for an insightful treatment of the relationship between gendered socialization and bureaucracy.

18. Dr Ron Davis, a Toronto clinical psychologist, estimated at a seminar on eating disorders that "five per cent of university women have full-blown eating disorders" and that more than 90 percent of those with eating disorders are women (Kirsch 1995, A3).

REFERENCES

Abele, Frances, and Daiva Stasiulis. 1989. "Canada as a 'White Settler Colony': What about Natives and Immigrants?" In *The New Canadian Political Economy*. Ed. Wallace Clement and Glen Williams, 240–77. Montreal: McGill-Queen's University Press.

Abella, Irving. 1982. *None Is Too Many: Canada and the Jews of Europe, 1933–1948*. Toronto: Lester & Orpen Dennys.

Abrams, Philip. 1982. *Historical Sociology*. Somerset, England: Open Books Publishing.

Adams, Kathleen Pirrie. 1993. "Back to Estrus: Thoughts on Lesbian Bar Scenes." *Fireweed* 38, 2: 29–35.

Adamson, Nancy. 1995. "Feminists, Libbers, Lefties and Radicals: The Emergence of the Women's Liberation Movement." In *A Diversity of Women: Ontario, 1945–1980*. Ed. Joy Parr, 252–80. Toronto: University of Toronto Press.

Adamson, Nancy, Linda Briskin, and Margaret McPhail. 1988. *Feminist Organizing for Change*. Toronto: Oxford University Press.

Akyeampong, Ernest R. 1995. "The Labour Market: Year-end Review." In *Perspectives on Labour and Income*. Ottawa: Statistics Canada.

Albo, Gregory, and Jane Jenson. 1989. "A Contested Concept: The Relative Autonomy of the State." In *The New Canadian Political Economy*. Ed. Wallace Clement and Glen Williams, 180–211. Montreal: McGill-Queen's University Press.

Anderson, Karen. 1987. "A Gendered World: Women, Men, and the Political Economy of the Seventeenth-Century Huron." In *Feminism and Political Economy: Women's Work, Women's Struggles*. Ed. Heather Jon Maroney and Meg Luxton, 121–38. Toronto: Methuen.

———. 1988. "As Gentle as Little Lambs: Images of Huron and Montagnais-Naskapi Women in the Writings of the 17th

Century Jesuits." *Canadian Review of Sociology and Anthropology* 25, 4: 560–76.

———. 1991. *Chain Her by One Foot.* London: Routledge.

Andrew, Caroline. 1984. "Women and the Welfare State." *Canadian Journal of Political Science* 17, 4: 667–83.

Arat-Koc, Sedef, 1989. "In the Privacy of Our Own Home: Foreign Domestic Workers as Solution to the Crisis in the Domestic Sphere in Canada." *Studies in Political Economy* 28 (Spring): 33–58.

Archibald, Kathleen. 1973. "Men, Women and Persons." *Canadian Public Administration* 16 (Spring): 14–24.

Arendt, Hannah. 1951. *Imperialism.* Part 2 of *The Origins of Totalitarianism.* New York: Harcourt, Brace & World.

Armstrong, Christopher, and H.V. Nelles. 1988. *Southern Exposure: Canadian Promoters in Latin America and the Caribbean, 1896–1930.* Toronto: University of Toronto Press.

Armstrong, Pat, and Hugh Armstrong. 1986. "Beyond Sexless Class and Classless Sex: Towards Feminist Marxism." In *The Politics of Diversity.* Ed. Roberta Hamilton and Michèle Barrett, 108–40. London: Verso.

———. 1988. "Women, Family and Economy." In *Reconstructing the Canadian Family: Feminist Perspectives.* Ed. Nancy Mandell and Ann Duffy, 143–74. Toronto: Butterworths.

———. 1990a. "Lessons from Pay Equity." *Studies in Political Economy* 32: 29–54.

———. 1990b. *Theorizing Women's Work.* Toronto: Garamond.

———. 1994. *The Double Ghetto: Canadian Women and their Segregated Work.* 3rd. ed. Toronto: McClelland & Stewart.

Arnopoulos, Sheila McLeod. 1979. *Problems of Immigrant Women in the Canadian Labour Force.* Ottawa: Canadian Advisory Council on the Status of Women.

Atwood, Margaret. 1988. *Cat's Eye.* Toronto: McClelland & Stewart.

Avery, Donald. 1979. *"Dangerous Foreigners": European Immigrant Workers and Labour Radicalism in Canada, 1896–1932.* Toronto: McClelland & Stewart.

Bacchi, Carol Lee. 1983. *Liberation Deferred? The Ideas of the English-Canadian Suffragists, 1877–1918.* Toronto: University of Toronto Press.

———. 1993. "Women and the Law." In *Changing Patterns: Women in Canada.* 2nd ed. Ed. Sandra Burt, Lorraine Code, and Lindsay Dorney, 243–78. Toronto: McClelland & Stewart.

Bakan, Abigail B., and Daiva K. Stasiulis. 1995. "Making the Match: Domestic Placement Agencies and the Racialization of Women's Household Work." *Signs* 20, 2: 303–335.

Bannerji, Himani. 1995. *Thinking Through: Essays on Feminism, Marxism and Anti-Racism.* Toronto: Women's Press.

Barber, Marilyn. 1985. "The Women Ontario Welcomed: Immigrant Domestics for Ontario Homes, 1870–1930." In *The Neglected Majority: Essays in Canadian Women's History.* Vol. 2. Ed. Alison Prentice and Susan Mann Trofimenkoff, 102–21. Toronto: McClelland & Stewart.

Barrett, Michèle. 1988. *Women's Oppression Today.* 2nd ed. London: Verso.

———. 1992. "Psychoanalysis and Feminism: A British Sociologist's View." *Signs* 17 (Winter): 455–66.

Bashevkin, Sylvia. 1989. "Free Trade and Canadian Feminism: The Case of the National Action Committee on the Status of Women." In *Canadian Public Policy/Analyse de Politiques* 15, 4: 363–75.

———. 1993. *Toeing the Lines: Women and Party Politics in English Canada.* 2nd ed. Toronto: Oxford University Press.

Batcher, Elaine. 1987. "Building the Barriers: Adolescent Girls Delimit the Future." In *Women and Men: Interdisciplinary Readings on Gender.* Ed. Greta Hofmann Nemiroff, 150–65. Richmond Hill, ON: Fitzhenry & Whiteside.

Baum, Gregory. 1986. *Liberation Theology and Marxism.* Montreal: McGill University.

Beattie, Chrisopher. 1975. *Minority Men in a Majority Setting: Middle-Level Francophones in the Canadian Public Service.* Toronto: McClelland & Stewart.

Beauvoir, Simone de. 1952. *The Second Sex.* New York: Knopf.

Bégin, Monique. 1992. "The Royal Commission on the Status of Women: Twenty Years Later." In *Challenging Times: The Women's Movement in Canada and the United States.* Ed. Constance Backhouse and David H. Flaherty, 21–38. Montreal: McGill-Queen's University Press.

Bell, Daniel. 1960. *The End of Ideology.* Glencoe, IL: Free Press.

Bell, Laurie, ed. 1987. *Good Girls Bad Girls: Sex Trade Workers and Feminists Face to Face.* Toronto: Women's Press.

Belsey, Catherine. 1980. *Critical Practice.* London: Methuen.

Benjamin, Jessica. 1988. *The Bonds of Love.* New York: Pantheon Books.

Berg, Maggie. 1991. "Luce Irigaray's 'Contradictions': Post-Structuralism and Feminism." *Signs* 17: 50–70.

Bernstein, Judy, Peggy Morton, Linda Seese, and Myrna Wood. 1972. "Sisters, Brothers, Lovers . . . Listen. . . ." In *Women Unite!* Toronto: Women's Press.

Bibby, Reginald, and Donald C. Posterski. 1992. *Teen Trends.* Toronto: Stoddart.

Bindman, Stephen. 1990. "Dismissed lesbian suing military." *Toronto Star*, 5 Feb., A3.

———. 1992. "Military gives OK to gays, lesbians." *Calgary Herald*, 28 Oct., A1.

Binkley, Marian. 1995. *Risks, Dangers, and Rewards in the Nova Scotia Offshore Fishery.* Montreal: McGill-Queen's University Press.

Black, Naomi. 1993. "The Canadian Women's Movement: The Second Wave." In *Changing Patterns: Women in Canada.* 2nd ed. Ed. Sandra Burt, Lorraine Code, and Lindsay Dorney, 151–76. Toronto: McClelland & Stewart.

Blackburn, Althea. 1995. "Fighting for the 'Family' Name: A Socio-legal Analysis of the Canadian Response to Same Sex Families in the Charter Era." MA thesis. Queen's University.

Borrows, John. 1994. "Contemporary Traditional Equality: The Effect of the Charter on First Nations Politics." *University of New Brunswick Law Journal* 43: 1–43.

Bose, Anuradha. 1972. "Consciousness Raising." In *Mother Was Not a Person.* Ed. Margret Andersen. Montreal: Black Rose Books.

Boyd, Monica. 1994. "Canada's Refugee Flows: Gender Inequality." *Canadian Social Trends* 32: 7–10.

Bradbury, Bettina. 1979. "The Family Economy and Work in an Industrializing City: Montreal in the 1870s." Canadian Historical Association *Papers.*

———. 1984. "Pigs, Cows and Boarders: Non-wage Forms of Survival Among Montreal Families, 1861–91." *Labour/Le Travail* 14: 9–46.

———. 1993. *Working Families: Age, Gender, and Daily Survival in Industrializing Montreal.* Toronto: McClelland & Stewart.

Brand, Dionne. 1984. "A Working Paper on Black Women in Toronto: Gender, Race and Class." *Fireweed* 19: 26–43.

———. 1991. *No Burden to Carry: Narratives of Black Working Women in Ontario, 1920s–1950s.* Toronto: Women's Press.

Brant, Beth. 1985. "Coming Out as Indian Lesbian Writers." In *In the Feminine: Women and Words/Les femmes et les mots.* Ed. Ann Dybikowski, Victoria Freeman, Daphne Marlatt, Barbara Pullman, and Betsy Warland. Edmonton: Longspoon Press.

———. 1991. *Food and Spirits.* Vancouver: Press Gang.

Bray, M. Phyllis. 1989. "'No Life for a Woman': An Examination and Feminist Critique of the Post-World War II Instant Town with Special Reference to Manitouwadge, Ontario." MA thesis, Queen's University.

———. 1991. "The Long-Distance Commute in the Mining Industry: The Human Dimension." *CIM Bulletin* 84, 953: 62–64.

———. 1993. "The 'Perfect' Mine Wife: The Sancta Barbara Order of Merit—A Retrospective." *Bulletin of the Canadian Institute of Mining and Metallurgy* (March): 99–102.

Briskin, Linda. 1993. "Union Women and Separate Organizing." In *Women Challenging Unions: Feminism, Democracy, and Militancy.* Ed. Linda Briskin and Patricia McDermott, 89–108. Toronto: University of Toronto Press.

Briskin, Linda, and Patricia McDermott, eds. 1993. *Women Challenging Unions: Feminism, Democracy, and Militancy.* Toronto: University of Toronto Press.

Brodie, Janine. 1989. "The Political Economy of Regionalism." In *The New Canadian Political Economy.* Ed. Wallace Clement and Glen Williams, 138–59. Montreal: McGill-Queen's University Press.

————. 1995. *Politics on the Margins: Restructuring and the Canadian Women's Movement.* Halifax: Fernwood.

Brodribb, Somer. 1992. *Nothing Mat(t)ers: A Feminist Critique of Postmodernism.* Toronto: Lorimer.

Brodsky, Gwen, and Shelagh Day. 1989. *Canadian Charter Equality Rights for Women: One Step Forward or Two Steps Back?* Ottawa: Canadian Advisory Council on the Status of Women.

Brouwer, Ruth Compton. 1990. *New Women for God: Canadian Presbyterian Women and India Missions, 1876–1914.* Toronto: University of Toronto Press.

Brown, Rosemary. 1989. *Being Brown: A Very Public Life.* Toronto: Random House.

Brunswick, Ruth. 1948. "The Preoedipal Phase of the Libido Development." In *The Psycho-analytic Reader.* Ed. Robert Fleiss. New York: International Universities Press.

Brym, Robert J., with Bonnie J. Fox. 1989. *From Culture to Power: The Sociology of English Canada.* Toronto: Oxford University Press.

Buckner, Philip. 1990. "CHR Dialogue—The Maritimes and Confederation: A Reassessment." *Canadian Historical Review* 71, 1.

Burnet, Jean, ed. 1986. *Looking in My Sister's Eyes: An Exploration in Women's History.* Toronto: Multicultural History Society of Ontario.

Burr, Catherine. 1995. "Ontario can't keep employment equity down." *Globe and Mail,* 29 June, A17.

Burstyn, Varda. 1983. "Economy, Sexuality, Politics: Engels and the Sexual Division of Labour." *Socialist Studies/Etudes Socialistes: A Canadian Annual.*

————. 1990. "The Waffle and the Women's Movement." *Studies in Political Economy* 33: 175–84.

Burstyn, Varda, and Judy Rebick. 1988. "How 'Women Against Free Trade' Came to Write Its Manifesto." *Resources for Feminist Research* 17, 3: 138–42.

Burt, Sandra. 1993. "The Changing Patterns of Public Policy." In *Changing Patterns: Women in Canada.* 2nd ed. Ed. Sandra Burt, Lorraine Code, and Lindsay Dorney, 212–42. Toronto: McClelland & Stewart.

Butler, Judith. 1993. *Bodies that Matter: On the Discursive Limits of "Sex."* New York: Routledge.

Byrne, John A. 1995. "Informed Consent." *Business Week,* 2 Oct., 104–16.

Cameron, Barb, and Cathy Pike. 1972. "Collective Child Care in a Class Society." In *Women Unite!,* 87–89. Toronto: Canadian Women's Educational Press.

Campbell, Marion. 1995. "Separation or Integration: A Case Study, the Ban Righ Board of Queen's University." MA thesis, Queen's University.

Canada Medical Record. 1890. "Co-education." 18: 118–20.

Canadian Parliamentary Guide. 1995. 23 Feb.: 201–3.

Canadian Practitioner. 1892. "Higher Education for Women." 17: 257–60.

Cannon, Martin. 1995. "(De)marginalizing the Intersection of 'Race' and 'Gender' in First Nations Politics." MA thesis, Queen's University.

Carpenter, Mary. 1996. "Female Grotesques in Academia: Ageism, Anti-Feminism and Feminists on the Faculty." In *Anti-Feminism in the Academy.* Ed. Vévé Clark, Shirley Nelson Garner, Margaret Higonmat, and Ketv Katrak. New York: Routledge.

Carr, Jim. 1994. "Immigration policy 'racist.'" *Winnipeg Free Press,* 15 Nov., A6.

Castellano, Marlene Brant. 1989. "Women in Huron and Ojibwa Societies." *Canadian Woman Studies/Les cahiers de la femme* 10, 2/3: 45–48.

Castellano, Marlene Brant, and Janice Hill. 1995. "First Nations Women: Reclaiming Our Responsibilities." In *A Diversity of Women: Ontario, 1945–1980.* Ed. Joy Parr, 232–51. Toronto: University of Toronto Press.

Cauchon, Paul. 1992. "Les mouvements de femmes donnent naissance à 'Québec féminin pluriel.'" *Le Devoir,* 1 June.

Cebarotov, E.A. (Nora). 1995. "From Domesticity to the Public Sphere: Farm Women, 1945–86." In *A Diversity of Women: Ontario, 1945–80.* Ed. Joy Parr, 200–31. Toronto: University of Toronto Press.

Chase, Gillean. 1996. "Strangers, Sisters." In *To Sappho, My Sister: Lesbian Sisters Write About Their Lives.* Ed. Lee Fleming, 59–68. Charlottetown: Gynergy Books.

Cheal, David. 1991. *Family and the State of Theory*. Toronto: University of Toronto Press.

Chenier, Elise Rose. 1995. "Tough Ladies and Troublemakers: Toronto's Public Lesbian Community, 1955–65." MA thesis, Queen's University.

Chunn, Dorothy. 1995. "Feminism, Law, and Public Policy: Politicizing the Personal." In *Canadian Families: Diversity, Conflict and Change*. Ed. Nancy Mandell and Ann Duffy, 177–210. Toronto: Harcourt Brace.

Clark, Alice. 1982 [1919]. *Working Life of Women in the Seventeenth Century*. London: Routledge and Kegan Paul.

Clark, Lorene, and Debra J. Lewis. 1977. *Rape: The Price of Coercive Sexuality*. Toronto: Women's Press.

Clement, Wallace. 1975. *The Canadian Corporate Elite: An Analysis of Economic Power*. Toronto: McClelland & Stewart.

Coates, Linda, Janet Beavin Bavelas, and James Gibson. 1994. "Anomalous Language in Sexual Assault Trial Judgements." *Discourse and Society* 5, 2: 189–206.

Cohen, Marjorie Griffin. 1987. *Free Trade and the Future of Women's Work: Manufacturing and Service Industries*. Toronto: Garamond Press and the Canadian Centre for Policy Alternatives.

———. 1988. *Women's Work, Markets and Economic Development in Nineteenth-Century Ontario*. Toronto: University of Toronto Press.

Cohen, Rina. 1994. "A Brief History of Racism in Immigration Policies for Recruiting Domestics." In *Canadian Woman Studies/Les cahiers de la femme* 14, 2: 83–86.

Collins, Patricia Hill. 1990. *Black Feminist Thought*. London: HarperCollins.

Connelly, Patricia. 1978. *Last Hired: First Fired*. Toronto: Women's Press.

Connelly, Patricia, and Martha MacDonald. 1986. "Women's Work: Domestic and Wage Labour in a Nova Scotia Community." In *The Politics of Diversity*. Ed. Roberta Hamilton and Michèle Barrett, 53–80. London: Verso.

Conrad, Margaret. 1986. "'Sundays Always Make Me Think of Home': Time and Place in Canadian Women's History." In *Rethinking Canada: The*

Promise of Women's History. Ed. Veronica Strong-Boag and Anita Clair Fellman, 67–81. Toronto: Copp Clark Pitman.

Cook, Sharon Anne. 1995. *"Through Sunshine and Shadow": The Woman's Christian Temperance Union, Evangelicalism, and Reform in Ontario, 1874–1930.* Montreal: McGill-Queen's University Press.

Cowan, Mary Rose. 1993. "When Will Justice Be Done?" *Herizons* 7, 12: 17–23.

Creese, Gillian. 1988. "The Politics of Dependence: Women, Work and Unemployment in the Vancouver Labour Movement Before World War II." In *Class, Gender, and Region: Essays in Canadian Historical Sociology.* Ed. Gregory S. Kealey, 121–42. St John's: Committee on Canadian Labour History.

Currie, Andrea. 1989. "A Roof is Not Enough: Feminism, Transition Houses and the Battle Against Abuse." *New Maritimes* (Sept./Oct.): 16–29.

Danylewycz, Marta. 1987. *Taking the Veil: An Alternative to Marriage, Motherhood, and Spinsterhood in Quebec, 1840–1920.* Toronto: McClelland & Stewart.

DeSève, Micheline. 1992. "The Perspectives of Quebec Feminists." In *Challenging Times: The Women's Movement in Canada and the United States.* Ed. Constance Backhouse and David H. Flaherty, 110–16. Montreal: McGill-Queen's University Press.

Dewar, Elaine. 1977. "Beyond Sisterhood: Is There Life after Liberation?" *Weekend Magazine, Winnipeg Free Press,* 1 April: 6–8, 10–11.

Dickie, Bonnie. 1993. *A Web Not a Ladder.* National Film Board, Women and Work Series.

Dodd, Dianne, and Deborah Gorham, eds. 1994. *Caring and Curing: Historical Perspectives on Women and Healing in Canada.* Ottawa: University of Ottawa Press.

Doucette, Joanne. 1989. "Redefining Difference: Disabled Lesbians Resist." *Resources for Feminist Research* 18, 2: 17–20.

Dubinsky, Karen. 1985. *Lament for a "Patriarchy Lost"? Anti-feminism, Anti-abortion, and REAL Women in Canada.* Ottawa: Canadian Research Institute for the Advancement of Women.

———. 1993. *Improper Advances: Rape and Heterosexual Conflict in Ontario, 1880–1929.* Chicago: University of Chicago Press.

DuBois, Ellen Carol. 1978. *Feminism and Suffrage: The Emergence of an Independent Women's Movement in America, 1848–1869.* Ithaca, NY: Cornell University Press.

Duffy, Ann. 1986. "Reformulating Power for Women." In *Canadian Review of Sociology and Anthropology* 23: 22–47.

Duffy, Ann, and Norene Pupo. 1992. *Part-Time Paradox: Connecting Gender, Work and Family.* Toronto: McClelland & Stewart.

Dumont, Micheline. 1992. "The Origins of the Women's Movement in Quebec." In *Challenging Times: The Women's Movement in Canada and the United States.* Ed. Constance Backhouse and David H. Flaherty, 72–89. Montreal: McGill-Queen's University Press.

———. 1995. "Women of Quebec and the Contemporary Constitutional Issue." In *Gender Politics.* Ed. François-Pierre Gingras, 153–74. Toronto: Oxford University Press.

Echols, Alice. 1989. *"Daring to Be Bad": Radical Feminism in America, 1967–1975.* Minneapolis: University of Minnesota Press.

Ehrenreich, Barbara. 1983. *The Hearts of Men: American Dreams and the Flight from Commitment.* New York: Doubleday.

Eichler, Margrit. 1988. *Families in Canada Today: Recent Changes and Their Policy Consequences.* 2nd ed. Toronto: Gage.

———. 1992. "Not Always an Easy Alliance: The Relationship Between Women's Studies and the Women's Movement in Canada." In *Challenging Times: The Women's Movement in Canada and the United States.* Ed. Constance Backhouse and David H. Flaherty, 71–102. Montreal: McGill-Queen's University Press.

———, ed. 1995. *Change of Plans: Towards a Non-sexist Sustainable City.* Toronto: Garamond.

Eisenstein, Hester. 1984. *Contemporary Feminist Thought.* London: Allen & Unwin.

Eisenstein, Zillah. 1981. *The Radical Future of Liberal Feminism.* Boston: Northeastern University Press.

Elliot, Pam. 1991. Letter to editor. *Ms.* 1, 4: 5.

Engels, F. 1948 [1884]. *The Origin of the Family, Private Property and the State.* Moscow: Progress Publishers.

Errington, Jane. 1993. "Pioneers and Suffragists." In *Changing Patterns: Women in Canada.* 2nd ed. Ed. Sandra Burt, Lorraine Code, and Lindsay Dorney, 59–91. Toronto: McClelland & Stewart.

———. 1996. *Wives and Mothers, Schoolmistresses and Scullery Maids: Working Women in Upper Canada, 1790–1840.* Montreal: McGill-Queen's University Press.

Evans, Sara. 1979. *Personal Politics: The Roots of Women's Liberation in the Civil Rights Movement and the New Left.* New York: Alfred A. Knopf.

Faderman, Lillian. 1981. *Surpassing the Love of Men: Romantic Friendship and Love Between Women from the Renaissance to the Present.* New York: Morrow.

Fahmy-Eid, Nadia, and Nicole Laurin-Frenette. 1986. "Theories of the Family and Family/Authority Relationships in the Educational Sector in Quebec and France, 1850–1960." In *The Politics of Diversity.* Ed. Roberta Hamilton and Michèle Barrett, 287–302. London: Verso.

Faludi, Susan. 1991. *Backlash: The Undeclared War Against American Women.* New York: Anchor Books.

Feminist Review. 1985–86. Vols. 20, 22, 23.

Fillmore, Nick. 1989. "The Big Oink: How Business Won the Free Trade Battle." *This Magazine* 22, 8 (March): 13–20.

Findlay, Deborah. 1995. "Discovering Sex: Medical Science, Feminism and Intersexuality." *Canadian Review of Sociology and Anthropology* 32, 1: 25–52.

Findlay, Sue. 1987. "Facing the State: The Politics of the Women's Movement Reconsidered." In *Feminism and Political Economy: Women's Work, Women's Struggles.* Ed. Heather Jon Maroney and Meg Luxton, 31–50. Toronto: Methuen.

Finkel, Alvin. 1993. "Populism and Gender: The UFA and Social Credit Experiences." *Journal of Canadian Studies* 27, 4: 76–97.

Firestone, Shulamith. 1970. *The Dialectic of Sex.* New York: William Morrow & Co.

Fiske, Jo-Anne. 1991. "Colonization and the Decline of Women's Status: The Tsimshian Case." *Feminist Studies* 17: 509–35.

Fleming, Lee, ed. 1996. *To Sappho, My Sister: Lesbian Sisters Write About Their Lives.* Charlottetown: Gynergy Books.

Forbes, Ernest R. 1979. *Maritime Rights—The Maritime Rights Movement, 1919–1927: A Study in Canadian Regionalism.* Montreal: McGill-Queen's University Press.

Fox, Bonnie J. 1989. "The Feminist Challenge: A Reconsideration of Social Inequality and Economic Development." In Robert Brym with Bonnie Fox, *From Culture to Power: The Sociology of English Canada.* Toronto: Oxford University Press.

Freud, Sigmund. 1965. *New Introductory Lectures on Psychoanalysis.* Trans. and ed. James Strachy. New York: W.W. Norton.

Friedan, Betty. 1963. *The Feminine Mystique.* New York: Dell Publishing.

Galloway, Priscilla. 1987. "Room to Grow." In *Still Running: Personal Stories of Queen's Women.* Ed Joy Parr, 108–20. Kingston: Queen's University Alumnae Association.

Gannagé, Charlene. 1986. *Double Day Double Bind: Women Garment Workers.* Toronto: Women's Press.

Gardiner, Judith. 1992. "Psychoanalysis and Feminism: An American Humanist's View." *Signs* 17 (Winter): 437–54.

Gaskell, Jane. 1986. "Conceptions of Skill and the Work of Women: Some Historical and Political Issues." In *The Politics of Diversity.* Ed. Roberta Hamilton and Michèle Barrett, 361–84. London: Verso.

———. 1988. "The Reproduction of Family Life: Perspectives of Male and Female Adolescents. In *Gender and Society: Creating a Canadian Women's Sociology.* Ed. Arlene Tigar McLaren, 146–68. Toronto: Copp Clark Pitman.

Gentile, Patrizia. 1995. "Defending Gender in the Security State: Beauty Contests and Fruit Machines, 1950–1972." Unpublished paper, Carleton University.

Gershbain, Nikki, and Aviva Rubin. 1994. "The Struggle Beneath the Struggle: Antisemitism in Toronto Anti-Racist Movements." In *Canadian Woman Studies/Les cahiers de la femme* 14, 2: 58–61.

Gibb-Clark, Margot, and Sean Fine. 1993. "Will 'slaves to the law' ever be free?" *Globe and Mail*, 27 Nov., A1, A10.

Gill, Judy, Diana Chastain, Linda Carmen, Mary Bolton, Jenny Robinson. 1972. Women's Liberation Movement Toronto, Ontario. September 1970. "Sexual Myths." In *Women Unite!* Toronto: Canadian Women's Educational Press, 162–69.

Gillett, Margaret. 1981. *"We Walked Very Warily": A History of Women at McGill*. Montreal: Eden Press.

Globe and Mail. 1976. "McLaughlin's long futile search." 11 Sept.

———. 1993. "Violence is not a women's issue." [Editorial]. 31 July, D6.

———. 1995. "Female refugees suffer abuse." 8 March, A10.

Gordon, Linda. 1976. *Woman's Body, Woman's Right: A Social History of Birth Control in America*. New York: Grossman.

Gorham, Deborah. 1979. "Flora MacDonald Denison: Canadian Feminist." In *A Not Unreasonable Claim: Women and Reform in Canada, 1880s–1920s*. Ed. Linda Kealey, 47–70. Toronto: Women's Press.

———. 1994. "'No Longer an Invisible Minority': Women Physicians and Medical Practice in Late Twentieth-Century North America." In *Caring and Curing: Historical Perspectives on Women and Healing in Canada*. Ed. Dianne Dodd and Deborah Gorham, 183–212. Ottawa: University of Ottawa Press.

Gough, Kathleen. 1973. *The Origin of the Family*. Toronto: New Hogtown Press.

Gray, Stan. 1987. "Sharing the Shop Floor." In *Women and Men: Interdisciplinary Readings on Gender*. Ed. Greta Hofmann Nemiroff, 377–402. Richmond Hill, ON: Fitzhenry & Whiteside.

Guindon, Hubert. 1988. *Tradition, Modernity, Nation*. Toronto: University of Toronto Press.

Haddad, Tony, and Lawrence Lam. 1988. "Canadian Families—Men's Involvement in Family Work: A Case Study of Immigrant Men in Toronto." In *International Journal of Comparative Sociology* 29, 3/4: 269–81.

Hale, Sylvia M. 1988. "Male Culture and Purdah for Women: The Social Construction of What Women Think Women Think." *Canadian Review of Sociology and Anthropology* 25, 2: 276–97.

Hamilton, Roberta. 1978. *The Liberation of Women: A Study of Patriarchy and Capitalism.* London: Allen and Unwin.

———. 1985. "Feminists in the Academy: Intellectuals or Political Subversives?" *Queen's Quarterly* 92, 1: 3–20.

———. 1986. "The Collusion with Patriarchy: A Psychoanalytic Account." In *The Politics of Diversity.* Ed. Roberta Hamilton and Michèle Barrett, 385–97. London: Verso.

———. 1988. *Feudalism and Colonization: The Historiography of New France.* Gananoque, ON: Langdale Press.

———. 1995. "Pro-Natalism, Feminism and Nationalism." In *Gender Politics.* Ed. François-Pierre Gingras, 135–52. Toronto: Oxford University Press.

———. 1996. "Theorizing Gender, Sexuality and Family: Feminism and Psychoanalysis Revisited." In *Feminism and Families.* Ed. Meg Luxton. Halifax: Fernwood.

Hansen, Karen V., and Ilene J. Philipson. 1990. *Women, Class, and the Feminist Imagination.* Philadelphia: Temple University Press.

Harding, Sandra. *The Science Question in Feminism.* Ithaca, NY: Cornell University Press, 1986.

Hartsock, Nancy. 1990. "Foucault on Power: A Theory for Women?" In *Feminism/Postmodernism.* Ed. Linda J. Nicholson, 157–75. New York: Routledge.

Henry, Frances. 1973. *Forgotten Canadians: The Blacks of Nova Scotia.* Don Mills, ON: Longman.

Henry, Frances, Carol Tator, Winston Mattis, and Tim Rees. 1995. *The Colour of Democracy: Racism in Canadian Society.* Toronto: Harcourt Brace.

Herman, Didi. 1995. *Rights of Passage: Struggles for Lesbian and Gay Equality.* Toronto: University of Toronto Press.

Hill, Christopher. 1969. *Reformation to Industrial Revolution.* Harmondsworth: Penguin Books.

hooks, bell. 1988. *thinking feminist, thinking black.* Toronto: Garamond Press.

Horn, Kahn-Tineta. 1991. "Beyond Oka: Dimensions of Mohawk Sovereignty" An Interview with Kahn-Tineta Horn. *Studies in Political Economy* 35: 29–41.

Horowitz, Gad. 1977. *Basic and Surplus Repression in Psychoanalytic Theory.* Toronto: University of Toronto Press.

Hrdy, Sarah. 1981. *The Woman Who Never Evolved.* Cambridge: Harvard University Press.

Hubbard, Ruth. 1990. "The Political Nature of 'Human Nature.'" In *Theoretical Perspectives on Sexual Differences.* Ed. Deborah L. Rhode, 63–73. New Haven, CT: Yale University Press.

Hughes, Mikaela, and Catherine Hughes. 1996. "The Hughes Family Chronicles." In *To Sappho, My Sister: Lesbian Sisters Write About Their Lives.* Ed. Lee Fleming, 135–50. Charlottetown: Gynergy Books.

Iacovetta, Franca. 1992. *Such Hardworking People: Italian Immigrants in Postwar Toronto.* Montreal: McGill-Queen's University Press.

———. 1995. "Remaking Their Lives: Women Immigrants, Survivors, and Refugees." In *A Diversity of Women: Ontario, 1945–80.* Ed. Joy Parr, 135–67. Toronto: University of Toronto Press.

Ibsen, Henrik. 1967. *Four Great Plays by Ibsen.* Trans. R. Farquharson Sharp. Intro. John Gassner. New York: Bantam.

Ingraham, Chrys. 1994. "The Heterosexual Imaginary: Feminist Sociology and Theories of Gender." *Sociological Theory* 12, 2: 201–19.

Jamieson, Kathleen. 1978. "Sex Discrimination and the Indian Act." In *Indian Women and the Law: Citizens Minus.* Ottawa: Minister of Supply and Services.

Kaufman, Michael, ed. 1987. *Beyond Patriarchy: Essays by Men on Pleasure, Power, and Change.* Toronto: Oxford University Press.

Kelly, Joan. 1984. "The Social Relation of the Sexes: Methodological Implications of Women's History." In *Women, History and Theory: The Essays of Joan Kelly.* Chicago: University of Chicago Press.

Kennedy, Elizabeth Lapovsky, and Madeline D. Davis. 1995. *Boots of Leather, Slippers of Gold: The History of a Lesbian Community.* New York: Routledge.

Killian, Melody. 1972. "Children are Only Littler People." In *Women Unite!* Toronto: Canadian Women's Educational Press, 90–98.

Kinsman, Gary. 1995. "'Character Weaknesses' and 'Fruit Machines': Towards an Analysis of the Anti-Homosexual Security Campaign in the Canadian Civil Service." *Labour/Le Travail* 35: 133–61.

Kirsch, Vik. 1995. "Eating disorders plague students: Hundreds now affected by dietary chaos says hospital psychologist." *Guelph Mercury,* 27 June, A3.

Klein, Alice, and Wayne Roberts. 1974. "Besieged Innocence: The 'Problem' and Problems of Working Women, Toronto, 1896–1914." In *Women at Work, Ontario, 1850–1930.* Ed. Janice Acton, Penny Goldsmith, and Bonnie Shepard, 211–60. Toronto: Canadian Women's Educational Press.

Koedt, Anne. 1973. "The Myth of the Vaginal Orgasm." In *Radical Feminism.* Ed. Anne Koedt, Ellen Levine, and Anita Rapone, 198–207. New York: Quadrangle.

Kome, Penney. 1983. *The Taking of Twenty Eight: Women Challenge the Constitution.* Toronto: Canadian Women's Educational Press.

Kostash, Myrna. 1980. *Long Way from Home. The Story of the Sixties Generation in Canada.* Toronto: Lorimer, 1980.

Kowaluk, Lucia. 1972. "The Status of Women in Canada." In *Mother Was Not a Person.* Montreal: Black Rose Books, 210–20.

Kreps, Bonnie. 1979. *No Life for a Woman.* Produced by Serendipity Films Ltd. for the National Film Board.

Kumar, Pradeep. 1993. "Collective Bargaining and Women's Workplace Concerns." In *Women Challenging Unions: Feminism, Democracy and Militancy.* Ed. Linda Briskin and Patricia McDermott, 207–30. Toronto: University of Toronto Press.

Ladurie, Emmanuel Le Roy. 1974. *The Peasants of Languedoc.* Trans. and intro. John Day. Chicago: University of Illinois Press.

LaMarsh, Judy. 1968. *Memoires of a Bird in a Gilded Cage.* Toronto: McClelland & Stewart.

Lamoureux, Diane. 1987. "Nationalism and Feminism in Quebec: An Impossible Attraction." In *Feminism and Political Economy: Women's*

Work, Women's Struggles. Ed. Heather Jon Maroney and Meg Luxton, 51–68. Toronto: Methuen.

Lavigne, Marie. 1979. "Feminist Reflections on the Fertility of Women in Quebec." In *The Politics of Diversity.* Ed. Roberta Hamilton and Michèle Barrett, 303–21. London: Verso.

Lavigne, Marie, Yolande Pinard, and Jennifer Stoddart. 1979. "The Fédération Nationale Saint-Jean-Baptiste and the Women's Movement in Quebec." In *A Not Unreasonable Claim: Women and Reform in Canada, 1880s–1920s.* Ed. Linda Kealey, 71–87. Toronto: Women's Press.

Leacock, Eleanor. 1981. *Myths of Male Dominance.* New York: Monthly Review Press.

———. 1986. "Montagnais Women and the Jesuit Program for Colonization." In *Rethinking Canada: The Promise of Women's History.* Ed. Veronica Strong-Boag and Anita Clair Fellman, 7–22. Toronto: Copp Clark Pitman.

Leslie, Genevieve. 1974. "Domestic Service in Canada, 1880–1920." In *Women at Work, Ontario, 1850–1930.* Ed. Janice Acton, Penny Goldsmith, and Bonnie Shepard, 71–126. Toronto: Canadian Women's Educational Press.

Lett, Dan. 1995. "Safe haven a nightmare for refugees." *Winnipeg Free Press,* 18 Sept., B3.

Liddington, Jill, and Jill Norris. 1978. *One Hand Tied Behind Us: The Rise of the Women's Suffrage Movement.* London: Virago.

Lippman, Abby. 1989. "Prenatal Diagnosis: Reproductive Choice? Reproductive Control?" In *The Future of Human Reproduction.* Ed. Christine Overall, 182–94. Toronto: Women's Press.

Lorde, Audre. 1984. *Sister Outsider.* Trumansburg, NY: Crossing Press Feminist Series.

Lowe, Graham S. 1987. *Women in the Administrative Revolution.* Toronto: University of Toronto Press.

Lowe, Mick. 1995. "Joan Kuyek vs. INCO." *Canadian Forum* 74 (Nov.): 14–20.

Luxton, Meg. 1980. *More than a Labour of Love.* Toronto: Women's Press.

MacGregor, Sherilyn. 1994. "Feminist Approaches to Planning Thought and Action: Practical Lessons from Women Plan Toronto." MA thesis, Queen's University.

Mackenzie, Suzanne. 1986. "Women's Responses to Economic Restructuring: Changing Gender, Changing Space." In *The Politics of Diversity.* Ed. Roberta Hamilton and Michèle Barrett, 81–100. London: Verso.

———. 1987. "The Politics of Restructuring: Gender and Economy in De-industrialized Areas." Paper presented to the Canadian Association of Geographers.

MacKinnon, Catharine A., and Andrea Dworkin. 1995. "In Defense of Themselves." *New York Times Book Review,* 7 May, 47.

Macpherson, Kay. 1994. *When in Doubt, Do Both: The Times of My Life.* Toronto: University of Toronto Press.

Marchak, Patricia. 1980. "The Two Dimensions of Canadian Regionalism." *Journal of Canadian Studies* 15, 2 (Summer): 88–97.

Mark, Ken. 1994. "Sharing the housework isn't a politial gesture, Ken Mark says. It just makes sense." *Globe and Mail,* 16 Feb. A24.

Maroney, Heather Jon. 1987. "Feminism at Work." In *Feminism and Political Economy: Women's Work, Women's Struggles.* Ed. Heather Jon Maroney and Meg Luxton, 85–108. Toronto: Methuen.

———. 1992. "'Who Has the Baby?' Nationalism, Pronatalism and the Construction of a 'Demographic Crisis' in Quebec, 1960–1988." *Studies in Political Economy* 39: 7–36.

Martindale, Kathleen. 1994. "Can I Get A Witness? My Lesbian Breast Cancer Story." *Fireweed* 42: 9–15.

———. 1995. "What Makes Lesbianism Thinkable: Theorizing Lesbianism from Adrienne Rich to Queer Theory." In *Feminist Issues: Race, Class and Sexuality.* Ed. Nancy Mandell. Scarborough, ON: Prentice-Hall.

Marx, Karl. 1969 [1869]. "The 18th Brumaire of Louis Bonaparte." In Karl Marx and Friedrich Engels, *Selected Works.* Vol. 1: 394–87. Moscow: Progress Publishers.

Marx, Karl, and Frederick Engels. 1969 [1848]. "Manifesto of the Communist Party." In *Selected Works,* 98–137. Moscow: Progress Publishers.

Matthews, Ralph. 1980. "The Significance and Explanation of Regional Divisions in Canada." *Journal of Canadian Studies* 15, 2: 43–61.

McBride, Joy, and Karen McBride. 1996. "Answering to My Sister's Name." In *To Sappho, My Sister: Lesbian Sisters Write About Their Lives.* Ed. Lee Fleming, 175–84. Charlottetown: Gynergy Books.

McCallum, Margaret E. 1986. "Keeping Women in Their Place: The Minimum Wage in Canada, 1910–25." *Labour/Le Travail* 17: 29–56.

McDaniel, Susan. 1993. "The Changing Canadian Family: Women's Roles and the Impact of Feminism." In *Changing Patterns: Women in Canada.* 2nd ed. Ed. Sandra Burt, Lorraine Code, and Lindsay Dorney, 422–51. Toronto: McClelland & Stewart.

McFarland, Joan. 1988. "The Construction of Women and Development Theory." *Canadian Review of Sociology and Anthropology* 25: 299–308.

McIntyre, Sheila. 1994. "Refining Reformism: The Consultations that Shaped Bill C-49." In *Confronting Sexual Assault: A Decade of Legal and Social Change.* Ed. Julian Roberts and Renate Mohr, 193–326. Toronto: University of Toronto Press.

———. 1995. "Gender Bias within the Law School: 'The Memo' and Its Impact." In *Breaking Anonymity: The Chilly Climate for Women Faculty.* Ed. the Chilly Collective, 211–64. Waterloo: Wilfrid Laurier University Press.

McKenna, Katherine M.J. 1994. *A Life of Propriety: Anne Murray Powell and Her Family, 1755–1849.* Montreal: McGill-Queen's University Press.

McLaren, Angus, and Arlene Tigar McLaren. 1986. *The Bedroom and the State: The Changing Practices and Politics of Contraception and Abortion in Canada, 1880–1980.* Toronto: McClelland & Stewart.

Messing, Karen. 1987. "Do Women Have Different Jobs Because of Their Biological Differences?" In *Women and Men: Interdisciplinary Readings on Gender.* Ed. Greta Hofmann Nemiroff, 341–53. Richmond Hill, ON: Fitzhenry & Whiteside.

Millett, Kate. 1971. *Sexual Politics.* New York: Avon Books.

Mills, C. Wright. 1959. *The Sociological Imagination.* London: Oxford University Press.

Mitchell, Juliet. 1971. *Women's Estate.* Harmondsworth: Penguin Books

————. 1974. *Psychoanalysis and Feminism.* New York: Pantheon Books.

Mitchell, Marjorie, and Anna Franklin. 1984. "When You Don't Know the Language, Listen to the Silence: An Historical Overview of Native Indian Women in B.C." In *Not Just Pin Money.* Ed. Barbara K. Latham and Roberta J. Pazdro, 17–34. Victoria: Camosun College.

Mitchinson, Wendy. 1979. "The WCTU: 'For God, Home and Native Land'—A Study in Nineteenth-Century Feminism." In *A Not Unreasonable Claim: Women and Reform in Canada, 1880s–1920s.* Ed. Linda Kealey, 151–68. Toronto: Women's Press.

Modleski, Tania. 1991. *Feminism Without Women: Culture and Criticism in a "Post-Feminist Age."* New York: Routledge.

Moghissi, Haideh. 1994. "Racism and Sexism in Academic Practice." In *The Dynamics of "Race" and Gender: Some Feminist Interventions.* Ed. Haleh Afshar and Mary Maynard, 222–34. London: Taylor and Francis.

Montreal Health Press. 1995. *A Book about Birth Control.* Montreal.

Monture-Angus, Patricia. 1995. *Thunder in My Soul: A Mohawk Woman Speaks.* Halifax: Fernwood Press.

Monture-Okanee, Patricia. 1995. "Introduction. Surviving the Contradictions: Personal Notes on Academia." In *Breaking Anonymity: The Chilly Climate for Women Faculty.* Ed. the Chilly Collective, 11–28. Waterloo: Wilfrid Laurier University Press.

Morris, Cerise. 1980. "'Determination and Thoroughness': The Movement for a Royal Commission on the Status of Women in Canada." *Atlantis* 5, 2: 1–21.

————. 1982. "No More than Simple Justice." PhD diss., McGill University.

Morton, Mary. 1988. "Dividing the Wealth, Sharing the Poverty: The (Re)formation of 'Family' in Law in Ontario." *Canadian Review of Sociology and Anthropology* 25, 2: 254–75.

Mosoff, Judith. 1993. "Reproductive Technology and Disability: Searching for the 'Rights' and Wrongs in Explanation." *Dalhousie Law Review* 16, 1: 97–126.

Mosse, Julia Cleves. 1993. *Half the World, Half a Chance.* Oxford: Oxfam.

Nakhaie, M.R. 1996a. "Class, Breadwinner Ideology and Housework." Unpublished paper.

———. 1996b."Vertical Mosaic Among the Elites: The New Imagery Revisited." *Canadian Review of Sociology and Anthropology* (forthcoming).

Nash, Catherine. 1995. "Siting Lesbians: Sexuality, Planning and Urban Space." MA thesis, Queen's University.

Nett, Emily. 1994. "Demure no more?" *Winnipeg Free Press,* 31 July, A7.

Newman Peter. 1969. *The Distemper of Our Times.* Toronto: McClelland & Stewart.

Newman, Roger. 1976. "Bank can't find woman qualified to serve as director." *Globe and Mail,* 10 Sept., 1.

Ng, Roxana. 1986. "The Social Construction of Immigrant Women." In *The Politics of Diversity.* Ed. Roberta Hamilton and Michèle Barrett, 269–86. London: Verso.

Nicholson, Linda J., ed. 1990. *Feminism/Postmodernism.* New York: Routledge.

Noble, Kimberly. 1991. "Being a bad sport about harassment." *Globe and Mail,* 29 Nov., A18

O'Brien, Mary. 1981. *The Politics of Reproduction.* London: Routledge & Kegan Paul.

Odette, Francine. 1992. "Body Beautiful/Body Perfect: Challenging the Status Quo. Where Do *Women with Disabilities* Fit In?" *Canadian Woman Studies/ Les cahiers de la femme* 14, 3: 41–43.

Ondaatje, Michael. 1992. *The English Patient.* Toronto: McClelland & Stewart.

O'Neil, Maureen, and Sharon Sutherland. 1990. "The Machinery of Women's Policy: Implementing the RCSW." Paper prepared for the conference Women and the Canadian State. Nov.

Osennontion and Skonaganleh:ra. 1989. "Our World." *Canadian Woman Studies/Les cahier de la femme* 10, 2/4: 7–19.

Ottawa Letter. 1993. "Campbell Sworn in as Prime Minister with Substantially Smaller Cabinet." 21 (28 June): 221–22.

Overall, Christine. 1992. "What's Wrong with Prostitution? Evaluating Sex Work." *Signs* 17, 4: 705–24.

————. 1993. *Human Reproduction: Principles, Practices, Policies.* Toronto: Oxford University Press.

Panitch, Leo. 1977. "The Role and Nature of the State." In *The Canadian State: Political Economy and Political Power.* Ed. Leo Panitch, 3–27. Toronto: University of Toronto Press.

Pal, Leslie A. 1993. *Interests of State: The Politics of Language, Multiculturalism, and Feminism in Canada.* Montreal: McGill-Queen's University Press.

Parr, Joy, ed. 1987. *Still Running: Personal Stories of Queen's Women Celebrating the Fiftieth Anniversary of the Marty Fellowship.* Kingston: Queen's University Alumnae Association.

————. 1990. *The Gender of Breadwinners.* Toronto: University of Toronto Press.

Parsons, Talcott. 1959. "The Social Structure of the Family." In *The Family: Its Function and Destiny.* Ed. R.N. Anshen. New York: Hayner.

Payette, Lise. 1982. *Le pouvoir? Connais pas.* Quebec: Québec/Amérique.

Peters, Evelyn. 1987. "Indians in Regina and Saskatoon, 1982: Some Strategies of Household Organization." PhD diss., Queen's University.

Phillips, David. 1995. "No difference, no deference." *Globe and Mail,* 10 Nov., A20.

Phillips, Susan D. 1991. "Meaning and Structure in Social Movements: Mapping the Network of National Canadian Women's Organizations." *Canadian Journal of Political Science* 24, 4: 755–82.

Philp, Margaret. 1995. "Male–female income gap widens." *Globe and Mail,* 20 Dec., A8.

Pierson, Ruth Roach. 1986. *"They're Still Women After All": The Second World War and Canadian Womanhood.* Toronto: McClelland & Stewart.

————. 1990. "Gender and the Unemployment Insurance Debates in Canada, 1934–1940." *Labour/Le Travail* 25: 77–103.

————. 1995. "The Politics of the Domestic Sphere." In *Canadian Women's Issues: Twenty-five Years of Women's Activism in English Canada.* Vol. 2. Ed. Ruth Roach Pierson and Marjorie Griffin Cohen, 1–33. Toronto: Lorimer.

Porter, John. 1965. *The Vertical Mosaic: An Analysis of Social Class and Power in Canada.* Toronto: University of Toronto Press.

Prentice, Alison, Paula Bourne, Gail Cuthbert Brandt, Beth Light, Wendy Mitchinson, and Naomi Black. 1988. *Canadian Women: A History.* Toronto: Harcourt, Brace, Jovanovich.

Prentice, Susan. 1995. "Workers, Mothers, Reds: Toronto's Postwar Daycare Fight." In *Social Welfare Policy in Canada.* Ed. Raymond B. Blake and Jeff Keshen, 258–76. Toronto: Copp Clark.

Ramkhalawansingh, Ceta. 1974. "Women During the Great War." In *Women at Work, Ontario, 1850–1930.* Ed. Janice Acton, Penny Goldsmith, and Bonnie Shepard, 261–308. Toronto: Canadian Women's Educational Press.

Rebick, Judy. 1994. "Interview with Judy Rebick." *Studies in Political Economy* 44, 39–71.

Report of the Royal Commission on the Status of Women in Canada. 1970. Ottawa: Information Canada.

Resources for Feminist Research. 1990. Special issue: Confronting Heterosexuality. 19, 3/4 (Sept.–Dec.).

Rich, Adrienne. 1980. "Compulsory Heterosexuality and Lesbian Existence." *Signs* 5 (Summer): 631–60.

Riddell, W.A. 1928. "Women's Franchise in Quebec a Century Ago." *Transactions of the Royal Society of Canada,* section 2: 85–98.

Riley, Denise. 1987. *"Am I that Name?" Feminism and the Category of "Women" in History.* Minneapolis: University of Minnesota Press.

Rinehart, Dianne. 1995. "Gender protection may harm refugees." *Winnipeg Free Press,* 17 March, B6.

Robertson, James R. 1995. *Sexual Orientation and Legal Rights.* Ottawa: Minister of Supply and Services.

Rodgers, Karen. 1994. "Wife Assault: The Findings of a National Survey." *Juristat* 14, 9: 1–22.

Rosenberg, Harriet. 1986. "The Home Is the Workplace: Hazards, Stresses and Pollutants." In *Through the Kitchen Window: The Politics of Home and*

Family. Ed. Meg Luxton and Harriet Rosenberg, 37–62. Toronto: Garamond.

———. 1987. "Motherwork, Stress, and Depression: The Costs of Privatized Social Reproduction." In *Feminism and Political Economy.* Ed. Heather Jon Maroney and Meg Luxton, 181–96. Toronto: Methuen.

Ross, Becki. 1995. *The House that Jill Built: A Lesbian Nation.* Toronto: University of Toronto Press.

Russell, Susan. 1987. "The Hidden Curriculum of School: Reproducing Gender and Class Hierarchies." In *Feminism and Political Economy: Women's Work, Women's Struggles.* Ed Heather Jon Maroney and Meg Luxton, 229–46. Toronto: Methuen.

———. 1989. "From Disability to Handicap: An Inevitable Response to Social Constraints?" *Canadian Review of Sociology and Anthropology* 26, 2: 276–93.

Sadlier, Rosemary. 1994. *Leading the Way: Black Women in Canada.* Toronto: Umbrella Press .

Sainte-Marie, Buffy. 1993. "Buffy Sainte-Marie: Lyrics of the Land." Interview with Fiona Muldrew and Suzanne McCloud. *Herizons* 7, 2: 30–32.

Saint-Onge, Nicole J.M. 1985. "The Dissolution of a Métis Community: Point à Grouette, 1860–1885." *Studies in Political Economy* 18: 149–72.

Salutin, Rick. 1993. "The sexual politics of Kim Campbell's future." *Globe and Mail,* 12 March, C1.

Sangster, Joan. 1979. "The 1907 Bell Telephone Strike: Organizing Women Workers." *Labour/Le Travailleur* 15.

———. 1989. *Dreams of Equality: Women on the Canadian Left, 1920–1950.* Toronto: McClelland & Stewart.

Scott, Joan Wallach. 1988. *Gender and the Politics of History.* New York: Columbia University Press.

Scriver, Jessie Boyd. 1984. "Memories." In *A Fair Shake: Autobiographical Essays by McGill Women.* Ed. Margaret Gillett and Kay Sibbald, 1–13. Montreal: Eden Press.

Seccombe, Wally. 1986. "Reflections on the Domestic Labour Debate and Prospects for Marxist-Feminist Synthesis." In *The Politics of Diversity.* Ed. Roberta Hamilton and Michèle Barrett, 190–207. London: Verso.

Seeley, John R., Alexander Sim, and Elizabeth Loosley. 1956. *Crestwood Heights: A Study of the Culture of Suburban Life.* New York: Wiley.

Sherfey, Mary-Jane. 1972. *The Nature and Evolution of Female Sexuality.* New York: Random House.

Silman, Janet. 1987. *Enough is Enough: Aboriginal Women Speak Out.* Toronto: Women's Press.

Silvera, Makeda. 1985. "How Far Have We Come." In *In the Feminine: Women and Words/les Femmes et les mots.* Ed. Ann Dybikowski, Victoria Freeman, Daphne Marlatt, Barbara Pullman, and Betsy Warland, 68–72. Edmonton: Longspoon Press.

———, ed. 1986. *Fireworks: The Best of Fireweed.* Toronto: Women's Press.

Simmons, Christina. 1991. "Helping the Poorer Sisters: The Women of the Jost Mission, Halifax, 1905–1945." In *Rethinking Canada: The Promise of Women's History.* 2nd ed. Ed. Veronica Strong-Boag and Anita Clair Fellman, 286–307. Toronto: Copp Clark Longman.

Smith, Dorothy. 1992. "Whistling Women: Reflections on Rage and Rationality." In *Fragile Truths: Twenty-five Years of Sociology and Anthropology in Canada.* Ed. William K. Carroll, Linda Christiansen-Ruffman, Raymond F. Currie, and Deborah Harrison, 207–26. Ottawa: Carleton University Press.

Smith, Vivian. 1993. "Women welcome victory, 'but it's still not an election.'" *Globe and Mail,* 15 June, A4.

Snitow, Ann. 1990. "A Gender Diary." In *Conflicts in Feminism.* Ed. Marianne Hirsch and Evelyn Fox Keller, 9–43. New York: Routledge.

Spock, Benjamin. 1957. *Baby and Child Care.* 3rd ed. New York: n.p.

———, and Michael B. Rothenberg. 1985. *Dr Spock's Baby and Child Care.* New York: E.P. Dutton.

Sprague, D.N. 1980. "The Manitoba Land Question 1870–1872." *Journal of Canadian Studies* 15, 3 (Autumn): 74–84.

Stacey-Moore, Gail. 1993. "In Our Own Voice." *Herizons* 6, 4: 21–23.

Statistics Canada. 1993. *Women in the Workplace.* 2nd ed. Ottawa: Ministry of Supply and Services.

————. 1995a. "Response to Allegations Made About the Violence Against Women Survey." Feb.

————. 1995b. "Unemployment." CANSIM (World Wide Web).

Stevenson, Garth. 1980. "Canadian Regionalism in Continental Perspective." *Journal of Canadian Studies* 15, 2: 16–28.

Stoddart, Jennifer. 1973. "The Woman Suffrage Bill in Quebec." In *Women in Canada.* Ed. Marylee Stephenson, 90–106. Toronto: New Press.

————. 1981. "Quebec's Legal Elite Looks at Women's Rights: The Dorion Commission, 1929–31." In *Essays in the History of Canadian Law.* Vol. 1. Ed. David H. Flaherty. Toronto: University of Toronto Press.

Strange, Carolyn. 1995. *Toronto's Girl Problem: The Perils and Pleasures of the City, 1880–1930.* Toronto: University of Toronto Press.

Strong-Boag, Veronica. 1976. *The Parliament of Women: The National Council of Women of Canada, 1893–1929.* Ottawa: National Museums of Canada.

————. 1979. "Canada's Women Doctors: Feminism Constrained." In *A Not Unreasonable Claim: Women and Reform in Canada, 1880s–1920s.* Ed. Linda Kealey, 109–30. Toronto: Women's Press.

————. 1983. "Mapping Women's Studies in Canada: Some Signposts." *Journal of Educational Thought* 17: 94–111.

————. 1986. "'Ever a Crusader': Nellie McClung, First-Wave Feminist." In *Rethinking Canada: The Promise of Women's History.* Ed. Veronica Strong-Boag and Anita Clair Fellman, 178–90. Toronto: Copp Clark Pitman.

————. 1988. *The New Day Recalled: Lives of Girls and Women in English Canada, 1919–1939.* Toronto: Copp Clark Pitman.

————. 1995. "'Their Side of the Story': Women's Voices from Ontario Suburbs." In *A Diversity of Women: Ontario, 1945–1980.* Ed. Joy Parr. Toronto: University of Toronto Press.

Sugiman, Pamela. 1994. *Labour's Dilemma: The Gender Politics of Auto Workers in Canada, 1937–1979.* Toronto: University of Toronto Press.

Swift, Jamie. 1995. *Wheel of Fortune: Work and Life in the Age of Falling Expectations.* Toronto: Between the Lines.

Sydie, Rosalind. 1991. "From Liberal to Radical: The Work and Life of Mary Wollstonecraft." *Atlantis* 17, 1: 36–71.

Tax, Meredith. 1980. *The Rising of the Women: Feminist Solidarity and Class Conflict, 1880–1917.* New York: Monthly Review Press.

Taylor, Barbara. 1979. "'The Men Are as Bad as Their Masters . . .': Socialism, Feminism, and Sexual Antagonism in the London Tailoring Trade in the Early 1830s." *Feminist Studies* 5, 1: 7–40.

———. 1983. *Eve and the New Jerusalem.* London: Virago.

Teeple, Gary, ed. 1972. *Capitalism and the National Question.* Toronto: University of Toronto Press.

Tennant, Paul. 1990. *Aboriginal Peoples and Politics: The Indian Land Question in British Columbia, 1849–1989.* Vancouver: University of British Columbia Press.

Thompson, Allan. 1995. "Immigrant women not protected, report says." *Toronto Star*, 23 May, A3.

Tiger, Lionel. 1969. *Men in Groups.* New York: Random House.

Todd, Douglas. 1993. "First openly gay minister ordained." *Vancouver Sun*, 20 Sept., A3.

Toronto Star. 1957. "Disqualified: 'Miss USA' Mother of 2." 19 July, 1.

Trigger, Bruce. 1991. "Early Native North American Responses to European Contact: Romantic versus Rationalist Interpretations." *Journal of American History* 77, 4 (March): 1195–215.

Trimble, Linda. 1995. "Politics Where We Live: Women and Cities." In *Canadian Metropolitics: Governing Our Cities.* Ed. James Lightbody, 92–114. Toronto: Copp Clark.

Trofimenkoff, Susan Mann. 1977. "Henri Bourassa and the Woman Question." In *The Neglected Majority: Essays in Canadian Women's History.* Ed. Susan Mann Trofimenkoff and Alison Prentice, 106–15. Toronto: McClelland & Stewart.

Turpel, M.E. (Aki-Kwe). 1993. "Patriarchy and Paternalism: The Legacy of the Canadian State for First Nations Women." *Canadian Journal of Women and the Law* 6, 1: 174–92.

Tynes, Maxine. 1987. *Borrowed Beauty*. Porters Lake, NS: Pottersfield Press.

———. 1990. *Woman Talking Woman*. Lawrencetown Beach, NS: Pottersfield Press.

Urquhart, M.C. and K.A.H. Buckley, ed. 1965. *Historical Statistics of Canada*. Toronto: Macmillan.

Valpy, Michael. 1992. "Lives of Canadian girls and women." *Globe and Mail*, 12 March, 2.

Valverde, Mariana. 1991. *The Age of Light, Soap and Water: Moral Reform in English Canada, 1885–1925*. Toronto: McClelland & Stewart.

Vancouver Women's Caucus. 1972. "Lesbians Belong in the Women's Movement." In *Women Unite!* Toronto: Canadian Women's Educational Press.

Van Kirk, Sylvia. 1980. *"Many Tender Ties": Women in Fur-Trade Society, 1670–1870*. Winnipeg: Watson and Dwyer.

———. 1986. "The Role of Native Women in the Fur Trade Society of Western Canada, 1670–1830." In *Rethinking Canada: The Promise of Women's History*. Ed. Veronica Strong-Boag and Anita Clair Fellman, 59–66. Toronto: Copp Clark Pitman.

———. 1987. *Towards a Feminist Perspective in Native History*. Toronto: Centre for Women's Studies in Education.

Vickers, Jill, 1987. "At His Mother's Knee: Sex/Gender and the Construction of National Identities." In *Women and Men: Interdisciplinary Readings on Gender*. Ed. Greta Hofmann Nemiroff, 478–92. Richmond Hill, ON: Fitzhenry & Whiteside.

Vickers, Jill, Pauline Rankin, and Christine Appelle. 1993. *Politics as if Women Mattered: A Political Analysis of the National Action Committee on the Status of Women*. Toronto: University of Toronto Press. 1993.

Vienneau, David. 1985. "Feminist movement is dead, REAL Women's group says." *Toronto Star*, 20 Nov., A12.

Walker, Gillian. 1990. *Family Violence and the Women's Movement: The Conceptual Politics of Struggle*. Toronto: University of Toronto Press.

Wallace, Bronwen. 1993. " . . . I couldn't separate the landscape from how I see my poems moving." Interview in *Sounding Differences: Conversations with Seventeen Canadian Women Writers*. Ed. Janice Williamson. Toronto: University of Toronto Press.

Warskett, Rosemary. 1988. "Bank Worker Unionization and the Law." *Studies in Political Economy* 25: 41–73.

Weaver, Sally. 1993. "First Nations Women and Government Policy, 1970–92: Discrimination and Conflict." In *Changing Patterns: Women in Canada*. 2nd ed. Ed. Sandra Burt, Lorraine Code, and Lindsay Dorney, 92–150. Toronto: McClelland & Stewart.

Weir, Lorna. 1987. "Socialist Feminism and the Politics of Sexuality." In *Feminism and Political Economy: Women's Work, Women's Struggles*. Ed. Heather Jon Maroney and Meg Luxton, 69–84. Toronto: Methuen.

Weissman, Aerlyn, and Lynne Fernie. 1993. *Forbidden Love*. National Film Board.

Wente, Margaret. 1994. "Success stories: Which ones really count?" *Globe and Mail*, 23 July, A2.

Whitaker, Reg. 1977. "Images of the State in Canada." In *The Canadian State: Political Economy and Political Power*. Ed. Leo Panitch, 28–68. Toronto: University of Toronto Press.

White, Julie. 1993. *Sisters and Solidarity: Women and Unions in Canada*. Toronto: Thompson.

Williams, Pam. 1994. "Handywoman: Powerful new role model is plugged in." *Globe and Mail*, 10 March, A24.

Williams, Patricia. 1991. *The Alchemy of Race and Rights*. Cambridge: Harvard University Press.

Williams, Raymond. 1976. *Keywords*. London: Fontana.

———. 1981. *Culture*. London: Fontana.

Williamson, Janice, and Deborah Gorham, eds. 1989. *Up and Doing: Canadian Women and Peace*. Toronto: Women's Press.

Winks, Robin. 1971. *The Blacks in Canada: A History.* Montreal: McGill-Queen's University Press.

Winnipeg Free Press. 1992a. "Passing the buck." 21 March, A6.

———. 1992b. "Wifebattering not funny, embarrassed MPs declare." 15 May, 14.

———. 1995. "Rules on refugee women faulted." 10 March, A12.

Wolf, Naomi. 1990. *The Beauty Myth.* Toronto: Vintage Books.

Wotherspoon, Terry, and Vic Satzewich. 1993. *First Nations: Race, Class and Gender Relations.* Scarborough, ON: Nelson.

Yetman, Lori, and Julie Yetman. 1996. "Peanut Butter and Jam." In *To Sappho, My Sister: Lesbian Sisters Write About Their Lives.* Ed. Lee Fleming, 211–24. Charlottetown: Gynergy Books.

York, Lorraine M. 1994. "Whirling Blindfolded in the House of Woman: Gender Politics in the Poetry and Fiction of Michael Ondaatje." In *Essays on Canadian Writing,* 71–91. Toronto: ECW Press.

Young, Claire, and Diana Majury. 1995. "Lesbian Perspectives." In *Breaking Anonymity: The Chilly Climate for Women Faculty.* Ed. the Chilly Collective, 345–58. Waterloo: Wilfrid Laurier University Press.

Young, Iris Marion. 1990. *Justice and the Politics of Difference.* Princeton: Princeton University Press.

Index

and class, 3, 22, 44, 126–27,
131–32, 174
and gender, 4, 79, 118
racialization, 3, 8, 10, 32, 148, 151,
164, 166, 178, 184, 197, 215,
217
racism, 4, 8, 9, 22, 27, 74, 75–76, 78,
83, 116–18, 126, 132, 136n,
137n, 148, 161, 163–66
Canadian state and, 5, 75–76,
88–89, 108, 112, 116–19,
127–33, 164–66
feminist theory and, 4, 8, 22, 32,
74–75, 79
radical feminism, 7, 18, 20–21, 22,
29, 31, 32, 52, 53, 55, 56, 59,
63–64, 65, 67, 70, 73, 77, 78,
96, 104, 153, 159, 175, 186–87,
188, 207, 219–20
rape, 54, 56, 57, 66–67, 74, 105, 129,
147, 197, 198, 216
REAL Women, 67
refugees, 76, 80, 129–30, 136n, 137n
regions, 5, 97–102, 115
religion, 25, 29, 31, 124, 141. *See
also* Catholic Church; United
Church of Canada
representation, 8, 9, 181–222
reproductive labour, 4, 169–70, 172
sexual division of, 20, 31, 35–39,
94
reproductive technologies, 38–39,
72, 74, 75
resource towns, 101–2
Rich, Adrienne, 21, 71
Riel, Louis, 97
Riley, Denise, 32, 33
Ritchie, Grace, 142
Rosenberg, Harriet, 170
Ross, Becki, 206
Royal Commission on the Relations
of Labour and Capital (1889),
148

Royal Commission on the Status of
Women, 42n, 51–52, 54–55,
63, 65, 72, 77, 87, 90, 104, 152,
172, 183
Rubin, Aviva, 132
Russell, Susan, 165, 221n

Sabia, Laura, 51
Sainte-Marie, Buffy, 78
Salutin, Rick, 191
Sappier, Sandra Lovelace, 120
Scriver, Jessie Boyd, 143–43
Seccombe, Wally, 180n
sexual assault. *See* Rape
sexual division of labour. *See*
Gendered division of labour
sexual harassment, 56, 166
sexual hierarchy. *See* Gender hierarchy
sexual objectification, 9, 154,
182–97, 206–7
critiques of feminist theory of,
74, 197–206
sexual orientation, 7, 23, 39, 53, 71,
156–57, 208. *See also*
Compulsory heterosexuality;
Homosexuality; Lesbians;
Sexuality
sexuality, 4, 9, 18, 24, 31, 64–65,
159–60, 189–90, 204–6, 207,
208, 210, 215
debate, 64–65
control of women's, 17, 20–21,
65, 66, 147–48
double standard, 56, 65, 166–67,
184
sexual subjects, women as,
189–90, 203
work and, 147–48, 166–69
Silvera, Makeda, 197
Sinclair, Margaret (Trudeau), 202
slavery, 22, 36, 39, 85, 126, 131, 164,
198